Praise for Reza Aslan's *Zealot*

"Meticulously researched ... This book challenges many long-held assumptions about the man whose life and teachings form the foundations of Christianity. Aslan is not the first author to consider the case of the historical Jesus, but his jargon-free, unprejudiced, reader-friendly presentation of both Scripture and history will ensure that this message will reach a large lay audience."
—*The Times of Israel*

"Aslan's insistence on human and historical actuality turns out to be far more interesting than dogmatic theology.... This tough-minded, deeply political book does full justice to the real Jesus, and honors him in the process." —*San Francisco Chronicle*

"A bold, powerfully argued revisioning of the most consequential life ever lived." —Lawrence Wright, Pulitzer Prize–winning author of *Going Clear: Scientology, Hollywood, and the Prison of Belief*

"Be advised, dear reader, Sunday school this isn't. Yet Aslan may come as close as one can to respecting those who revere Jesus as the peace-loving, turn-the-other-cheek, true son of God depicted in modern Christianity, even as he knocks down that image.... Aslan is steeped in the history, languages and scriptural foundation of the biblical scholar and is a very clear writer with an authoritative, but not pedantic, voice. Those of us who wade into this genre often know how rare that is.... Fascinatingly and convincingly drawn."
—*The Seattle Times*

"Fascinating . . . [Aslan's] literary talent is as essential to the effect of *Zealot: The Life and Times of Jesus of Nazareth* as are his scholarly and journalistic chops. . . . A vivid, persuasive portrait of the world and societies in which Jesus lived and the role he most likely played in both."
—*Salon*

"Reza Aslan's powerful new *Zealot* paints a vivid, accessible portrait of Jesus. . . . a coherent and often convincing portrait of who Jesus was and what he wanted."
—*Tablet*

"The story of Jesus of Nazareth is arguably the most influential narrative in human history. Here Reza Aslan writes vividly and insightfully about the life and meaning of the figure who has come to be seen by billions as the Christ of faith. This is a special and revealing work, one that believer and skeptic alike will find surprising, engaging, and original."
—Jon Meacham, Pulitzer Prize-winning author
of *Thomas Jefferson: The Art of Power*

"Aslan brings a fine popular style, shorn of all jargon, to bear on the presentation of Jesus of Nazareth. . . . He isn't interested in attacking religion or even the church, much less in comparing Christianity unfavorably to another religion. He would have us admire Jesus as one of the many would-be messiahs who sprang up during Rome's occupation of Palestine, animated by zeal for "strict adherence to the Torah and the Law," refusal to serve a human master, and devotion to God, and therefore dedicated to throwing off Rome and repudiating Roman religion. . . . You don't have to lose your religion to learn much that's vitally germane to its history from Aslan's absorbing, reader-friendly book."
—*Booklist* (starred review)

"Jesus of Nazareth is not the same as Jesus Christ. The Gospels are not historical documents. . . . Why has Christianity taken hold

BY REZA ASLAN

BOOKS

God

Zealot

Beyond Fundamentalism (originally published as
How to Win a Cosmic War)

No god but God

EDITED COLLECTIONS

Tablet & Pen

Muslims and Jews in America
(with Aaron J. Hahn Tapper)

and flourished? This book will give you the answers.... A well-researched, readable biography of Jesus of Nazareth."

—*Kirkus Reviews* (starred review)

"Parts an important curtain that has long hidden from view the man Jesus.... Aslan develops a convincing and coherent story of how the Christian church, and in particular Paul, reshaped Christianity's essence, obscuring the very real man who was Jesus of Nazareth. Compulsively readable and written at a popular level, this superb work is highly recommended."

—*Publishers Weekly* (starred review)

"In *Zealot*, Reza Aslan doesn't just synthesize research and reimagine a lost world, though he does those things very well. He does for religious history what Bertolt Brecht did for playwriting. Aslan rips Jesus out of all the contexts we thought he belonged in and holds him forth as someone entirely new. This is Jesus as a passionate Jew, a violent revolutionary, a fanatical ideologue, an odd and scary and extraordinarily interesting man."

—Judith Shulevitz, author of *The Sabbath World*

ZEALOT

ZEALOT

The Life and Times of Jesus of Nazareth

Reza Aslan

RANDOM HOUSE TRADE PAPERBACKS

NEW YORK

For my wife, Jessica Jackley, and the entire Jackley clan,

whose love and acceptance have taught me more about Jesus

than all my years of research and study.

Do not think that I have come to bring peace on earth. I have not come to bring peace, but the sword.

MATTHEW 10:34

Contents

PART II

PART III

First-Century
Palestine

Illustration by Laura Hartman maestro ©2013

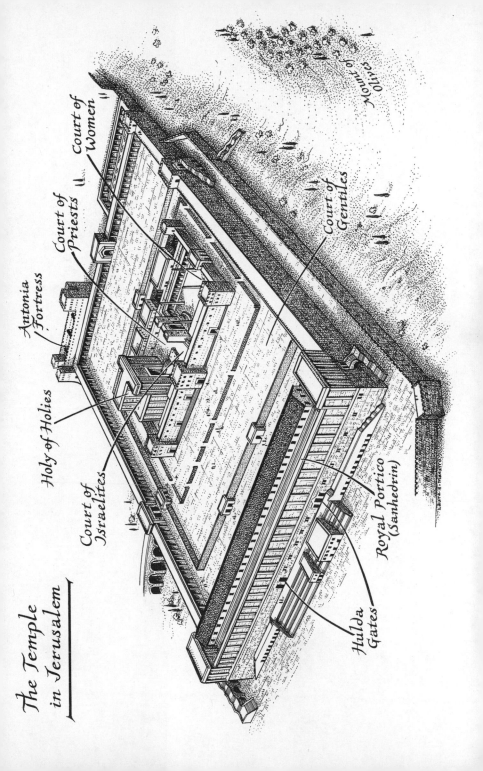

The Temple
in Jerusalem

Court of
Women

Court of
Priests

Autonia
Fortress

Holy of Holies

Court of
Israelites

Court of
Gentiles

Mount of
Olives

Royal Portico
(Sanhedrin)

Hulda
Gates

Author's Note

When I was fifteen years old, I found Jesus.

I spent the summer of my sophomore year at an evangelical youth camp in Northern California, a place of timbered fields and boundless blue skies, where, given enough time and stillness and soft-spoken encouragement, one could not help but hear the voice of God. Amidst the man-made lakes and majestic pines my friends and I sang songs, played games, and swapped secrets, rollicking in our freedom from the pressures of home and school. In the evenings, we gathered in a firelit assembly hall at the center of the camp. It was there that I heard a remarkable story that would change my life forever.

Two thousand years ago, I was told, in an ancient land called Galilee, the God of heaven and earth was born in the form of a helpless child. The child grew into a blameless man. The man became the Christ, the savior of humanity. Through his words and miraculous deeds, he challenged the Jews, who thought they were the chosen of God, and in return the Jews had him nailed to a cross. Though he could have saved himself from that gruesome death, he freely chose to die. His death was the point of it all, for his sacrifice freed us all from the burden of our sins. But the story did not end there, because three days later, he rose again, exalted and divine, so that now, all who believe in him and accept him into their hearts will also never die, but have eternal life.

For a kid raised in a motley family of lukewarm Muslims and exuberant atheists, this was truly the greatest story ever told. Never before had I felt so intimately the pull of God. In Iran, the place of my birth, I was Muslim in much the way I was Persian. My religion and my ethnicity were mutual and linked. Like most people born into a religious tradition, my faith was as familiar to me as my skin, and just as disregardable. After the Iranian revolution forced my family to flee our home, religion in general, and Islam in particular, became taboo in our household. Islam was shorthand for every-thing we had lost to the mullahs who now ruled Iran. My mother still prayed when no one was looking, and you could still find a stray Quran or two hidden in a closet or a drawer somewhere. But, for the most part, our lives were scrubbed of all trace of God.

That was just fine with me. After all, in the America of the 1980s, being Muslim was like being from Mars. My faith was a bruise, the most obvious symbol of my otherness; it needed to be concealed.

Jesus, on the other hand, *was* America. He was the central figure in America's national drama. Accepting him into my heart was as close as I could get to feeling truly American. I do not mean to say that mine was a conversion of convenience. On the contrary, I burned with absolute devotion to my newfound faith. I was pre-sented with a Jesus who was less "Lord and Savior" than he was a best friend, someone with whom I could have a deep and personal relationship. As a teenager trying to make sense of an indetermi-nate world I had only just become aware of, this was an invitation I could not refuse.

The moment I returned home from camp, I began eagerly to share the good news of Jesus Christ with my friends and family, my neighbors and classmates, with people I'd just met and with strang-ers on the street: those who heard it gladly, and those who threw it back in my face. Yet something unexpected happened in my quest to save the souls of the world. The more I probed the Bible to arm myself against the doubts of unbelievers, the more distance I discovered between the Jesus of the gospels and the Jesus of history—between Jesus the Christ and Jesus of Nazareth. In college, where I began my formal study of the history of religions, that initial discomfort soon ballooned into full-blown doubts of my own.

The bedrock of evangelical Christianity, at least as it was taught to me, is the unconditional belief that every word of the Bible is God-breathed and true, literal and inerrant. The sudden realization that this belief is patently and irrefutably false, that the Bible is replete with the most blatant and obvious errors and contradictions—just as one would expect from a document written by hundreds of hands across thousands of years—left me confused and spiritually unmoored. And so, like many people in my situation, I angrily discarded my faith as if it were a costly forgery I had been duped into buying. I began to rethink the faith and culture of my forefathers, finding in them as an adult a deeper, more intimate familiarity than I ever had as a child, the kind that comes from reconnecting with an old friend after many years apart.

Meanwhile, I continued my academic work in religious studies, delving back into the Bible not as an unquestioning believer but as an inquisitive scholar. No longer chained to the assumption that the stories I read were literally true, I became aware of a more meaningful truth in the text, a truth intentionally detached from the exigencies of history. Ironically, the more I learned about the life of the historical Jesus, the turbulent world in which he lived, and the brutality of the Roman occupation that he defied, the more I was drawn to him. Indeed, the Jewish peasant and revolutionary who challenged the rule of the most powerful empire the world had ever known and lost became so much more real to me than the detached, unearthly being I had been introduced to in church.

Today, I can confidently say that two decades of rigorous aca-

demic research into the origins of Christianity has made me a
more genuinely committed disciple of Jesus of Nazareth than I
ever was of Jesus Christ. My hope with this book is to spread the
good news of the Jesus of history with the same fervor that I once
applied to spreading the story of the Christ.

There are a few things to keep in mind before we begin our
examination. For every well-attested, heavily researched, and emi-
nently authoritative argument made about the historical Jesus,
there is an equally well-attested, equally researched, and equally
authoritative argument opposing it. Rather than burden the reader
with the centuries-long debate about the life and mission of Jesus
of Nazareth, I have constructed my narrative upon what I believe
to be the most accurate and reasonable argument, based on my two
decades of scholarly research into the New Testament and early
Christian history. For those interested in the debate, I have exhaus-
tively detailed my research and, whenever possible, provided the
arguments of those who disagree with my interpretation in the
lengthy notes section at the end of this book.

All Greek translations of the New Testament are my own (with
a little help from my friends Liddell and Scott). In those few cases
in which I do not directly translate a passage of the New Testament, I rely on the translation provided by the New Revised Standard Version of the Bible. All Hebrew and Aramaic translations are
provided by Dr. Ian C. Werrett, associate professor of religious
studies at St. Martin's University.

Throughout the text, all references to the Q source material
(the material unique to the gospels of Matthew and Luke) will be
marked thus: (Matthew | Luke), with the order of the books indi-
cating which gospel I am most directly quoting. The reader will
notice that I rely primarily on the gospel of Mark and the Q material in forming my outline of the story of Jesus. That is because
these are the earliest and thus most reliable sources available to us
about the life of the Nazarean. In general I have chosen not to
delve too deeply into the so-called Gnostic Gospels. While these

texts are incredibly important in outlining the wide array of opinions among the early Christian community about who Jesus was and what his teachings meant, they do not shed much light on the historical Jesus himself.

It may appear to the casual reader that I am haphazardly choosing which gospel verses are historically reliable and which are not. But in fact, the methodological tools for determining the historical accuracy of any given passage in the gospels have been in place for nearly two centuries. For example, there is broad consensus among scholars that an earlier passage (say, from the gospel of Mark) is more reliable than a later one (say, from the gospel of John). If a passage appears in all four canonized gospels—a phenomenon known as "multiple attestations"—then it, too, is more likely to be historically accurate. The same is true of a verse or passage that seems to contradict basic church doctrine. For instance, those passages in which Jesus emphasizes the exclusivity rather than the universality of his message are widely acknowledged to be historically reliable because they conflict with the early church's emphasis on the universality of Christianity. There are many more rules that have been adopted by scholars to help place the gospels in their historical context, but to put it in the simplest way possible: those passages that coincide with what we know about the political, social, and religious milieu of first-century Palestine are generally accepted as historical, while those that do not are rejected.

Although it is almost unanimously agreed that, with the possible exception of Luke-Acts, the gospels were not written by the people for whom they are named, for ease and the sake of clarity, I will continue to refer to the gospel writers by the names by which we now know and recognize them.

Finally, in keeping with scholarly designations, this text employs C.E., or Common Era, instead of A.D. in its dating, and B.C.E. instead of B.C. It also more properly refers to the Old Testament as the Hebrew Bible or the Hebrew Scriptures.

Introduction

It is a miracle that we know anything at all about the man called Jesus of Nazareth. The itinerant preacher wandering from village to village clamoring about the end of the world, a band of ragged followers trailing behind, was a common sight in Jesus's time—so common, in fact, that it had become a kind of caricature among the Roman elite. In a farcical passage about just such a figure, the Greek philosopher Celsus imagines a Jewish holy man roaming the Galilean countryside, shouting to no one in particular: "I am God, or the servant of God, or a divine spirit. But I am coming, for the world is already in the throes of destruction. And you will soon see me coming with the power of heaven."

The first century was an era of apocalyptic expectation among the Jews of Palestine, the unofficial Roman designation for the vast tract of land encompassing modern-day Israel/Palestine as well as large parts of Jordan, Syria, and Lebanon (the land would not be officially called Palestine until after 135 C.E.). Countless prophets, preachers, and messiahs tramped through the Holy Land delivering messages of God's imminent judgment. Many of these so-called false messiahs we know by name. A few are even mentioned in the New Testament. The prophet Theudas, according to the book of

Acts, had four hundred disciples before Rome captured him and cut off his head. A mysterious charismatic figure known only as "the Egyptian" raised an army of followers in the desert, nearly all of whom were massacred by Roman troops. In 4 B.C.E., the year in which most scholars believe Jesus of Nazareth was born, a poor shepherd named Athronges put a diadem on his head and crowned himself "King of the Jews"; he and his followers were brutally cut down by a legion of soldiers. Another messianic aspirant, called simply "the Samaritan," was crucified by Pontius Pilate even though he raised no army and in no way challenged Rome—an indication that the authorities, sensing the apocalyptic fever in the air, had become extremely sensitive to any hint of sedition. There was Hezekiah the bandit chief, Simon of Peraea, Judas the Galilean, his grandson Menahem, Simon son of Giora, and Simon son of Kochba—all of whom declared messianic ambitions and all of whom were killed for doing so. Add to this list the Essene sect, some of whose members lived in seclusion atop the dry plateau of Qumran on the northwestern shore of the Dead Sea; the first-century Jewish revolutionary party known as the Zealots, who helped launch a bloody war against Rome; and the fearsome bandit-assassins whom the Romans dubbed the Sicarii (the Daggermen), and the picture that emerges of first-century Palestine is of an era awash in messianic energy.

It is difficult to place Jesus of Nazareth squarely within any of the known religiopolitical movements of his time. He was a man of profound contradictions, one day preaching a message of racial exclusion ("I was sent solely to the lost sheep of Israel"; Matthew 15:24), the next, of benevolent universalism ("Go and make disciples of all nations"; Matthew 28:19); sometimes calling for unconditional peace ("Blessed are the peacemakers for they shall be called the sons of God"; Matthew 5:9), sometimes promoting violence and conflict ("If you do not have a sword, go sell your cloak and buy one"; Luke 22:36).

The problem with pinning down the historical Jesus is that, outside of the New Testament, there is almost no trace of the man who would so permanently alter the course of human history. The earliest and most reliable nonbiblical reference to Jesus comes from the first-century Jewish historian Flavius Josephus (d. 100 C.E.). In a brief throwaway passage in the *Antiquities,* Josephus writes of a fiendish Jewish high priest named Ananus who, after the death of the Roman governor Festus, unlawfully condemned a certain "James, the brother of Jesus, the one they call messiah," to stoning for transgression of the law. The passage moves on to relate what happened to Ananus after the new governor, Albinus, finally arrived in Jerusalem.

Fleeting and dismissive as this allusion may be (the phrase "the one they call messiah" is clearly meant to express derision), it nevertheless contains enormous significance for those searching for any sign of the historical Jesus. In a society without surnames, a common name like James required a specific appellation—a place of birth or a father's name—to distinguish it from all the other men named James roaming around Palestine (hence, Jesus *of Nazareth*). In this case, James's appellative was provided by his fraternal connection to someone with whom Josephus assumes his audience would be familiar. The passage proves not only that "Jesus, the one they call messiah" probably existed, but that by the year 94 C.E., when the *Antiquities* was written, he was widely recognized as the founder of a new and enduring movement.

It is that movement, not its founder, that receives the attention of second-century historians like Tacitus (d. 118) and Pliny the Younger (d. 113), both of whom mention Jesus of Nazareth but reveal little about him, save for his arrest and execution—an important historical note, as we shall see, but one that sheds little light on the details of Jesus's life. We are therefore left with whatever information can be gleaned from the New Testament.

The first written testimony we have about Jesus of Nazareth comes from the epistles of Paul, an early follower of Jesus who died sometime around 66 C.E. (Paul's first epistle, 1 Thessalonians, can be dated between 48 and 50 C.E., some two decades after Jesus's death.)

The trouble with Paul, however, is that he displays an extraordinary lack of interest in the historical Jesus. Only three scenes from Jesus's life are ever mentioned in his epistles: the Last Supper (1 Corinthians 11:23–26), the crucifixion (1 Corinthians 2:2), and, most crucially for Paul, the resurrection, without which, he claims, "our preaching is empty and your faith is in vain" (1 Corinthians 15:14). Paul may be an excellent source for those interested in the early formation of Christianity, but he is a poor guide for uncovering the historical Jesus.

That leaves us with the gospels, which present their own set of problems. To begin with, with the possible exception of the gospel of Luke, none of the gospels we have were written by the person after whom they are named. That actually is true of most of the books in the New Testament. Such so-called *pseudepigraphical* works, or works attributed to but not written by a specific author, were extremely common in the ancient world and should by no means be thought of as forgeries. Naming a book after a person was a standard way of reflecting that person's beliefs or representing his or her school of thought. Regardless, the gospels are not, nor were they ever meant to be, a historical documentation of Jesus's life. These are not eyewitness accounts of Jesus's words and deeds recorded by people who knew him. They are testimonies of faith composed by communities of faith and written many years after the events they describe. Simply put, the gospels tell us about Jesus the Christ, not Jesus the man.

The most widely accepted theory on the formation of the gospels, the "Two-Source Theory," holds that Mark's account was written first sometime after 70 C.E., about four decades after Jesus's death. Mark had at his disposal a collection of oral and perhaps a handful of written traditions that had been passed around by Jesus's earliest followers for years. By adding a chronological narrative to this jumble of traditions, Mark created a wholly new literary genre popularly called *gospel,* derived from the Old English *god-spell,* meaning "good news." Yet Mark's gospel is a short and somewhat unsatisfying one for many Christians. There is no infancy narrative; Jesus simply arrives one day on the banks of the Jordan River to be baptized by John the Baptist. There are no resurrection appearances. Jesus is crucified. His body is placed in a tomb. A few days later, the tomb is empty.* Even the earliest Christians were left wanting by Mark's brusque account of Jesus's life and ministry, and so it was left to Mark's successors, Matthew and Luke, to improve upon the original text.

Two decades after Mark, between 90 and 100 C.E., the authors of Matthew and Luke, working independently of each other and with Mark's manuscript as a template, updated the gospel story by adding their own unique traditions, including two different and conflicting infancy narratives as well as a series of elaborate resurrection stories to satisfy their Christian readers. Matthew and Luke also relied on what must have been an early and fairly well distributed collection of Jesus's sayings that scholars have termed Q (German for *Quelle,* or "source"). Although we no longer have any physical copies of this document, we can infer its contents by compiling those verses that Matthew and Luke share in common but that do not appear in Mark.

Together, these three gospels—Mark, Matthew, and Luke—became known as the *Synoptics* (Greek for "viewed together") because they more or less present a common narrative and chronology about the life and ministry of Jesus, one that is greatly at odds with the fourth gospel, John, which was likely written soon after the close of the first century, between 100 and 120 C.E.

These, then, are the canonized gospels. But they are not the only gospels. We now have access to an entire library of noncanonical scriptures written mostly in the second and third centuries that provides a vastly different perspective on the life of Jesus of Nazareth. These include the Gospel of Thomas, the Gospel of Philip, the Secret Book of John, the Gospel of Mary Magdalene,

---

* It is unanimously agreed that the original version of Mark ended with 16:8.

and a host of other so-called Gnostic writings discovered in Upper Egypt, near the town of Nag Hammadi, in 1945. Though they were left out of what would ultimately become the New Testament, these books are significant in that they demonstrate the dramatic divergence of opinion that existed over who Jesus was and what Jesus meant, even among those who claimed to walk with him, who shared his bread and ate with him, who heard his words and prayed with him.

In the end, there are only two hard historical facts about Jesus of Nazareth upon which we can confidently rely: the first is that Jesus was a Jew who led a popular Jewish movement in Palestine at the beginning of the first century C.E.; the second is that Rome crucified him for doing so. By themselves these two facts cannot provide a complete portrait of the life of a man who lived two thousand years ago. But when combined with all we know about the tumultuous era in which Jesus lived—and thanks to the Romans, we know a great deal—these two facts can help paint a picture of Jesus of Nazareth that may be more historically accurate than the one painted by the gospels. Indeed, the Jesus that emerges from this historical exercise—a zealous revolutionary swept up, as all Jews of the era were, in the religious and political turmoil of first-century Palestine—bears little resemblance to the image of the gentle shepherd cultivated by the early Christian community.

Consider this: Crucifixion was a punishment that Rome reserved almost exclusively for the crime of sedition. The plaque the Romans placed above Jesus's head as he writhed in pain—"King of the Jews"—was called a *titulus* and, despite common perception, was not meant to be sarcastic. Every criminal who hung on a cross received a plaque declaring the specific crime for which he was being executed. Jesus's crime, in the eyes of Rome, was striving for kingly rule (i.e., treason), the same crime for which nearly every other messianic aspirant of the time was killed. Nor did Jesus die alone. The gospels claim that on either side of Jesus hung men who in Greek are called *lestai,* a word often rendered into English as "thieves" but which actually means "bandits" and was the most common Roman designation for an insurrectionist or rebel.

Three rebels on a hill covered in crosses, each cross bearing the racked and bloodied body of a man who dared defy the will of Rome. That image alone should cast doubt upon the gospels' portrayal of Jesus as a man of unconditional peace almost wholly insulated from the political upheavals of his time. The notion that the leader of a popular messianic movement calling for the imposition of the "Kingdom of God"—a term that would have been understood by Jew and gentile alike as implying revolt against Rome—could have remained uninvolved in the revolutionary fervor that had gripped nearly every Jew in Judea is simply ridiculous.

Why would the gospel writers go to such lengths to temper the revolutionary nature of Jesus's message and movement? To answer this question we must first recognize that almost every gospel story written about the life and mission of Jesus of Nazareth was composed *after* the Jewish rebellion against Rome in 66 C.E. In that year, a band of Jewish rebels, spurred by their zeal for God, roused their fellow Jews in revolt. Miraculously, the rebels managed to liberate the Holy Land from the Roman occupation. For four glorious years, the city of God was once again under Jewish control. Then, in 70 C.E., the Romans returned. After a brief siege of Jerusalem, the soldiers breached the city walls and unleashed an orgy of violence upon its residents. They butchered everyone in their path, heaping corpses on the Temple Mount. A river of blood flowed down the cobblestone streets. When the massacre was complete, the soldiers set fire to the Temple of God. The fires spread beyond the Temple Mount, engulfing Jerusalem's meadows, the farms, the olive trees. Everything burned. So complete was the devastation wrought upon the holy city that Josephus writes there was nothing left to prove Jerusalem had ever been inhabited. Tens of thousands of Jews were slaughtered. The rest were marched out of the city in chains.

The spiritual trauma faced by the Jews in the wake of that catastrophic event is hard to imagine. Exiled from the land promised them by God, forced to live as outcasts among the pagans of the Roman Empire, the rabbis of the second century gradually and deliberately divorced Judaism from the radical messianic nationalism that had launched the ill-fated war with Rome. The Torah replaced the Temple in the center of Jewish life, and rabbinic Judaism emerged.

The Christians, too, felt the need to distance themselves from the revolutionary zeal that had led to the sacking of Jerusalem, not only because it allowed the early church to ward off the wrath of a deeply vengeful Rome, but also because, with the Jewish religion having become pariah, the Romans had become the primary target of the church's evangelism. Thus began the long process of transforming Jesus from a revolutionary Jewish nationalist into a pacifistic spiritual leader with no interest in any earthly matter. That was a Jesus the Romans could accept, and in fact did accept three centuries later when the Roman emperor Flavius Theodosius (d. 395) made the itinerant Jewish preacher's movement the official religion of the state, and what we now recognize as orthodox Christianity emerged.

This book is an attempt to reclaim, as much as possible, the Jesus of history, the Jesus *before* Christianity: the politically conscious Jewish revolutionary who, two thousand years ago, walked across the Galilean countryside, gathering followers for a messianic movement with the goal of establishing the Kingdom of God but whose mission failed when, after a provocative entry into Jerusalem and a brazen attack on the Temple, he was arrested and executed by Rome for the crime of sedition. It is also about how, in the aftermath of Jesus's failure to establish God's reign on earth, his followers reinterpreted not only Jesus's mission and identity, but also the very nature and definition of the Jewish messiah.

There are those who consider such an endeavor to be a waste of time, believing the Jesus of history to be irrevocably lost and incapable of recovery. Long gone are the heady days of "the quest for the historical Jesus," when scholars confidently proclaimed that modern scientific tools and historical research would allow us to uncover Jesus's true identity. The *real* Jesus no longer matters, these scholars argue. We should focus instead on the only Jesus that is accessible to us: Jesus *the Christ*.

Granted, writing a biography of Jesus of Nazareth is not like writing a biography of Napoleon Bonaparte. The task is somewhat akin to putting together a massive puzzle with only a few of the pieces in hand; one has no choice but to fill in the rest of the puzzle based on the best, most educated guess of what the completed image should look like. The great Christian theologian Rudolf Bultmann liked to say that the quest for the historical Jesus is ultimately an internal quest. Scholars tend to see the Jesus they want to see. Too often they see *themselves*—their own reflection—in the image of Jesus they have constructed.

And yet that best, most educated guess may be enough to, at the very least, question our most basic assumptions about Jesus of Nazareth. If we expose the claims of the gospels to the heat of historical analysis, we can purge the scriptures of their literary and theological flourishes and forge a far more accurate picture of the Jesus of history. Indeed, if we commit to placing Jesus firmly within the social, religious, and political context of the era in which he lived—an era marked by the slow burn of a revolt against Rome that would forever transform the faith and practice of Judaism—then, in some ways, his biography writes itself.

The Jesus that is uncovered in the process may not be the Jesus we expect; he certainly will not be the Jesus that many modern Christians would recognize. But in the end, he is the only Jesus that we can access by historical means.

Everything else is a matter of faith.

Chronology

PART I

Arise! Arise!
Put on your strength, O Zion!
Put on your beautiful garments, Jerusalem, the holy city;
for the uncircumcised and the unclean
shall never again enter you.
Shake off the dust from yourself, stand up,
O captive Jerusalem;
release the bonds from your neck,
O captive daughter of Zion.

ISAIAH 52:1–2

A Different Sort of Sacrifice

The war with Rome begins not with a clang of swords but with the lick of a dagger drawn from an assassin's cloak.

Festival season in Jerusalem: a time when Jews from across the Mediterranean converge upon the holy city bearing fragrant offerings to God. There are in the ancient Jewish religion a host of annual observances and celebrations that can only be performed here, inside the Temple of Jerusalem, in the presence of the high priest, who hoards the most sacred feast days—Passover, Pentecost, the harvest festival of Sukkot—for himself, all the while pocketing a healthy fee, or *tithe,* as he would call it, for his trouble. And what trouble it is! On such days the city's population can swell to more than a million people. It takes the full force of the porters and lower priests to squeeze the crush of pilgrims through the Hulda Gates at the Temple's southern wall, to herd them along the dark and cavernous galleries beneath the Temple plaza and guide them up the double flight of stairs that lead to the public square and marketplace known as the Court of Gentiles.

The Temple of Jerusalem is a roughly rectangular structure, some five hundred meters long and three hundred meters wide, balanced atop Mount Moriah, on the eastern edge of the holy city.

Its outer walls are rimmed with covered porticos whose slab-topped roofs, held up by row after row of glittering white stone columns, protect the masses from the merciless sun. On the Temple's southern flank sits the largest and most ornate of the porticoes, the Royal Portico—a tall, two-story, basilica-like assembly hall built in the customary Roman style. This is the administrative quarters of the Sanhedrin, the supreme religious body and highest judicial court of the Jewish nation. It is also where a clatter of merchants and grubby money changers lie in wait as you make your way up the underground stairs and onto the spacious sunlit plaza.

The money changers play a vital role in the Temple. For a fee, they will exchange your foul foreign coins for the Hebrew shekel, the only currency permitted by the Temple authorities. The money changers will also collect the half-shekel Temple tax that all adult males must pay to preserve the pomp and spectacle of all you see around you: the mountains of burning incense and the ceaseless sacrifices, the wine libations and the first-fruits offering, the Levite choir belting out psalms of praise and the accompanying orchestra thrumming lyres and banging cymbals. Someone must pay for these necessities. Someone must bear the cost of the burnt offerings that so please the Lord.

With the new currency in hand, you are now free to peruse the pens lining the periphery walls to purchase your sacrifice: a pigeon, a sheep—it depends on the depth of your purse, or the depth of your sins. If the latter transcends the former, do not despair. The money changers are happy to offer the credit you need to enhance your sacrifice. There is a strict legal code regulating the animals that can be purchased for the blessed occasion. They must be free of blemish. Domesticated, not wild. They cannot be beasts of burden. Whether ox or bull or ram or sheep, they must have been reared for this purpose alone. They are not cheap. Why should they be? The sacrifice is the Temple's primary purpose. It is the very reason for the Temple's being. The songs, the prayers, the readings—every ritual that takes place here arose in service of this singular and most vital ritual. The blood libation not only wipes away your sins, it cleanses the earth. It feeds the earth, renewing and sustaining it, protecting us all from drought or famine or worse. The cycle of life and death that the Lord in his omnificence has decreed is wholly dependent upon your sacrifice. This is not the time for thrift.

So purchase your offering, and make it a good one. Pass it on to any of the white-robed priests roaming the Temple plaza. They are the descendants of Aaron, the brother of Moses, responsible for maintaining the Temple's daily rites: the burning of incense, the lighting of lamps, the sounding of trumpets, and, of course, the sacrificial offerings. The priesthood is a hereditary position, but there is no shortage of them, certainly not during festival season, when they arrive in droves from distant lands to assist in the festivities. They cram the Temple in twenty-four-hour shifts to ensure that the fires of sacrifice are kept aflame day and night.

The Temple is constructed as a series of tiered courtyards, each smaller, more elevated, and more restrictive than the last. The outermost courtyard, the Court of Gentiles, where you purchased your sacrifice, is a broad piazza open to everyone, regardless of race or religion. If you are a Jew—one free of any physical affliction (no lepers, no paralytics) and properly purified by a ritual bath—you may follow the priest with your offering through a stone-lattice fence and proceed into the next courtyard, the Court of Women (a plaque on the fence warns all others to proceed no farther than the outer court on pain of death). Here is where the wood and oil for the sacrifices are stored. It is also the farthest into the Temple that any Jewish woman may proceed; Jewish men may continue up a small semicircular flight of stairs through the Nicanor Gate and into the Court of Israelites.

This is as close as you will ever be to the presence of God. The stink of carnage is impossible to ignore. It clings to the skin, the hair, becoming a noisome burden you will not soon shake off. The priests burn incense to ward off the fetor and disease, but the mixture of myrrh and cinnamon, saffron and frankincense cannot mask the insufferable stench of slaughter. Still, it is important to stay where you are and witness your sacrifice take place in the next courtyard, the Court of Priests. Entry into this court is permitted solely to the priests and Temple officials, for this is where the Temple's altar stands: a four-horned pedestal made of bronze and wood—five cubits long, five cubits wide—belching thick black clouds of smoke into the air.

The priest takes your sacrifice to a corner and cleanses himself in a nearby basin. Then, with a simple prayer, he slits the animal's throat. An assistant collects the blood in a bowl to sprinkle on the four horned corners of the altar, while the priest carefully disembowels and dismembers the carcass. The animal's hide is his to keep; it will fetch a handsome price in the marketplace. The entrails and the fatty tissue are torn out of the corpse, carried up a ramp to the altar, and placed directly atop the eternal fire. The meat of the beast is carved away carefully and put to the side for the priests to feast upon after the ceremony.

The entire liturgy is performed in front of the Temple's innermost court, the Holy of Holies—a gold-plated, columnar sanctuary at the very heart of the Temple complex. The Holy of Holies is the highest point in all Jerusalem. Its doors are draped in purple and scarlet tapestries embroidered with a zodiac wheel and a panorama of the heavens. This is where the glory of God physically dwells. It is the meeting point between the earthly and heavenly realms, the center of all creation. The Ark of the Covenant containing the commandments of God once stood here, but that was lost long ago. There is now nothing inside the sanctuary. It is a vast, empty space that serves as a conduit for the presence of God, channeling his divine spirit from the heavens, flowing it out in concentric waves across the Temple's chambers, through the Court of Priests and the Court of Israelites, the Court of Women and the Court of Gentiles, over the Temple's porticoed walls and down into the city of Jerusalem, across the Judean countryside to Samaria and Idumea, Peraea and Galilee, through the boundless empire of mighty Rome and on to the rest of the world, to all peoples and nations, all of them—Jew and gentile alike—nourished and sustained by the spirit of the Lord of Creation, a spirit that has one sole source and no other: the inner sanctuary, the Holy of Holies, tucked within the Temple, in the sacred city of Jerusalem.

Entrance to the Holy of Holies is barred to all save the high priest, who at this time, 56 C.E., is a young man named Jonathan son of Ananus. Like most of his recent predecessors, Jonathan purchased his office directly from Rome, and for a hefty price, no doubt. The office of high priest is a lucrative one, limited to a handful of noble families who pass the position between them like a legacy (the lower priests generally come from more modest backgrounds).

The role of the Temple in Jewish life cannot be overstated. The Temple serves as calendar and clock for the Jews; its rituals mark the cycle of the year and shape the day-to-day activities of every inhabitant of Jerusalem. It is the center of commerce for all Judea, its chief financial institution and largest bank. The Temple is as much the dwelling place of Israel's God as it is the seat of Israel's nationalist aspirations; it not only houses the sacred writings and scrolls of law that maintain the Jewish religion, it is the main repository for the legal documents, historical notes, and genealogical records of the Jewish nation.

Unlike their heathen neighbors, the Jews do not have a multiplicity of temples scattered across the land. There is only one cultic center, one unique source for the divine presence, one singular place and no other where a Jew can commune with the living God. Judea is, for all intents and purposes, a temple-state. The very term "theocracy" was coined specifically to describe Jerusalem. "Some people have entrusted the supreme political powers to monarchies," wrote the first-century Jewish historian Flavius Josephus, "others to oligarchies, yet others to the masses [democracy]. Our lawgiver [God], however, was attracted by none of these forms of polity, but gave to his constitution the form of what—if a forced expression be permitted—may be termed a 'theocracy' [*theokratia*], placing all sovereignty and authority in the hands of God."

Think of the Temple as a kind of feudal state, employing thousands of priests, singers, porters, servants, and ministers while maintaining vast tracts of fertile land tilled by Temple slaves on behalf of the high priest and for his benefit. Add to this the revenue raked in by the Temple tax and the constant stream of gifts and offerings from visitors and pilgrims—not to mention the huge sums that pass through the hands of the merchants and money changers, of which the Temple takes a cut—and it is easy to see why so many Jews view the entire priestly nobility, and the high priest in particular, as nothing but a band of avaricious "lovers of luxury," to quote Josephus.

Picture the high priest Jonathan standing at the altar, incense smoldering in his hand, and it is easy to see where this enmity comes from. Even his priestly garments, passed down to him by his wealthy predecessors, attest to the high priest's opulence. The long, sleeveless robe dyed purple (the color of kings) and fringed with dainty tassels and tiny golden bells sewn to the hem; the hefty breastplate, speckled with twelve precious gems, one for each of the tribes of Israel; the immaculate turban sitting upon his head like a tiara, fronted by a gold plate on which is engraved the unutterable name of God; the *urim* and *thummim*, a sort of sacred dice made of wood and bone that the high priest carries in a pouch near his breast and through which he reveals the will of God by casting lots—all of these symbols of ostentation are meant to represent the high priest's exclusive access to God. They are what make the high priest different; they set him apart from every other Jew in the world.

It is for this reason that only the high priest can enter the Holy of Holies, and on only one day a year, Yom Kippur, the Day of Atonement, when all the sins of Israel are wiped clean. On this day, the high priest comes into the presence of God to atone for the

whole nation. If he is worthy of God's blessing, Israel's sins are for-
given. If he is not, a rope tied to his waist ensures that when God
strikes him dead, he can be dragged out of the Holy of Holies
without anyone else defiling the sanctuary.

Of course, on this day, the high priest does die, though not, it
would seem, by the hand of God.

The priestly blessings complete and the *shema* sung ("Hear, O
Israel: the Lord is our God, the Lord alone!"), the high priest Jonathan steps away from the altar and walks down the ramp into the
Temple's outer courts. The moment he arrives at the Court of
Gentiles he is swallowed up by a frenzy of exaltation. The Temple
guards form a barrier of purity around him, protecting the high
priest from the contaminating hands of the masses. Yet it is easy for
the assassin to track him. He does not need to follow the blinding
glare of his bejeweled vestments. He need only listen for the jingle
of the bells dangling from the hem of his robe. The peculiar melody is the surest sign that the high priest is coming. The high
priest is near.

The assassin elbows through the crowd, pushing close enough
to Jonathan to reach out an invisible hand, to grasp the sacred vestments, to pull him away from the Temple guards and hold him in
place, just for an instant, long enough to unsheathe a short dagger
and slide it across his throat. A different sort of sacrifice.

Before the high priest's blood spills onto the Temple floor, before the guards can react to the broken rhythm of his stride, before
anyone in the courtyard knows what has happened, the assassin has
melted back into the crowd.

You should not be surprised if he is the first to cry, "Murder!"

Chapter One

A Hole in the Corner

Who killed Jonathan son of Ananus as he strode across the Temple Mount in the year 56 C.E.? No doubt there were many in Jerusalem who longed to slay the rapacious high priest, and more than a few who would have liked to wipe out the bloated Temple priesthood in its entirety. For what must never be forgotten when speaking of first-century Palestine is that this land—this hallowed land from which the spirit of God flowed to the rest of the world—was occupied territory. Legions of Roman troops were stationed throughout Judea. Some six hundred Roman soldiers resided atop the Temple Mount itself, within the high stone walls of the Antonia Fortress, which buttressed the northwest corner of the Temple wall. The unclean centurion in his red cape and polished cuirass who paraded through the Court of Gentiles, his hand hovering over the hilt of his sword, was a not so subtle reminder, if any were needed, of who really ruled this sacred place.

Roman dominion over Jerusalem began in 63 B.C.E., when Rome's master tactician, Pompey Magnus, entered the city with his conquering legions and laid siege to the Temple. By then, Jerusalem had long since passed its economic and cultural zenith. The Canaanite settlement that King David had recast into the seat of his kingdom, the city he had passed to his wayward son, Solomon, who built the first Temple to God—sacked and destroyed by the Babylonians in 586 B.C.E.—the city that had served as the religious, economic, and political capital of the Jewish nation for a thousand years, was, by the time Pompey strode through its gates, recognized less for its beauty and grandeur than for the religious fervor of its troublesome population.

Situated on the southern plateau of the shaggy Judean mountains, between the twin peaks of Mount Scopus and the Mount of Olives, and flanked by the Kidron Valley in the east and the steep, forbidding Valley of Gehenna in the south, Jerusalem, at the time of the Roman invasion, was home to a settled population of about a hundred thousand people. To the Romans, it was an inconsequential speck on the imperial map, a city the wordy statesman Cicero dismissed as "a hole in the corner." But to the Jews this was the navel of the world, the axis of the universe. There was no city more unique, more holy, more venerable in all the world than Jerusalem. The purple vineyards whose vines twisted and crawled across the level plains, the well-tilled fields and viridescent orchards bursting with almond and fig and olive trees, the green beds of papyrus floating lazily along the Jordan River—the Jews not only knew and deeply loved every feature of this consecrated land, they laid claim to all of it. Everything from the farmsteads of Galilee to the low-lying hills of Samaria and the far outskirts of Idumea, where the Bible says the accursed cities of Sodom and Gomorrah once stood, was given by God to the Jews, though in fact the Jews ruled none of it, not even Jerusalem, where the true God was worshipped. The city that the Lord had clothed in splendor and glory and placed, as the prophet Ezekiel declared, "in the center of all nations"—the eternal seat of God's kingdom on earth—was, at the dawn of the first century C.E., just a minor province, and a vexing one at that, at the far corner of the mighty Roman Empire.

It is not that Jerusalem was unaccustomed to invasion and occupation. Despite its exalted status in the hearts of the Jews, the truth is that Jerusalem was little more than a trifle to be passed among a succession of kings and emperors who took turns plundering and despoiling the sacred city on their way to far grander ambitions. In 586 B.C.E. the Babylonians—masters of Mesopotamia—rampaged through Judea, razing both Jerusalem and its Temple to the ground. The Babylonians were conquered by the Persians, who allowed the Jews to return to their beloved city and rebuild their temple, not because they admired the Jews or took their religion seriously, but because they considered Jerusalem an irrelevant backwater of little interest or concern to an empire that stretched the length of Central Asia (though the prophet Isaiah would thank the Persian king Cyrus by anointing him messiah). The Persian Empire, and Jerusalem with it, fell to the armies of Alexander the Great, whose descendants imbued the city and its inhabitants with Greek culture and ideas. Upon Alexander's untimely death in 323 B.C.E., Jerusalem was passed as spoils to the Ptolemaic dynasty and ruled from distant Egypt, though only briefly. In 198 B.C.E., the city was wrested from Ptolemaic control by the Seleucid king Antiochus the Great, whose son Antiochus Epiphanes fancied himself god incarnate and strove to put an end once and for all to the worship of the Jewish deity in Jerusalem. But the Jews responded to this blasphemy with a relentless guerrilla war led by the stouthearted sons of Mattathias the Hasmonaean—the Maccabees—who reclaimed the holy city from Seleucid control in 164 B.C.E. and, for the first time in four centuries, restored Jewish hegemony over Judea.

For the next hundred years, the Hasmonaeans ruled God's land with an iron fist. They were priest-kings, each sovereign serving as both King of the Jews and high priest of the Temple. But when civil war broke out between the brothers Hyrcanus and Aristobulus over control of the throne, each brother foolishly reached out to Rome for support. Pompey took the brothers' entreaties as an invitation to seize Jerusalem for himself, thus putting an end to the brief period of direct Jewish rule over the city of God. In 63 B.C.E.,

Judea became a Roman protectorate, and the Jews were made once again a subject people.

Roman rule, coming as it did after a century of independence, was not warmly received by the Jews. The Hasmonaean dynasty was abolished, but Pompey allowed Hyrcanus to maintain the position of high priest. That did not sit well with the supporters of Aristobulus, who launched a series of revolts to which the Romans responded with characteristic savagery—burning towns, massacring rebels, enslaving populations. Meanwhile, the chasm between the starving and indebted poor toiling in the countryside and the wealthy provincial class ruling in Jerusalem grew even wider. It was standard Roman policy to forge alliances with the landed aristocracy in every captured city, making them dependent on the Roman overlords for their power and wealth. By aligning their interests with those of the ruling class, Rome ensured that local leaders remained wholly vested in maintaining the imperial system. Of course, in Jerusalem, "landed aristocracy" more or less meant the priestly class, and specifically, that handful of wealthy priestly families who maintained the Temple and who, as a result, were charged by Rome with collecting the taxes and tribute and keeping order among the increasingly restive population—tasks for which they were richly compensated.

The fluidity that existed in Jerusalem between the religious and political powers made it necessary for Rome to maintain close supervision over the Jewish cult and, in particular, over the high priest. As head of the Sanhedrin and "leader of the nation," the high priest was a figure of both religious and political renown with the power to decide all religious matters, to enforce God's law, and even to make arrests, though only in the vicinity of the Temple. If the Romans wanted to control the Jews, they had to control the Temple. And if they wanted to control the Temple, they had to control the high priest, which is why, soon after taking control over Judea, Rome took upon itself the responsibility of appointing and deposing (either directly or indirectly) the high priest, essentially

transforming him into a Roman employee. Rome even kept custody of the high priest's sacred garments, handing them out only
on the sacred festivals and feast days and confiscating them immediately after the ceremonies were complete.

Still, the Jews were better off than some other Roman subjects.
For the most part, the Romans humored the Jews, allowing them
to conduct their rituals and sacrifices without interference. The
Jews were even excused from the direct worship of the emperor,
which Rome imposed upon nearly every other religious community under its dominion. All that Rome asked of Jerusalem was a
twice-daily sacrifice of one bull and two lambs on behalf of the
emperor and for his good health. Continue making the sacrifice,
keep up with the taxes and tribute, follow the provincial laws, and
Rome was happy to leave you, your god, and your temple alone.

The Romans were, after all, fairly proficient in the religious
beliefs and practices of subject peoples. Most of the lands they conquered were allowed to maintain their temples unmolested. Rival
gods, far from being vanquished or destroyed, were often assimi-
lated into the Roman cult (that is how, for example, the Canaanite
god Baal became associated with the Roman god Saturn). In some
cases, under a practice called *evocatio,* the Romans would take possession of an enemy's temple—and therefore its god, for the two
were inextricable in the ancient world—and transfer it to Rome,
where it would be showered with riches and lavish sacrifices. Such
displays were meant to send a clear signal that the hostilities were
directed not toward the enemy's god but toward its fighters; the
god would continue to be honored and worshipped in Rome if
only his devotees would lay down their arms and allow themselves
to be absorbed into the empire.

As generally tolerant as the Romans may have been when it
came to foreign cults, they were even more lenient toward the Jews
and their fealty to their One God—what Cicero decried as the
"barbarian superstitions" of Jewish monotheism. The Romans
may not have understood the Jewish religion, with its strange ob-

servances and its overwhelming obsession with ritual purity—"The Jews regard as profane all that we hold sacred," Tacitus wrote, "while they permit all that we abhor"—but they nevertheless tolerated it.

What most puzzled Rome about the Jews was not their unfamiliar rites or their strict devotion to their laws, but rather what the Romans considered to be their unfathomable sense of superiority. The notion that an insignificant Semitic tribe residing in a distant corner of the mighty Roman Empire demanded, and indeed received, special treatment from the emperor was, for many Romans, simply incomprehensible. How dare they consider their god to be the sole god in the universe? How dare they keep themselves separate from all other nations? Who do these backward and superstitious tribesmen think they are? The Stoic philosopher Seneca was not alone among the Roman elite in wondering how it had possibly come to pass in Jerusalem that "the vanquished have given laws to the victors."

What the Romans could not understand was that this Jewish exceptionalism was not a matter of arrogance or pride. It was a direct commandment from a jealous God who tolerated no foreign presence in the land he had set aside for his chosen people. That is why, when the Jews first came to this land a thousand years earlier, God had decreed that they massacre every man, woman, and child they encountered, that they slaughter every ox, goat, and sheep they came across, that they burn every farm, every field, every crop, every living thing without exception so as to ensure that the land would belong solely to those who worshipped this one God and no other.

"As for the towns of these people that the Lord your God is giving you as an inheritance," God told the Israelites, "you must not let anything that breathes remain alive. You shall annihilate them all—the Hittites and the Amorites, the Canaanites and the Perizzites, the Hivites and the Jebusites—just as the Lord your God has commanded" (Deuteronomy 20:17–18).

It was, the Bible claims, only after the Jewish armies had "utterly destroyed all that breathed" in the cities of Libnah and Lachish and Eglon and Hebron and Debir, in the hill country and in the Negeb, in the lowlands and in the slopes—only after every single previous inhabitant of this land was eradicated, "as the Lord God of Israel had commanded" (Joshua 10: 28–42)—that the Jews were allowed to settle here.

And yet, a thousand years later, this same tribe that had shed so much blood to cleanse the Promised Land of every foreign element so as to rule it in the name of its God now found itself laboring under the boot of an imperial pagan power, forced to share the holy city with Gauls, Spaniards, Romans, Greeks, and Syrians—all of them foreigners, all of them heathens—obligated by law to make sacrifices in God's own Temple on behalf of a Roman idolater who lived more than a thousand kilometers away.

How would the heroes of old respond to such humiliation and degradation? What would Joshua or Aaron or Phineas or Samuel do to the unbelievers who had defiled the land set aside by God for his chosen people?

They would drown the land in blood. They would smash the heads of the heathens and the gentiles, burn their idols to the ground, slaughter their wives and their children. They would slay the idolaters and bathe their feet in the blood of their enemies, just as the Lord commanded. They would call upon the God of Israel to burst forth from the heavens in his war chariot, to trample upon the sinful nations and make the mountains writhe at his fury.

As for the high priest—the wretch who betrayed God's chosen people to Rome for some coin and the right to prance about in his spangled garments? His very existence was an insult to God. It was a blight upon the entire land.

It had to be wiped away.

Chapter Two

King of the Jews

In the years of tumult that followed the Roman occupation of Judea, as Rome became enmeshed in a debilitating civil war between Pompey Magnus and his erstwhile ally Julius Caesar, even while remnants of the Hasmonaean Dynasty continued vying for the favors of both men, the situation for the Jewish farmers and peasants who harrowed and sowed God's land steadily worsened. The small family farms that for centuries had served as the primary basis of the rural economy were gradually swallowed up by large estates administered by landed aristocracies flush with freshly minted Roman coins. Rapid urbanization under Roman rule fueled mass internal migration from the countryside to the cities. The agriculture that had once sustained the meager village populations was now almost wholly focused on feeding the engorged urban centers, leaving the rural peasants hungry and destitute. The peasantry were not only obligated to continue paying their taxes and their tithes to the Temple priesthood, they were now forced to pay a heavy tribute to Rome. For farmers, the total could amount to nearly half their annual yield.

At the same time, successive droughts had left large swaths of the countryside fallow and in ruin as much of the Jewish peasantry was reduced to slavery. Those who managed to remain on their wasted fields often had no choice but to borrow heavily from the landed aristocracy, at exorbitant interest rates. Never mind that Jewish law forbade the charging of interest on loans; the massive fines that were levied on the poor for late payments had basically the same effect. In any case, the landed aristocracy expected the peasants to default on their loans; they were banking on it. For if the loan was not promptly and fully repaid, the peasant's land could be confiscated and the peasant kept on the farm as a tenant toiling on behalf of its new owner.

Within a few years after the Roman conquest of Jerusalem, an entire crop of landless peasants found themselves stripped of their property with no way to feed themselves or their families. Many of these peasants immigrated to the cities to find work. But in Galilee, a handful of displaced farmers and landowners exchanged their plows for swords and began fighting back against those they deemed responsible for their woes. From their hiding places in the caves and grottoes of the Galilean countryside, these peasant-warriors launched a wave of attacks against the Jewish aristocracy and the agents of the Roman Republic. They roamed through the provinces, gathering to themselves those in distress, those who were dispossessed and mired in debt. Like Jewish Robin Hoods, they robbed the rich and, on occasion, gave to the poor. To the faithful, these peasant gangs were nothing less than the physical embodiment of the anger and suffering of the poor. They were heroes: symbols of righteous zeal against Roman aggression, dispensers of divine justice to the traitorous Jews. The Romans had a different word for them. They called them *lestai*. Bandits.

"Bandit" was the generic term for any rebel or insurrectionist who rose up against Rome or its Jewish collaborators. To some, the word "bandit" was synonymous with "thief" or "rabble-rouser." But these were no common criminals. The bandits represented the first stirrings of what would become a nationalist resistance movement against the Roman occupation. This may have been a peasant revolt; the bandit gangs hailed from impoverished villages like Emmaus, Beth-horon, and Bethlehem. But it was something else, too. The bandits claimed to be agents of God's retribution. They cloaked their leaders in the emblems of biblical kings and heroes and presented their actions as a prelude for the restoration of God's kingdom on earth. The bandits tapped into the widespread apocalyptic expectation that had gripped the Jews of Palestine in the wake of the Roman invasion. One of the most fearsome of all the bandits, the charismatic bandit chief Hezekiah, openly declared himself to be the messiah, the promised one who would restore the Jews to glory.

Messiah means "anointed one." The title alludes to the practice of pouring or smearing oil on someone charged with divine office: a king, like Saul, or David, or Solomon; a priest, like Aaron and his sons, who were consecrated to do God's work; a prophet, like Isaiah or Elisha, who bore a special relationship with God, an intimacy that comes with being designated God's representative on earth. The messiah was popularly believed to be the descendant of King David, and so his principal task was to rebuild David's kingdom and reestablish the nation of Israel. Thus, to call oneself the messiah at the time of the Roman occupation was tantamount to declaring war on Rome. Indeed, the day would come when these angry bands of peasant gangs would form the backbone of an army of zealous revolutionaries that would force the Romans to flee Jerusalem in humiliation. In those early years of the occupation, however, the bandits were little more than a nuisance. Still, they needed to be stopped; someone had to restore order in the countryside.

That someone turned out to be a clever young Jewish nobleman from Idumea named Herod. Herod's father, Antipater, had the good fortune of being on the right side in the civil war between Pompey Magnus and Julius Caesar. Caesar rewarded Antipater for his loyalty by granting him Roman citizenship in 48 B.C.E. and giving him administrative powers on behalf of Rome over all of

Judea. Before his death a few years later, Antipater cemented his position among the Jews by appointing his sons Phasael and Herod as governors over Jerusalem and Galilee, respectively. Herod was probably only fifteen years old at the time, but he immediately distinguished himself as an effective leader and energetic supporter of Rome by launching a bloody crusade against the bandit gangs. He even captured the bandit chief Hezekiah and cut off his head, putting an end (temporarily) to the bandit menace.

While Herod was clearing Galilee of the bandit gangs, Antigonus, the son of Aristobulus, who had lost the throne and the high priesthood to his brother Hyrcanus after the Roman invasion, was stirring up trouble in Jerusalem. With the help of Rome's avowed enemies, the Parthians, Antigonus besieged the holy city in 40 B.C.E., taking both the high priest Hyrcanus and Herod's brother Phasael prisoner. Hyrcanus was mutilated, rendering him ineligible, according to Jewish law, to serve any longer as high priest; Herod's brother Phasael committed suicide while in captivity.

The Roman Senate determined that the most effective way to retake Jerusalem from Parthian control was to make Herod its client-king and let him accomplish the task on Rome's behalf. The naming of client-kings was standard practice during the early years of the Roman Empire, allowing Rome to expand its borders without expending valuable resources administering conquered provinces directly.

In 37 B.C.E., Herod marched to Jerusalem with a massive Roman army under his command. He expelled the Parthian forces from the city and wiped out the remnants of the Hasmonaean dynasty. In recognition of his services, Rome named Herod "King of the Jews," granting him a kingdom that would ultimately grow larger than that of King Solomon.

Herod's was a profligate and tyrannical rule marked by farcical excess and bestial acts of cruelty. He was ruthless to his enemies and tolerated no hint of revolt from the Jews under his reign. Upon ascending the throne, he massacred nearly every member of the Sanhedrin and replaced the Temple priests with a claque of fawning admirers who purchased their positions directly from him. This act effectively neutered the political influence of the Temple and redistributed power to a new class of Jews whose reliance on the favors of the king transformed them into a sort of nouveau riche aristocracy. Herod's penchant for violence and his highly publicized domestic disputes, which bordered on the burlesque, led him to execute so many members of his own family that Caesar Augustus once famously quipped, "I would rather be Herod's pig than his son."

In truth, being King of the Jews in Herod's time was no enviable task. There were, according to Josephus, twenty-four fractious Jewish sects in and around Jerusalem. Although none enjoyed unfettered dominance over the others, three sects, or rather *schools,* were particularly influential in shaping Jewish thought at the time: the Pharisees, who were primarily lower- and middle-class rabbis and scholars who interpreted the laws for the masses; the Sadducees, more conservative and, with regard to Rome, more accommodating priests from wealthier landowning families; and the Essenes, a predominantly priestly movement that separated itself from the authority of the Temple and made its base on a barren hilltop in the Dead Sea valley called Qumran.

Charged with pacifying and administering an unruly and heterogeneous population of Jews, Greeks, Samaritans, Syrians, and Arabs—all of whom hated him more than they hated each other—Herod did a masterful job of maintaining order on behalf of Rome. His reign ushered in an era of political stability among the Jews that had not been seen for centuries. He initiated a monumental building and public works project that employed tens of thousands of peasants and day laborers, permanently changing the physical landscape of Jerusalem. He built markets and theaters, palaces and ports, all modeled on the classical Hellenic style.

To pay for his colossal construction projects and to satisfy his own extravagance, Herod imposed a crushing tax rate upon his subjects, from which he continued to dispatch a hefty tribute to Rome, and with pleasure, as an expression of his esteem for his Roman masters. Herod was not just the emperor's client-king. He was a close and personal friend, a loyal citizen of the Republic who wanted more than to emulate Rome; he wanted to remake it in the sands of Judea. He instituted a forced Hellenization program upon the Jews, bringing gymnasia, Greek amphitheaters, and Roman baths to Jerusalem. He made Greek the language of his court and minted coins bearing Greek letters and pagan insignia.

Yet Herod was also a Jew, and as such he understood the importance of appealing to the religious sensibilities of his subjects. That is why he embarked on his most ambitious project: the rebuilding and expansion of the Temple of Jerusalem. It was Herod who had the Temple raised on a platform atop Mount Moriah—the highest point in the city—and embellished with wide Roman colonnades and towering marble columns that gleamed in the sun. Herod's Temple was meant to impress his patrons in Rome, but he also wanted to please his fellow Jews, many of whom did not consider the King of the Jews to be himself a Jew. Herod was a convert, after all. His mother was an Arab. His people, the Idumeans, had come to Judaism only a generation or two earlier. The rebuilding of the Temple was, for Herod, not only a means of solidifying his political dominance; it was a desperate plea for acceptance by his Jewish subjects.

It did not work.

Despite the rebuilding of the Temple, Herod's unabashed Hellenism and his aggressive attempts to "Romanize" Jerusalem enraged pious Jews who seem never to have ceased viewing their king as a slave to foreign masters and a devotee of foreign gods. Not even the Temple, the supreme symbol of Jewish identity, could mask Herod's infatuation with Rome. Shortly before its completion, Herod placed a golden eagle—the sign of Roman dominion—over its main portal and forced his handpicked high priest to offer two sacrifices a day on behalf of Caesar Augustus as "the Son of God." Nevertheless, it is a sign of how firmly Herod held his kingdom in his grip that the general odium of the Jews toward his reign never rose to the level of insurrection, at least not in his lifetime.

When Herod the Great died in 4 B.C.E., Augustus split his realm among his three sons: Archelaus was given Judea, Samaria, and Idumea; Herod Antipas—known as "the Fox"—reigned over Galilee and Peraea (a region in the Transjordan northeast of the Dead Sea); and Philip was handed control over Gaulanitis (modern day Golan) and the lands northeast of the Sea of Galilee. None of Herod's three sons were given the title of king: Antipas and Philip were each named *tetrarch,* meaning "ruler of a quarter," and Archelaus was named *ethnarch,* or "ruler of a people"; both titles were deliberately meant to signal the end of unified kingship over the Jews.

The division of Herod's kingdom proved a disaster for Rome, as the dam of anger and resentment that had been built during his long and oppressive reign burst into a flood of riots and violent protests that his nebbish sons, dulled by a life of idleness and languor, could hardly contain. The rioters burned down one of Herod's palaces on the Jordan River. Twice, the Temple itself was overrun: first during Passover, then again at Shavuot or the Festival of Weeks. In the countryside, the bandit gangs that Herod had beaten into submission once again began tearing through Galilee, slaughtering the former king's associates. In Idumea, Herod's home region, two thousand of his soldiers mutinied. Even Herod's allies, including his own cousin Achiab, joined the rebellion.

These uprisings were no doubt fueled by the messianic expectations of the Jews. In Peraea, a former slave of Herod's—an imposing giant of a man named Simon—crowned himself messiah and rallied together a group of bandits to plunder the royal palaces at Jericho. The rebellion ended when Simon was captured and beheaded. A short while later, another messianic aspirant, a poor shepherd boy named Athronges, placed a crown upon his head and launched a foolhardy attack against Roman forces. He, too, was caught and executed.

The chaos and bloodshed continued unabated until Caesar Augustus finally ordered his own troops into Judea to put an end to the uprising. Although the emperor allowed Philip and Antipas to remain in their posts, he sent Archelaus into exile, placed Jerusalem under a Roman governor, and, in the year 6 C.E., transformed all of Judea into a province ruled directly by Rome. There would be no more semi-independence. No more client-kings. No more King of the Jews. Jerusalem now belonged wholly to Rome.

According to tradition, Herod the Great died on the eve of Passover in 4 B.C.E., at the ripe age of seventy, having reigned over the Jews for thirty-seven years. Josephus writes that on the day of Herod's death, there was an eclipse of the moon, an inauspicious sign, perhaps presaging the tumult that would follow. There is, of course, another tradition told about the demise of Herod the Great: that sometime between his death in 4 B.C.E. and the Roman takeover of Judea in 6 C.E., in an obscure hillside village in Galilee, a child was born who would one day claim for himself Herod's mantle as King of the Jews.

Chapter Three

You Know Where I Am From

Ancient Nazareth rests on the jagged brow of a windy hilltop in lower Galilee. No more than a hundred Jewish families live in this tiny village. There are no roads, no public buildings. There is no synagogue. The villagers share a single well from which to draw fresh water. A single bath, fed by a trickle of rainfall captured and stored in underground cisterns, serves the entire population. It is a village of mostly illiterate peasants, farmers, and day laborers; a place that does not exist on any map.

The homes in Nazareth are simple affairs: a single windowless room, divided in two—one room for the family, the other for the livestock—made of whitewashed mud and stone and crowned with a flat-topped roof where the householders gather to pray, where they lay out their wash to dry, where they take their meals on temperate evenings, and where, in the hot summer months, they roll out their dusty mats and sleep. The lucky inhabitants have a courtyard and a tiny patch of soil to grow vegetables, for no matter their occupation or skill, every Nazarean is a farmer. The peasants who call this secluded village home are, without exception, cultivators of the land. It is agriculture that feeds and sustains the meager population. Everyone raises their own livestock, everyone plants their own crops: a bit of barley, some wheat, a few stalks of millet and oats. The manure collected from the animals feeds the earth, which in turn feeds the villagers, who then feed the livestock. Self-sufficiency is the rule.

The hillside hamlet of Nazareth is so small, so obscure, that its name does not appear in any ancient Jewish source before the third century C.E.—not in the Hebrew Bible, not in the Talmud, not in the Midrash, not in Josephus. It is, in short, an inconsequential and utterly forgettable place. It is also the city in which Jesus was likely born and raised. That he came from this tightly enclosed village of a few hundred impoverished Jews may very well be the only fact concerning Jesus's childhood about which we can be fairly confident. So identified was Jesus with Nazareth that he was known throughout his life simply as "the Nazarean." Considering how common a first name Jesus (Yeshua) was, the city of his birth became his principal sobriquet. It was the one thing about which everyone who knew him—his friends and his enemies alike—seemed to agree.

Why, then, do Matthew and Luke—and *only* Matthew (2:1–9) and Luke (2:1–21)—claim that Jesus was born not in Nazareth but in Bethlehem, even though the name Bethlehem does not appear anywhere else in the entire New Testament (not even anywhere else in Matthew or Luke, both of which repeatedly refer to Jesus as "the Nazarean"), save for a single verse in the gospel of John (7:42)?

The answer may be found in that verse from John.

It was, the evangelist writes, early in Jesus's ministry. Up to this point, Jesus had, for the most part, restricted himself to preaching his message to the poor farmers and fishermen of Galilee—his friends and neighbors. But now that the Feast of Tabernacles has arrived, Jesus's family urge him to travel with them to Judea to celebrate the joyous harvest festival together, and to reveal himself to the masses.

"Come," they say. "Show yourself to the world."

Jesus refuses. "You go," he tells them. "I am not going to this festival. It is not yet my time."

Jesus's family leave him behind and head off to Judea together. Yet, unbeknownst to them, Jesus decides to follow them down to Judea after all, if for no other reason than to secretly roam through the assembled crowd and hear what people are saying about him.

"He is a good man," someone whispers.

"No. He is leading the people astray," says another.

Sometime later, after Jesus has revealed himself to the crowd, a few begin to make guesses about his identity. "Surely, he is a prophet."

And then someone finally says it. Everyone is clearly thinking it; how could they not be, what with Jesus standing tall amid the crowd declaring, "Let he who thirsts come to me and drink?" How are they to understand such heretical words? Who else would dare say such a thing openly and within earshot of the scribes and the teachers of the law, many of whom, we are told, would like nothing more than to silence and arrest this irksome preacher?

"This man is the messiah!"

This is no simple declaration. It is, in fact, an act of treason. In first-century Palestine, simply saying the words "This is the messiah," aloud and in public, can be a criminal offense, punishable by crucifixion. True, the Jews of Jesus's time had somewhat conflicting views about the role and function of the messiah, fed by a score of messianic traditions and popular folktales that were floating around the Holy Land. Some believed the messiah would be a restorative figure who would return the Jews to their previous position of power and glory. Others viewed the messiah in more apocalyptic and utopian terms, as someone who would annihilate the present world and build a new, more just world upon its ruins. There were those who thought the messiah would be a king, and those who thought he'd be a priest. The Essenes apparently awaited two separate messiahs—one kingly, the other priestly—though most Jews thought of the messiah as possessing a combination of both traits. Nevertheless, among the crowd of Jews gathered for the Feast of Tabernacles, there seems to have been a fair consensus about who the messiah is supposed to be and what the messiah is supposed to do: he is the descendant of King David; he comes to restore Israel, to free the Jews from the yoke of occupation, and to establish God's rule in Jerusalem. To call Jesus the messiah, there- fore, is to place him inexorably upon a path—already well trodden by a host of failed messiahs who came before him—toward con- flict, revolution, and war against the prevailing powers. Where that path would ultimately lead, no one at the festival could know for sure. But there was some sense of where the path must begin.

"Does not the scripture say that the messiah is of David's seed?" someone in the crowd asks. "That he comes from the village where David lived? From Bethlehem?"

"But we know where this man comes from," claims another. Indeed, the crowd seems to know Jesus well. They know his broth- ers, who are there with him. His entire family is present. They traveled to the festival together from their home in Galilee. From Nazareth.

"Look into it," says a Pharisee with the confidence that comes from a lifetime of scrutinizing the scriptures. "You will see: the prophet does not come out of Galilee."

Jesus does not dispute their claim. "Yes, you all know me," he admits. "And you know where I am from." Instead, he deflects the matter of his earthly home entirely, choosing instead to empha- size his heavenly origins. "I have not come here on my own; the one who sent me is true. And he, you do not know. But I know him. I am from him. He is the one who sent me" (John 7:1–29).

Such statements are commonplace in John, the last of the four canonized gospels, composed between 100 and 120 C.E. John shows no interest at all in Jesus's physical birth, though even he acknowledges that Jesus was a "Nazarean" (John 18:5–7). In John's view, Jesus is an eternal being, the *logos* who was with God from the beginning of time, the primal force through whom all creation sprang and without whom nothing came into being (John 1:3).

A similar lack of concern about Jesus's earthly origins can be found in the first gospel, Mark, written just after 70 C.E. Mark's focus is kept squarely on Jesus's ministry; he is uninterested either in Jesus's birth or, perhaps surprisingly, in Jesus's resurrection, as he writes nothing at all about either event.

The early Christian community appears not to have been particularly concerned about any aspect of Jesus's life before the launch of his ministry. Stories about his birth and childhood are conspicuously absent from the earliest written documents. The Q material, which was compiled around 50 C.E., makes no mention of anything that happened before Jesus's baptism by John the Baptist. The letters of Paul, which make up the bulk of the New Testament, are wholly detached from any event in Jesus's life save his crucifixion and resurrection (though Paul does mention the Last Supper).

But as interest in the person of Jesus increased after his death, an urgent need arose among some in the early Christian community to fill in the gaps of Jesus's early years and, in particular, to address the matter of his birth in Nazareth, which seems to have been used by his Jewish detractors to prove that Jesus could not possibly have been the messiah, at least not according to the prophecies. Some kind of creative solution was required to push back against this criticism, some means to get Jesus's parents to Bethlehem so that he could be born in the same city as David.

For Luke, the answer lies in a census. "In those days," he writes, "there came a decree from Caesar Augustus that the entire Roman world should be registered. This was the first registration to take place while Quirinius was governor of Syria. Everyone went to his own town to be registered. Joseph also went up from the town of Nazareth in Galilee to Judea, to Bethlehem, the city of David." Then, in case his readers may have missed the point, Luke adds, "because Joseph belonged to the house and the lineage of David" (Luke 2:1–4).

Luke is right about one thing and one thing only. Ten years after the death of Herod the Great, in the year 6 C.E., when Judea officially became a Roman province, the Syrian governor, Quirinius, did call for a census to be taken of all the people, property, and slaves in Judea, Samaria, and Idumea—not "the entire Roman world," as Luke claims, and definitely not Galilee, where Jesus's family lived (Luke is also wrong to associate Quirinius's census in 6 C.E. with the birth of Jesus, which most scholars place closer to 4 B.C.E., the year given in the gospel of Matthew). However, because the sole purpose of a census was taxation, Roman law assessed an individual's property in the place of residence, not in the place of one's birth. There is nothing written in any Roman document of the time (and the Romans were quite adept at documentation, particularly when it came to taxation) to indicate otherwise. Luke's suggestion that the entire Roman economy would periodically be placed on hold as every Roman subject was forced to uproot himself and his entire family in order to travel great distances to the place of his father's birth, and then wait there patiently, perhaps for months, for an official to take stock of his family and his possessions, which, in any case, he would have left behind in his place of residence, is, in a word, preposterous.

What is important to understand about Luke's infancy narrative is that his readers, still living under Roman dominion, would have known that Luke's account of Quirinius's census was factually inaccurate. Luke himself, writing a little more than a generation after the events he describes, knew that what he was writing was technically false. This is an extremely difficult matter for modern readers of the gospels to grasp, but Luke never meant for his story about Jesus's birth at Bethlehem to be understood as historical fact. Luke would have had no idea what we in the modern world even mean when we say the word "history." The notion of history as a critical analysis of observable and verifiable events in the past is a product of the modern age; it would have been an altogether foreign concept to the gospel writers for whom history was not a matter of uncovering *facts,* but of revealing *truths.*

The readers of Luke's gospel, like most people in the ancient world, did not make a sharp distinction between myth and reality; the two were intimately tied together in their spiritual experience. That is to say, they were less interested in what actually happened than in what it meant. It would have been perfectly normal—indeed, expected—for a writer in the ancient world to tell tales of gods and heroes whose fundamental facts would have been recognized as false but whose underlying message would be seen as true.

Hence, Matthew's equally fanciful account of Jesus's flight into Egypt, ostensibly to escape Herod's massacre of all the sons born in and around Bethlehem in a fruitless search for the baby Jesus, an event for which there exists not a shred of corroborating evidence in any chronicle or history of the time whether Jewish, Christian, or Roman—a remarkable fact considering the many chronicles and narratives written about Herod the Great, who was, after all, the most famous Jew in the whole of the Roman Empire (the King of the Jews, no less!).

As with Luke's account of Quirinius's census, Matthew's account of Herod's massacre was not intended to be read as what we would now consider *history,* certainly not by his own community, who would surely have remembered an event as unforgettable as the massacre of its own sons. Matthew needs Jesus to come out of Egypt for the same reason he needs him to be born in Bethlehem: to fulfill the scattered prophecies left behind by his ancestors for him and his fellow Jews to decipher, to place Jesus in the footsteps of the kings and prophets who came before him, and, most of all, to answer the challenge made by Jesus's detractors that this simple peasant who died without fulfilling the single most important of the messianic prophecies—the restoration of Israel—was in fact the "anointed one."

The problem faced by Matthew and Luke is that there is simply no single, cohesive prophetic narrative concerning the messiah in the Hebrew Scriptures. The passage from the gospel of John quoted above is a perfect example of the general confusion that existed among the Jews when it came to the messianic prophecies. For even as the scribes and teachers of the law confidently proclaim that Jesus could not be the messiah because he is not, as the prophecies demand, from Bethlehem, others in the crowd argue that the Nazarean could not be the messiah because the prophecies say "When the messiah comes, no one will know where he is from" (John 7:27).

The truth is that the prophecies say *both* things. In fact, were one to take the advice given to the festival crowd by the skeptical Pharisee and "look into it," one would discover a host of contradictory prophecies about the messiah, collected over hundreds of years by dozens of different hands. A great many of these prophecies are not even actually prophecies. Prophets such as Micah, Amos, and Jeremiah, who appear to be predicting the coming of a future salvific character from the line of King David that would one day restore Israel to its former glory, are in fact making veiled criticisms of their *current* king and the *present* order, which the prophets imply have fallen short of the Davidic ideal. (There is, however, one thing about which all the prophecies seem to agree: the messiah is a human being, not divine. The idea of a divine messiah is anathema to Judaism, which is why, without exception, every text in the Hebrew Bible dealing with the messiah presents him as performing his messianic functions on earth, not in heaven.) So then, if you wish to fit your preferred messianic candidate into this jumbled prophetic tradition, you must first decide which of the many texts, oral traditions, popular stories, and folktales you want to consider. How you answer that question depends largely on what it is you want to say about your messiah.

Matthew has Jesus flee to Egypt to escape Herod's massacre not because it happened, but because it fulfills the words of the prophet Hosea: "Out of Egypt I have called my son" (Hosea 11:1). The story is not meant to reveal any fact about Jesus; it is meant to reveal this truth: that Jesus is the new Moses, who survived Pharaoh's massacre of the Israelites' sons, and emerged from Egypt with a new law from God (Exodus 1:22).

Luke places Jesus's birth in Bethlehem not because it took place there, but because of the words of the prophet Micah: "And you Bethlehem . . . from you shall come to me a ruler in Israel" (Micah 5:2). Luke means that Jesus is the new David, the King of the Jews, placed on God's throne to rule over the Promised Land. Simply put, the infancy narratives in the gospels are not historical accounts, nor were they meant to be read as such. They are theological affirmations of Jesus's status as the anointed of God. The descendant of King David. The promised messiah.

That Jesus—the eternal *logos* from whom creation sprang, the Christ who sits at the right hand of God—you will find swaddled in a filthy manger in Bethlehem, surrounded by simple shepherds and wise men bearing gifts from the east.

But the real Jesus—the poor Jewish peasant who was born some time between 4 B.C.E. and 6 C.E. in the rough-and-tumble Galilean countryside—look for him in the crumbling mud and loose brick homes tucked within the windswept hamlet of Nazareth.

Chapter Four

The Fourth Philosophy

Here is what we know about Nazareth at the time of Jesus's birth: there was little there for a woodworker to do. That is, after all, what tradition claims was Jesus's occupation: a *tekton*—a woodworker or builder—though it bears mentioning that there is only one verse in the whole of the New Testament in which this claim about him is made (Mark 6:3). If that claim is true, then as an artisan and day laborer, Jesus would have belonged to the lowest class of peasants in first-century Palestine, just above the indigent, the beggar, and the slave. The Romans used the term *tekton* as slang for any uneducated or illiterate peasant, and Jesus was very likely both.

Illiteracy rates in first-century Palestine were staggeringly high, particularly for the poor. It is estimated that nearly 97 percent of the Jewish peasantry could neither read nor write, a not unexpected figure for predominantly oral societies such as the one in which Jesus lived. Certainly the Hebrew Scriptures played a prominent role in the lives of the Jewish people. But the overwhelming majority of Jews in Jesus's time would have had a rudimentary grasp of Hebrew, enough to understand the scriptures when they were read to them at the synagogue. Hebrew was the language of the scribes and scholars of the law—the language of learning. Peasants like Jesus would have had enormous difficulty communicating in Hebrew, even in its colloquial form, which is why much of the scriptures had been translated into Aramaic, the primary language of the Jewish peasantry: the language of Jesus. It is possible that Jesus had some basic knowledge of Greek, the lingua franca of the Roman Empire (ironically, Latin was the language least used in the lands occupied by Rome), enough perhaps to negotiate contracts and deal with customers, but certainly not enough to preach. The only Jews who could communicate comfortably in Greek were the Hellenized Herodian elite, the priestly aristocracy in Judea, and the more educated Diaspora Jews, not the peasants and day laborers of Galilee.

Whatever languages Jesus may have spoken, there is no reason to think he could read or write in any of them, not even Aramaic. Luke's account of the twelve-year-old Jesus standing in the Temple of Jerusalem debating the finer points of the Hebrew Scriptures with rabbis and scribes (Luke 2:42–52), or his narrative of Jesus at the (nonexistent) synagogue in Nazareth reading from the Isaiah scroll to the astonishment of the Pharisees (Luke 4:16–22), are both fabulous concoctions of the evangelist's own devising. Jesus would not have had access to the kind of formal education necessary to make Luke's account even remotely credible. There were no schools in Nazareth for peasant children to attend. What education Jesus did receive would have come directly from his family and, considering his status as an artisan and day laborer, it would have been almost exclusively focused on learning the trade of his father and his brothers.

That Jesus *had* brothers is, despite the Catholic doctrine of his mother Mary's perpetual virginity, virtually indisputable. It is a fact attested to repeatedly by both the gospels and the letters of Paul. Even Josephus references Jesus's brother James, who would become the most important leader of the early Christian church after Jesus's death. There is no rational argument that can be made against the notion that Jesus was part of a large family that included at least four brothers who are named in the gospels—James, Joseph, Simon, and Judas—and an unknown number of sisters who, while mentioned in the gospels, are unfortunately not named.

Far less is known about Jesus's father, Joseph, who quickly disappears from the gospels after the infancy narratives. The consensus is that Joseph died while Jesus was still a child. But there are those who believe that Joseph never actually existed, that he was a creation of Matthew and Luke—the only two evangelists who mention him—to account for a far more contentious creation: the virgin birth.

On the one hand, the fact that both Matthew and Luke recount the virgin birth in their respective infancy narratives, despite the belief that they were completely unaware of each other's work, indicates that the tradition of the virgin birth was an early one, perhaps predating the first gospel, Mark. On the other hand, outside of Matthew and Luke's infancy narratives, the virgin birth is never even hinted at by anyone else in the New Testament: not by the evangelist John, who presents Jesus as an otherworldly spirit without earthly origins, nor by Paul, who thinks of Jesus as literally God incarnate. That absence has led to a great deal of speculation among scholars over whether the story of the virgin birth was invented to mask an uncomfortable truth about Jesus's parentage—namely, that he was born out of wedlock.

This is in actuality an old argument, one made by opponents of the Jesus movement from its earliest days. The second-century writer Celsus recounts a scurrilous story he claims to have heard from a Palestinian Jew that Jesus's mother was impregnated by a soldier named Panthera. Celsus's story is so clearly polemical that it cannot be taken seriously. However, it does indicate that, less than a hundred years after Jesus's death, rumors about his illegitimate birth were already circulating throughout Palestine. Such rumors may have been current even in Jesus's lifetime. When Jesus first begins preaching in his hometown of Nazareth, he is confronted with the murmuring of neighbors, one of whom bluntly asks, "Is this not Mary's son?" (Mark 6:3). This is an astonishing statement, one that cannot be easily dismissed. Calling a first-born Jewish male in Palestine by his mother's name—that is, Jesus *bar Mary,* instead of Jesus *bar Joseph*—is not just unusual, it is egregious. At the very least it is a deliberate slur with implications so obvious that later redactions of Mark were compelled to insert the phrase "son of the carpenter, and Mary" into the verse.

An even more contentious mystery about Jesus involves his marital status. Although there is no evidence in the New Testament to indicate whether Jesus was married, it would have been almost unthinkable for a thirty-year-old Jewish male in Jesus's time not to have a wife. Celibacy was an extremely rare phenomenon in first-century Palestine. A handful of sects such as the aforementioned Essenes and another called the Therapeutae practiced celibacy, but these were quasimonastic orders; they not only refused to marry, they completely divorced themselves from society. Jesus did nothing of the sort. Yet while it may be tempting to assume that Jesus was married, one cannot ignore the fact that nowhere in all the words ever written about Jesus of Nazareth—from the canonical gospels to the gnostic gospels to the letters of Paul or even the Jewish and pagan polemics written against him—is there ever any mention of a wife or children.

In the end, it is simply impossible to say much about Jesus's early life in Nazareth. That is because before Jesus was declared messiah, it did not matter what kind of childhood a Jewish peasant from an insignificant hamlet in Galilee may or may not have had. After Jesus was declared messiah, the only aspects of his infancy and childhood that did matter were those that could be creatively imagined to buttress whatever theological claim one was trying to make about Jesus's identity as Christ. For better or worse, the only access one can have to the real Jesus comes not from the stories that were told about him after his death, but rather from the smattering of facts we can gather from his life as part of a large Jewish family of woodworkers/builders struggling to survive in the small Galilean village of Nazareth.

The problem with Nazareth is that it was a city of mud and brick. Even the most elaborate buildings, such as they were, would have been constructed of stone. There were wooden beams in the roofs, and surely the doors would have been made of wood. A handful of Nazareans may have been able to afford wooden furniture—a table, some stools—and perhaps a few could have owned wooden yokes and plows with which to sow their meager plots of land. But even if one considers *tekton* to mean an artisan who deals in any aspect of the building trade, the hundred or so impoverished families of a modest and utterly forgettable village such as Nazareth, most of whom themselves lived barely above subsistence level, could in no way have sustained Jesus's family. As with most artisans and day laborers, Jesus and his brothers would have had to go to bigger towns or cities to ply their trade. Fortunately, Nazareth was just a short walk from one of the largest and most affluent cities in Galilee—the capital city, Sepphoris.

Sepphoris was a sophisticated urban metropolis, as rich as Nazareth was poor. Whereas Nazareth had not a single paved road, the roads in Sepphoris were wide avenues surfaced with polished slabs of stone and lined with two-story homes boasting open courtyards and private rock-cut cisterns. The Nazareans shared a single public bath. In Sepphoris, two separate aqueducts merged in the center of the city, providing ample water to the large lavish baths and public latrines that served nearly the entire population of some forty thousand inhabitants. There were Roman villas and palatial mansions in Sepphoris, some covered in colorful mosaics featuring sprightly nudes hunting fowl, garlanded women bearing baskets of fruit, young boys dancing and playing musical instruments. A Roman theater in the center of town seated forty-five hundred people, while an intricate web of roads and trade routes connected Sepphoris to Judea and the rest of the towns of Galilee, making the city a major hub of culture and commerce.

Although Sepphoris was a predominantly Jewish city, as evidenced by the synagogues and ritual bath houses that have been unearthed there, these were a wholly different class of Jews than those found in much of Galilee. Rich, cosmopolitan, deeply influenced by Greek culture, and surrounded by a panoply of races and religions, the Jews of Sepphoris were the product of the Herodian social revolution—the nouveaux riches who rose to prominence after Herod's massacre of the old priestly aristocracy. The city itself had been a major landmark for years; after Jerusalem, it is the most frequently mentioned city in rabbinic literature. Sepphoris served as the administrative center of Galilee throughout the Hasmonaean Dynasty. During the reign of Herod the Great, it became a vital military outpost where weapons and war provisions were stored. However, it was not until Herod's son Antipas ("the Fox") chose it as the royal seat of his tetrarchy, probably sometime around the turn of the first century C.E., that the stalwart city of Sepphoris became known throughout Palestine as "the Ornament of Galilee."

Like his father, Antipas had a passion for large-scale building projects, and in Sepphoris he found a blank slate upon which to design a city in his own image. That is because when Antipas arrived at Sepphoris with a cohort of Roman soldiers in tow, the city was no longer the central hub of Galilee it had been under his father's rule. It was a still smoldering heap of ash and stone, a victim of Roman retribution for the rebellions that had broken out across Palestine in the wake of Herod the Great's death in 4 B.C.E.

When Herod died, he left behind far more than a seething populace eager to exact revenge on his friends and allies. He also left a mob of jobless poor who had flooded into Jerusalem from the rural villages to build his palaces and theaters. Herod's monumental building spree, and especially his Temple expansion project, had employed tens of thousands of peasants and day laborers, many of whom had been driven off their land by drought or famine or, often enough, the malevolent persistence of the debt collector. But

with the end of the building boom in Jerusalem and the completion of the Temple shortly before Herod's death, these peasants
and day laborers suddenly found themselves unemployed and cast
out of the holy city to fend for themselves. As a result of the mass
rustication, the countryside once again became a hotbed of revolutionary activity, just as it had been before Herod was declared
king.

It was around this time that a new and far more fearsome group
of bandits arose in Galilee, led by a magnetic teacher and revolutionary known as Judas the Galilean. The traditions say that Judas
was the son of the famed bandit chief Hezekiah, the failed messiah
whom Herod had captured and beheaded forty years earlier as part
of his campaign to clear the countryside of the bandit menace.
After Herod's death, Judas the Galilean joined forces with a mysterious Pharisee named Zaddok to launch a wholly new independence movement that Josephus terms the "Fourth Philosophy," so
as to differentiate it from the other three "philosophies": the Pharisees, the Sadducees, and the Essenes. What set the members of the
Fourth Philosophy apart from the rest was their unshakable commitment to freeing Israel from foreign rule and their fervent insistence, even unto death, that they would serve no lord save the One
God. There was a well-defined term for this type of belief, one
that all pious Jews, regardless of their political stance, would have
recognized and proudly claimed for themselves: *zeal*.

Zeal implied a strict adherence to the Torah and the Law, a refusal to serve any foreign master—to serve any human master at
all—and an uncompromising devotion to the sovereignty of God.
To be zealous for the Lord was to walk in the blazing footsteps of
the prophets and heroes of old, men and women who tolerated no
partner to God, who would bow to no king save the King of the
World, and who dealt ruthlessly with idolatry and with those who
transgressed God's law. The very land of Israel was claimed through
zeal, for it was the zealous warriors of God who cleansed it of all
foreigners and idolaters, just as God demanded. "Whoever sacri-

fices to any god but the Lord alone shall be utterly annihilated"
(Exodus 22:20).

Many Jews in first-century Palestine strove to live a life of zeal,
each in his or her own way. But there were some who, in order to
preserve their zealous ideals, were willing to resort to extreme acts
of violence if necessary, not just against the Romans and the uncircumcised masses, but against their fellow Jews, those who dared
submit to Rome. They were called *zealots*.

These zealots should not be confused with the Zealot Party
that would arise sixty years later, after the Jewish Revolt in 66 C.E.
During Jesus's lifetime, zealotry did not signify a firm sectarian
designation or political party. It was an idea, an aspiration, a model
of piety inextricably linked to the widespread sense of apocalyptic
expectation that had seized the Jews in the wake of the Roman
occupation. There was a feeling, particularly among the peasants
and the pious poor, that the present order was coming to an end,
that a new and divinely inspired order was about to reveal itself.
The Kingdom of God was at hand. Everyone was talking about it.
But God's reign could only be ushered in by those with the *zeal* to
fight for it.

Such ideas had existed long before Judas the Galilean came
along. But Judas was perhaps the first revolutionary leader to fuse
banditry and zealotry into a single revolutionary force, making resistance to Rome a religious duty incumbent on all Jews. It was
Judas's fierce determination to do whatever it took to free the Jews
from foreign rule and cleanse the land in the name of Israel's God
that made the Fourth Philosophy a model of zealous resistance for
the numerous apocalyptic revolutionaries who would, a few decades later, join forces to expel the Romans from the Holy Land.

In 4 B.C.E., with Herod the Great dead and buried, Judas and his
small army of zealots made a daring assault on the city of Sepphoris. They broke open the city's royal armory and seized for themselves the weapons and provisions that were stored inside. Now
fully armed and joined by a number of sympathetic Sepphoreans,

the members of the Fourth Philosophy launched a guerrilla war throughout Galilee, plundering the homes of the wealthy and powerful, setting villages ablaze, and meting out the justice of God upon the Jewish aristocracy and those who continued to pledge their loyalty to Rome.

The movement grew in size and ferocity throughout the following decade of violence and instability. Then, in the year 6 C.E., when Judea officially became a Roman province and the Syrian governor, Quirinius, called for a census to tally, register, and properly tax the people and property in the newly acquired region, the members of the Fourth Philosophy seized their opportunity. They used the census to make a final appeal to the Jews to stand with them against Rome and fight for their freedom. The census, they argued, was an abomination. It was affirmation of the slavery of the Jews. To be voluntarily tallied like sheep was, in Judas's view, tantamount to declaring allegiance to Rome. It was an admission that the Jews were not the chosen tribe of God but the personal property of the emperor.

It was not the census itself that so enraged Judas and his followers; it was the very notion of paying any tax or tribute to Rome. What more obvious sign was needed of the subservience of the Jews? The tribute was particularly offensive as it implied that the land belonged to Rome, not God. Indeed, the payment of tribute became, for the zealots, a test of piety and allegiance to God. Simply put, if you thought it lawful to pay tribute to Caesar, then you were a traitor and apostate. You deserved to die.

Inadvertently helping Judas's cause was the bumbling high priest at the time, a Roman lackey named Joazar, who happily went along with Quirinius's census and encouraged his fellow Jews to do the same. The collusion of the high priest was all the proof Judas and his followers needed that the Temple itself had been defiled and must be forcibly rescued from the sinful hands of the priestly aristocracy. As far as Judas's zealots were concerned, Joazar's acceptance of the census was his death warrant. The fate of the

Jewish nation depended on killing the high priest. Zeal demanded it. Just as the sons of Mattathias "showed zeal for the law" by killing those Jews who sacrificed to any but God (Maccabees 2:19–28), just as Josiah, King of Judah, butchered every uncircumcised man in his land because of his "zeal for the Mighty One" (2 Baruch 66:5), so now must these zealots turn back the wrath of God upon Israel by ridding the land of treasonous Jews like the high priest.

It is clear from the fact that the Romans removed the high priest Joazar from his post not long after he had encouraged the Jews to obey the census that Judas won the argument. Josephus, who has very little positive to say about Judas the Galilean (he calls him a "sophist," a pejorative that to Josephus signifies a trouble-maker, a disturber of the peace, a deceiver of the young), notes somewhat cryptically that Joazar was "overpowered" by the argument of the zealots.

Josephus's problem with Judas seems not to have been his "sophistry" or his use of violence, but rather what he derisively calls Judas's "royal aspirations." What Josephus means is that in fighting against the subjugation of the Jews and preparing the way for the establishment of God's reign on earth, Judas, like his father Hezekiah before him, was claiming for himself the mantle of the messiah, the throne of King David. And, like his father before him, Judas would pay the price for his ambition.

Not long after he led the charge against the census, Judas the Galilean was captured by Rome and killed. As retribution for the city's having given up its arms to Judas's followers, the Romans marched to Sepphoris and burned it to the ground. The men were slaughtered, the women and children auctioned off as slaves. More than two thousand rebels and sympathizers were crucified en masse. A short time later, Herod Antipas arrived and immediately set to work transforming the flattened ruins of Sepphoris into an extravagant royal city fit for a king.

Jesus of Nazareth was likely born the same year that Judas the Galilean—Judas the failed messiah, son of Hezekiah the failed messiah—rampaged through the countryside, burning with zeal. He would have been about ten years old when the Romans captured Judas, crucified his followers, and destroyed Sepphoris. When Antipas began to rebuild Sepphoris in earnest, Jesus was a young man ready to work in his father's trade. By then practically every artisan and day laborer in the province would have poured into Sepphoris to take part in what was the largest restoration project of the time, and one can be fairly certain that Jesus and his brothers, who lived a short distance away in Nazareth, would have been among them. In fact, from the time he began his apprenticeship as a *tekton* to the day he launched his ministry as an itinerant preacher, Jesus would have spent most of his life not in the tiny hamlet of Nazareth, but in the cosmopolitan capital of Sepphoris: a peasant boy in a big city.

Six days a week, from sunup to sundown, Jesus would have toiled in the royal city, building palatial houses for the Jewish aristocracy during the day, returning to his crumbling mud-brick home at night. He would have witnessed for himself the rapidly expanding divide between the absurdly rich and the indebted poor. He would have mingled with the city's Hellenized and Romanized population: those wealthy, wayward Jews who spent as much time praising the emperor of Rome as they did the Lord of the Universe. He certainly would have been familiar with the exploits of Judas the Galilean. For while the population of Sepphoris seems to have been tamed and transformed after Judas's rebellion into the model of Roman cooperation—so much so that in 66 C.E., as most of Galilee was joining the revolt against Rome, Sepphoris immediately declared its loyalty to the emperor and became a Roman garrison during the battle to reclaim Jerusalem—the memory of Judas the Galilean and what he accomplished did not fade in Sepphoris: not for the drudge and the dispossessed; not for those, like Jesus, who spent their days slogging bricks to build yet another mansion for yet another Jewish nobleman. And no doubt Jesus would have been aware of the escapades of Herod Antipas—"that

Fox," as Jesus calls him (Luke 13:31)—who lived in Sepphoris until around 20 C.E., when he moved to Tiberias, on the coast of the Sea of Galilee. Indeed, Jesus may have regularly set eyes upon the man who would one day cut off the head of his friend and mentor, John the Baptist, and seek to do the same to him.

Chapter Five

Where Is Your Fleet to Sweep
the Roman Seas?

Prefect Pontius Pilate arrived in Jerusalem in the year 26 C.E. He was the fifth prefect, or governor, Rome had sent to oversee the occupation of Judea. After the death of Herod the Great and the dismissal of his son Archelaus as ethnarch in Jerusalem, Rome decided it would be best to govern the province directly, rather than through yet another Jewish client-king.

The Pontii were Samnites, descended from the mountainous domain of Samnium in southern Rome, a hard country of stone and blood and brutal men that had been broken and forcibly absorbed into the Roman Republic in the third century B.C.E. The surname Pilatus meant "skilled with a javelin," a tribute perhaps to Pilate's father, whose glory as a Roman soldier under Julius Caesar had allowed the Pontii to advance from their humble origins into the Roman knightly class. Pilate, like all Roman knights, performed his expected military service to the empire. But he was not a soldier like his father; he was an administrator, more comfortable with accounts and tallies than with swords and spears. Yet Pilate was no less hard a man. The sources describe him as cruel, cold-hearted, and rigid: a proudly imperious Roman with little regard for the sensitivities of subject peoples.

Pilate's disdain for the Jews was obvious from the very first day he arrived in Jerusalem, bedecked in a white tunic and golden breastplate, a red cape draped over his shoulders. The new governor announced his presence in the holy city by marching through Jerusalem's gates trailed by a legion of Roman soldiers carrying standards bearing the emperor's image—an ostentatious display of contempt for Jewish sensibilities. Later, he introduced a set of gilded Roman shields dedicated to Tiberius, "son of the divine Augustus," into the Temple of Jerusalem. The shields were an offering on behalf of the Roman gods, their presence in the Jewish Temple a deliberate act of blasphemy. Informed by his engineers that Jerusalem needed to rebuild its aging aqueducts, Pilate simply took the money to pay for the project from the Temple's treasury. When the Jews protested, Pilate sent his troops to slaughter them in the streets.

The gospels present Pilate as a righteous yet weak-willed man so overcome with doubt about putting Jesus of Nazareth to death that he does everything in his power to save his life, finally washing his hands of the entire episode when the Jews demand his blood. That is pure fiction. What Pilate was best known for was his extreme depravity, his total disregard for Jewish law and tradition, and his barely concealed aversion to the Jewish nation as a whole. During his tenure in Jerusalem he so eagerly, and without trial, sent thousands upon thousands of Jews to the cross that the people of Jerusalem felt obliged to lodge a formal complaint with the Roman emperor.

Despite, or perhaps because of, his cold, hard cruelty to the Jews, Pontius Pilate became one of the longest-serving Roman governors in Judea. It was a perilous and volatile job. The governor's most important task was to ensure the uninterrupted flow of tax revenues back to Rome. But to do so he had to maintain a functional, if fragile, relationship with the high priest; the governor would administer the civil and economic affairs of Judea, while the high priest maintained the Temple cult. The tenuous bond between the two offices meant that no Roman governor or Jewish high priest lasted very long, especially in those first few decades after Herod's death. The five governors before Pilate served only a couple of years each, the lone exception being Pilate's immediate predecessor, Valerius Gratus. But whereas Gratus appointed and dismissed five different high priests in his time as governor, throughout Pilate's decade-long tenure in Jerusalem, he had only one high priest to contend with: Joseph Caiaphas.

Like most high priests, Caiaphas was an extremely wealthy man, though his wealth may have come through his wife, who was the daughter of a previous high priest named Ananus. Caiaphas likely was appointed to the office of high priest not because of his own merit but through the influence of his father-in-law, a larger-than-life character who managed to pass the position to five of his own sons while remaining a significant force throughout Caiaphas's tenure. According to the gospel of John, after Jesus was arrested in the Garden of Gethsemane, he was first brought to Ananus for questioning before being dragged to Caiaphas for judgment (John 18:13).

Gratus had appointed Caiaphas as high priest in the year 18 C.E., meaning he had already served eight years in the office by the time Pilate arrived in Jerusalem. Part of the reason Caiaphas was able to hold the position of high priest for an unprecedented eighteen years was because of the close relationship he ended up forging with Pontius Pilate. The two men worked well together. The period of their combined rule, from 26 C.E. to 36 C.E., coincided with the most stable period in the entire first century. Together they managed to keep a lid on the revolutionary impulse of the Jews by dealing ruthlessly with any hint of political disturbance, no matter how small.

Yet despite their best efforts, Pilate and Caiaphas were unable to extinguish the zeal that had been kindled in the hearts of the Jews by the messianic uprisings that took place at the turn of the century—those of Hezekiah the bandit chief, Simon of Peraea, Athronges the shepherd boy, and Judas the Galilean. Not long after Pilate arrived in Jerusalem, a new crop of preachers, prophets, bandits, and messiahs began traipsing through the Holy Land, gathering disciples, preaching liberation from Rome, and promising the coming of the Kingdom of God. In 28 C.E., an ascetic preacher named John began baptizing people in the waters of the Jordan River, initiating them into what he believed was the true nation of Israel. When John the Baptist's popularity became too great to control, Pilate's tetrarch in Peraea, Herod Antipas, had him imprisoned and executed sometime around 30 C.E. A couple of years later, a peasant day laborer from Nazareth named Jesus led a band of disciples on a triumphant procession into Jerusalem, where he assaulted the Temple, overturned the tables of the money changers, and broke free the sacrificial animals from their cages. He, too, was captured and sentenced to death by Pilate. Three years after that, in 36 C.E., a messiah known only as "the Samaritan" gathered a group of followers atop Mount Gerizim, where he claimed he would reveal "sacred vessels" hidden there by Moses. Pilate responded with a detachment of Roman soldiers who climbed Gerizim and cut the Samaritan's faithful multitude to pieces.

It was that final act of unrestrained violence on Mount Gerizim that ended Pilate's governorship in Jerusalem. Summoned to Rome to explain his actions to the emperor Tiberius, Pilate never returned to Judea. He was exiled to Gaul in 36 C.E. Considering their close working relationship, it may be no coincidence that Joseph Caiaphas was dismissed from his position as high priest in the same year.

With Pilate and Caiaphas gone, there was no longer any hope of stifling the revolutionary passions of the Jews. By midcentury the whole of Palestine was buzzing with messianic energy. In 44 C.E., a wonder-working prophet named Theudas crowned himself messiah and brought hundreds of followers to the Jordan,

promising to part the river just as Moses had done at the Sea of
Reeds a thousand years earlier. This, he claimed, would be the first
step in reclaiming the Promised Land from Rome. The Romans,
in response, dispatched an army to lop off Theudas's head and scat-
ter his followers into the desert. In 46 C.E., two sons of Judas the
Galilean, Jacob and Simon, launched their own revolutionary
movement in the footsteps of their father and grandfather; both
were crucified for their actions.

What Rome required to keep these messianic stirrings in check
was a steady, sensible hand, someone who would respond to the
grumblings of the Jews while still maintaining peace and order in
the Judean and Galilean countryside. What Rome sent to Jerusalem instead was a series of bumbling governors—each more vicious and greedy than the last—whose corruption and ineptitude
would transform the anger, resentment, and apocalyptic mania that
had been steadily building throughout Palestine into a full-scale
revolution.

It started with Ventidius Cumanus, who was stationed in Jerusalem in 48 C.E., two years after the uprising by Judas's sons had
been quelled. As governor, Cumanus was little more than a thief
and a fool. Among his first acts was the posting of Roman soldiers
on the roofs of the Temple's porticoes, ostensibly to guard against
chaos and disorder during the feast of Passover. In the midst of the
holy celebrations, one of these soldiers thought it would be amus-
ing to pull back his garment and display his bare ass to the congregation below, all the while shouting what Josephus, in his decorum,
describes as "such words as you might expect upon such a posture."

The crowd was incensed. A riot broke out in the Temple plaza.
Rather than calming the situation, Cumanus sent a cohort of
Roman soldiers up to the Temple Mount to butcher the panicked
crowd. The pilgrims who escaped the slaughter were trapped by
the narrow exits leading out of the Temple courtyard. Hundreds
were trampled underfoot. Tensions escalated further after one of
Cumanus's legionaries grabbed hold of a Torah scroll and tore it to

pieces in front of a Jewish assembly. Cumanus had the soldier hast-
ily executed, but it was not enough to quell the growing anger and
disaffection among the Jews.

Things came to a head when a group of Jewish travelers from
Galilee were attacked while passing through Samaria on their way
to Jerusalem. When Cumanus dismissed the Jews' appeal for justice, allegedly because the Samaritans had bribed him, a group of
bandits, led by a man named Eleazar son of Dinaeus, took justice
into their own hands and went on a rampage throughout Samaria,
killing every Samaritan they came across. This was more than an
act of bloody vengeance; it was an assertion of freedom by a people
fed up with allowing law and order to rest in the hands of a crooked
and fickle administrator from Rome. The outbreak of violence
between the Jews and Samaritans was the last straw for the emperor. In 52 C.E., Ventidius Cumanus was sent into exile and Antonius Felix was shipped off to Jerusalem in his stead.

As governor, Felix fared no better than his predecessor. Like
Cumanus, he treated the Jews under his control with utter contempt. He used the power of the purse to play the different Jewish
factions in Jerusalem against one another, always to his benefit. He
seemed at first to have enjoyed a close relationship with the high
priest Jonathan, one of the five sons of Ananus who served in the
position. Felix and Jonathan worked together to suppress the bandit gangs in the Judean countryside; Jonathan may have even played
a role in Felix's capture of the bandit chief Eleazar son of Dinaeus,
who was sent to Rome and crucified. But once the high priest had
served Felix's purpose, he was cast aside. Some say Felix had a hand
in what happened next, for it was under his governorship that a
new kind of bandit arose in Jerusalem: a shadowy group of Jewish
rebels that the Romans dubbed *Sicarii,* or "Daggermen," due to
their penchant for small, easy-to-conceal daggers, called *sicae,* with
which they assassinated the enemies of God.

The Sicarii were zealots fueled by an apocalyptic worldview
and a fervent devotion to establishing God's rule on earth. They

were fanatical in their opposition to the Roman occupation, though they reserved their vengeance for those Jews, particularly among the wealthy priestly aristocracy, who submitted to Roman rule. Fearless and unstoppable, the Sicarii murdered their opponents with impunity: in the middle of the city, in broad daylight, in the midst of great hordes, during feast days and festivals. They blended into assemblies and crowds, their daggers tucked inside their cloaks, until they were close enough to strike. Then, as the dead man collapsed to the ground, covered in blood, the Sicarii would sheath their daggers stealthily and join their voices in the cries of indignation from the panicked crowd.

The leader of the Sicarii at the time was a young Jewish revolutionary named Menahem, the grandson of none other than the failed messiah Judas the Galilean. Menahem shared his grandfather's hatred for the wealthy priestly aristocracy in general, and the unctuous high priests in particular. To the Sicarii, Jonathan son of Ananus was an imposter: a thief and a swindler who had grown rich by exploiting the suffering of the people. He was as responsible for the bondage of the Jews as the heathen emperor in Rome. His presence on the Temple Mount defiled the entire nation. His very existence was an abomination to the Lord. He had to die.

In the year 56 C.E., the Sicarii under Menahem's leadership were finally able to achieve what Judas the Galilean could only dream of accomplishing. During the feast of Passover, a Sicarii assassin pushed his way through the mass of pilgrims packed into the Temple Mount until he was close enough to the high priest Jonathan to pull out a dagger and swipe it across his throat. He then melted back into the crowd.

The murder of the high priest threw all of Jerusalem into a panic. How could the leader of the Jewish nation, God's representative on earth, be killed in broad daylight, in the middle of the Temple courtyard, and seemingly with impunity? Many refused to believe that the culprit could have been a Jew. There were whispers that the Roman governor, Felix, had ordered the assassination himself. Who else could have been so profane as to spill the high priest's blood on the Temple grounds?

Yet the Sicarii had only just begun their reign of terror. Shouting their slogan "No lord but God!" they began attacking the members of the Jewish ruling class, plundering their possessions, kidnapping their relatives, and burning down their homes. By these tactics they sowed terror into the hearts of the Jews so that, as Josephus writes, "More terrible than their crimes was the fear they aroused, every man hourly expecting death, as in war."

With Jonathan's death, the messianic ardor in Jerusalem reached fever pitch. There was a widespread sense among the Jews that something profound was happening, a feeling born of desperation, nurtured by a people yearning for freedom from foreign rule. Zeal, the spirit that had fueled the revolutionary fervor of the bandits, prophets, and messiahs, was now coursing through the population like a virus working its way through the body. No longer could it be contained in the countryside; its influence was being felt in the towns and cities, even in Jerusalem. It was not just the peasants and outcasts who were whispering about the great kings and prophets who had freed Israel from her enemies in the past. The wealthy and upwardly mobile were also becoming increasingly animated by the fervent desire to cleanse the Holy Land of the Roman occupation. The signs were everywhere. The scriptures were about to be fulfilled. The end of days was at hand.

In Jerusalem, a holy man named Jesus son of Ananias suddenly appeared, prophesying the destruction of the city and the imminent return of the messiah. Another man, a mysterious Jewish sorcerer called "the Egyptian," declared himself King of the Jews and gathered thousands of followers on the Mount of Olives, where he vowed that, like Joshua at Jericho, he would bring the walls of Jerusalem tumbling down at his command. The crowd was massacred by Roman troops, though, as far as anyone knows, the Egyptian escaped.

Felix's bumbling reaction to these events ultimately led to his sacking and replacement with another man, Porcius Festus. But

Festus proved no better in dealing with the restive Jewish population, either in the countryside, where the number of prophets and messiahs gathering followers and preaching liberation from Rome was growing out of control, or in Jerusalem, where the Sicarii, buoyed by their success in killing the high priest Jonathan, were now murdering and pillaging at will. So overwhelmed was Festus by the stress of the position that he died soon after taking the office. He was followed by Lucceius Albinus, a notorious degenerate, swindler, and incompetent who spent his two years in Jerusalem enriching himself by plundering the wealth of the populace. After Albinus came Gessius Florus, whose brief, turbulent tenure was remembered because first, it made the years under Albinus seem positively peaceful in comparison, and second, he would be the last Roman governor Jerusalem would know.

It was now 64 C.E. In two years' time the anger, resentment, and messianic zeal that had been steadily building throughout the land would erupt into a full-scale revolt against Rome. Cumanus, Felix, Festus, Albinus, Florus—each of these governors contributed through his malfeasance to the Jewish uprising. Rome itself was to blame for its mismanagement and severe overtaxation of the beleaguered population. Certainly the Jewish aristocracy, with their incessant conflicts and their sycophantic efforts to gain power and influence by bribing Roman officials, shared responsibility for the deteriorating social order. And no doubt the Temple leadership played a role in fostering the widespread sense of injustice and crushing poverty that had left so many Jews with no choice but to turn to violence. Add to all this the seizure of private lands, the high levels of unemployment, the displacement and forced urbanization of the peasantry, and the drought and famine that devastated the Judean and Galilean countryside, and it was only a matter of time before the fires of rebellion would engulf the whole of Palestine. It seemed that the entire Jewish nation was ready to erupt into open revolt at the slightest provocation—which Florus was foolish enough to provide.

In May of 66 C.E., Florus suddenly announced that the Jews owed Rome a hundred thousand dinarii in unpaid taxes. Trailed by an army of bodyguards, the Roman governor marched into the Temple and broke into the treasury, plundering the money that the Jews had offered as a sacrifice to God. Riots ensued, to which Florus responded by sending a thousand Roman soldiers into the upper city to murder at will. The soldiers killed women and children. They broke into homes and slaughtered people in their beds. The city was thrown into chaos. War was on the horizon.

To calm the situation, the Romans sent the Jews one of their own: Agrippa II, whose father, Agrippa I, was a beloved Jewish leader who had managed to maintain a close bond with Rome. Although the son did not share his late father's popularity, he was the best hope the Romans had for defusing the tension in Jerusalem.

The young Agrippa rushed to the holy city in a last-ditch effort to stave off war. Standing on the roof of the royal palace with his sister Bernice at his side, he pleaded with the Jews to face the reality of the situation. "Will you defy the whole Roman Empire?" he asked. "What is the army, where is the weapon on which you rely? Where is your fleet to sweep the Roman seas? Where is your treasury to meet the cost of your campaigns? Do you really suppose that you are going to war with Egyptians or Arabs? Will you shut your eyes to the might of the Roman Empire? Will you not measure your own weakness? Are you wealthier than the Gauls, stronger than the Germans, more intelligent than the Greeks, more numerous than all the peoples of the world? What is it which inspires you with confidence to defy the Romans?"

Of course, the revolutionaries had an answer to Agrippa's question. It was zeal that inspired them. The same zeal that had led the Maccabees to throw off Seleucid control two centuries before—the zeal that had helped the Israelites conquer the Promised Land in the first place—would now help this ragtag band of Jewish revolutionaries to throw off the shackles of Roman occupation.

Derided and ignored by the crowd, Agrippa and Bernice had

no choice but to flee the city. Still, up to this point, war with Rome could have been avoided if it had not been for the actions of a young man named Eleazar, who, as the Temple captain, was the priestly official with powers to police disturbances in the Temple vicinity. Backed by a group of lower-class priests, Eleazar seized control of the Temple and put an end to the daily sacrifices on behalf of the emperor. The signal sent to Rome was clear: Jerusalem had declared its independence. In a short time, the rest of Judea and Galilee, Idumea and Peraea, Samaria and all the villages scattered across the Dead Sea valley would follow.

Menahem and the Sicarii rallied to the Temple captain's side. Together, they expelled all the non-Jews from Jerusalem, just as the scriptures demanded. They tracked down and killed the high priest, who had gone into hiding as soon as the fighting began. Then, in an act of profound symbolism, they set fire to the public archives. The ledgers of the debt collectors and moneylenders, the property deeds and public records—all of it went up in flames. There would be no more record of who was rich and who was poor. Everyone in this new and divinely inspired world order would begin anew.

With the lower city under their control, the rebels began fortifying themselves for the inevitable Roman assault. Yet rather than sending a massive army to retake Jerusalem, Rome inexplicably dispatched a small force to the city, which the rebels easily repelled before turning their attention to the upper city, where the few remaining soldiers left in Jerusalem were holed up in a Roman garrison. The Roman soldiers agreed to surrender in exchange for safe passage out of the city. But when they laid down their arms and came out of their stronghold, the rebels turned on them, slaughtering every last soldier, removing utterly the scourge of Roman occupation from the city of God.

After that, there was no turning back. The Jews had just declared war on the greatest empire the world had ever known.

Chapter Six

Year One

In the end, it came down to just a thousand men, women, and children—the last of the rebels to survive the Roman onslaught. The year was 73 C.E. Fitting that what had begun with the Sicarii should end with the Sicarii. The city of Jerusalem had already been burned to the ground, its walls toppled, its population slaughtered. The whole of Palestine was once more under Roman control. All that remained of the rebellion were these last few Sicarii who had fled Jerusalem with their wives and children to hole themselves up inside the fortress of Masada, on the western shore of the Dead Sea. Now here they were, stuck on top of an isolated rock cliff in the middle of a barren desert, watching helplessly as a phalanx of Roman soldiers gradually made its way up the face of the cliff—shields up, swords drawn—ready to put a definitive end to the rebellion that had begun seven years earlier.

The Sicarii originally came to Masada in the first few days after the launch of the war with Rome. As a naturally fortified and virtually impregnable fortress situated more than a thousand feet above the Dead Sea, Masada had long served as a refuge for the Jews. David came here to hide from King Saul when he sent his men to hunt down the shepherd boy who would one day take the crown from him. The Maccabees used Masada as a military base during their revolt against the Seleucid Dynasty. A century later, Herod the Great transformed Masada into a veritable fortress city, flattening the boat-shaped summit and enclosing it with a massive wall made of white Jerusalem stone. Herod added storerooms and grain houses, rainwater cisterns, even a swimming pool. He also placed in Masada a huge cache of weapons sufficient, it was said, to arm a thousand men. For himself and his family, Herod constructed a monumental three-tiered palace that hung from the northern prow of the cliff face, just below the lip of the summit, complete with baths, glittering colonnades, multihued mosaics, and a dazzling 180-degree view of the briny-white Dead Sea valley.

After Herod's death, the fortress and palaces at Masada, and the cache of weapons stored therein, fell into Roman hands. When the Jewish rebellion began in 66 C.E., the Sicarii, under the leadership of Menahem, seized Masada from Roman control and took its weapons back to Jerusalem to join forces with Eleazar the Temple captain. Having seized control over the city and destroyed the Temple archives, the rebels began minting coins to celebrate their hard-won independence. These were etched with symbols of victory—chalices and palm branches—and inscribed with slogans like "Freedom of Zion" and "Jerusalem Is Holy," written not in Greek, the language of the heathens and idolaters, but in Hebrew. Each coin was self-consciously dated "Year One," as though a wholly new era had begun. The prophets had been right. Surely, this was the Kingdom of God.

Yet in the midst of the celebrations, as Jerusalem was being secured and a fragile calm was slowly descending upon the city, Menahem did something unexpected. Draping himself in purple robes, he made a triumphal entry into the Temple courtyard, where, flanked by his armed devotees among the Sicarii, he openly declared himself messiah, King of the Jews.

In some ways, Menahem's actions made perfect sense. After all, if the Kingdom of God had indeed been established, then it was time for the messiah to appear so as to rule over it in God's name. And who else should don the kingly robes and sit upon the throne but Menahem, grandson of Judas the Galilean, great-grandson of Hezekiah the bandit chief? Menahem's messianic assumption was, for his followers, merely the realization of the prophecies: the final step in ushering in the last days.

That is not how Eleazar the Temple captain saw it. He and his associates among the lower priests were incensed at what they viewed as a blatant power grab by the Sicarii. They put together a plan to kill the self-proclaimed messiah and rid the city of his meddlesome followers. While Menahem was prancing about the Temple in his royal garb, Eleazar's men suddenly rushed the Temple Mount and overpowered his guards. They dragged Menahem out into the open and tortured him to death. The surviving Sicarii barely fled Jerusalem with their lives. They reassembled at their base atop the fortress of Masada, where they waited out the rest of the war.

Seven years the Sicarii waited. As the Romans regrouped and returned to wrest Palestine from rebel control, as one after another the towns and villages of Judea and Galilee were razed and their populations tamed by the sword, as Jerusalem itself was surrounded and its inhabitants slowly starved to death, the Sicarii waited in their mountain fortress. Only after every rebellious city had been destroyed and the land once again placed under their control did the Romans turn their sights toward Masada.

The Roman regiment arrived at the foot of Masada in 73 C.E., three years after Jerusalem fell. Because the soldiers could not attack the fortress outright, they first built a massive wall around the entire base of the mountain, ensuring that no rebel could escape undetected. With the area secured, the Romans constructed a steep ramp up the yawning chasm on the western side of the cliff face, slowly scraping away tens of thousands of pounds of earth and stone for weeks on end, even as the rebels hurled rocks at them from above. The soldiers then pushed a huge siege tower up the ramp, from which they spent days bombarding the rebels with arrows and ballista balls. Once Herod's perimeter wall finally gave, all that separated the Romans from the last of the Jewish rebels was a hurriedly built interior wall. The Romans set fire to the wall, then returned to their encampments and patiently waited for it to collapse on its own.

Huddled together inside Herod's palace, the Sicarii knew the end had come. The Romans would surely do to them and their families what they had done to the inhabitants of Jerusalem. Amid the steely silence, one of the Sicarii leaders stood and addressed the rest.

"My friends, since we resolved long ago never to be servants to the Romans, nor to any other than to God himself, who alone is the true and just Lord of mankind, the time has now come to make that resolution true in practice." Drawing his dagger, he made a final plea. "God has granted us the power to die bravely, and in a state of freedom, which was not the case for those [in Jerusalem] who were conquered unexpectedly."

The speech had its desired effect. As the Romans prepared for their final assault on Masada, the rebels drew lots among them to decide the order with which they would proceed with their gruesome plan. They then pulled out their daggers—the same daggers that had given them their identity, the daggers that had, with a swipe across the high priest's throat, launched the ill-fated war with Rome—and began to kill their wives and their children, before turning the knives upon each other. The last ten men chose one among them to kill the remaining nine. The final man set the entire palace ablaze. Then he killed himself.

The following morning, as the Romans stood triumphantly atop the hitherto impregnable fortress of Masada, all they encountered was a ghostly calm: nine hundred and sixty dead men, women, and children. The war was finally over.

The question is why it took so long.

News of the Jewish Revolt had traveled swiftly to Emperor

Nero, who immediately tapped one of his most trusted men, Titus Flavius Vespasianus—Vespasian, as he was known—to retake Jerusalem. Taking command of a massive army of more than sixty thousand fighting men, Vespasian set off at once for Syria, while his son Titus went to Egypt to collect the Roman legions stationed in Alexandria. Titus would lead his troops north through Idumea as Vespasian pushed south into Galilee. The plan was for father and son to squeeze the Jews between their two armies and choke the life out of the rebellion.

One by one the rebellious cities gave way to the might of Rome as Titus and Vespasian carved a trail of destruction across the Holy Land. By 68 C.E., all of Galilee, as well as Samaria, Idumea, Peraea, and the entire Dead Sea region, save for Masada, were firmly back under Roman control. All that remained was for Vespasian to send his armies into Judea to lay waste to the seat of the rebellion: Jerusalem.

As he was preparing for the final assault, however, Vespasian received word that Nero had committed suicide. Rome was in turmoil. Civil war was tearing through the capital. In the span of a few short months, three different men—Galba, Otho, and Vitellius—declared themselves emperor, each in turn violently overthrown by his successor. There was a complete breakdown of law and order in Rome as thieves and hooligans plundered the population without fear of consequence. Not since the war between Octavian and Mark Antony a hundred years earlier had the Romans experienced such civil unrest. Tacitus described it as a period "rich in disasters, terrible with battles, torn by civil struggles, horrible even in peace."

Spurred by the legions under his command, Vespasian halted his campaign in Judea and hastened to Rome to stake his own claim to the throne. The haste, it seems, was unnecessary. Long before he reached the capital in the summer of 70 C.E., his supporters had taken control of the city, murdered his rivals, and declared Vespasian sole emperor.

Yet the Rome that Vespasian now found himself ruling had undergone a profound transformation. The mass civil unrest had given rise to a great deal of consternation about the decline of Roman power and influence. The situation in distant Judea was particularly galling. It was bad enough that the lowly Jews had rebelled in the first place; it was inconceivable that after three long years, the rebellion still had not been crushed. Other subject peoples revolted, of course. But these were not Gauls or Britons; they were superstitious peasants hurling rocks. The very scale of the Jewish Revolt, and the fact that it had come at a time of profound social and political distress in Rome, had created something akin to an identity crisis among the Roman citizenry.

Vespasian knew that to consolidate his authority and address the malaise that had descended upon Rome, he needed to focus the people's attention away from their domestic troubles and toward a spectacular foreign conquest. A small victory would not do. What the emperor required was an absolute pummeling of an enemy force. He needed a Triumph: a fabulous display of Roman might replete with captives, slaves, and spoils to win over his disgruntled citizens and strike terror into the hearts of his subjects. And so, immediately upon taking the throne, Vespasian set out to complete the task he had left unfinished in Judea. He would not simply quash the Jewish rebellion; that would be insufficient to make his point. He would utterly annihilate the Jews. He would wipe them from the earth. Devastate their lands. Burn their temple. Destroy their cult. Kill their god.

From his perch in Rome, Vespasian sent word to his son Titus to march at once to Jerusalem and spare no expense in bringing the rebellion of the Jews to a swift and decisive end. What the emperor could not have known was that the rebellion was on the verge of collapsing on its own.

Not long after Menahem was murdered and the Sicarii banished from Jerusalem, the rebels began preparing for the Roman invasion they were certain was on the horizon. The walls sur-

rounding the city were fortified, and preparations were made to
gather as much military equipment as was available. Swords and
arrows were collected, suits of armor forged, catapults and ballista
balls stacked along the city's perimeter. Young boys were hurriedly
trained in hand-to-hand combat. The whole city was in a panic as
the rebels manned their positions and waited for the Romans to
return and reclaim Jerusalem.

But the Romans never came. The rebels were certainly aware
of the devastation taking place around them. Every day a horde of
bruised and bloodied refugees poured into Jerusalem; the city was
bursting at its borders. But the Roman reprisals were thus far focused solely on the countryside and major rebel strongholds such
as Tiberias, Gamala, and Gischala. The longer the rebels waited for
the Romans to arrive in Jerusalem, the more fractured and unsta-
ble the city's leadership became.

Early on, a transitional government of sorts had been formed,
made up mostly of those among Jerusalem's priestly aristocracy
who had joined the rebellion, many of them reluctantly. This so-
called "moderate" faction was in favor of coming to terms with
Rome, if that was still possible. They wanted to surrender uncon-
ditionally, beg for mercy, and submit once more to Roman rule.
The moderates enjoyed a good deal of support in Jerusalem, particularly among the wealthier Jews who were looking for a way to
preserve their status and property, not to mention their lives.

But an even larger and more vocal faction in Jerusalem was
convinced that God had led the Jews into war against Rome and
that God would lead them to victory. Things may have seemed
bleak at the moment, and the enemy invincible. But that was part
of God's divine plan. Did not the prophets warn that in the final
days "the sown places shall appear unsown and the storehouses
shall be found empty" (2 Esdras 6:22)? Yet if the Jews would only
remain loyal to the Lord, then very soon they would see Jerusalem
clothed in glory. The trumpets would sound and all who heard

them would be struck with fear. The mountains would flatten and the earth would open up to swallow God's enemies. All that was required was faithfulness. Faithfulness and zeal.

At the head of this camp was a coalition of peasants, lower-class priests, bandit gangs, and recently arrived refugees who came together to form a distinct revolutionary faction called the Zealot Party. Poor, pious, and antiaristocratic, the members of the Zealot Party wanted to remain true to the original intention of the revolt: to purify the Holy Land and establish God's rule on earth. They were violently opposed to the transitional government and its plans to surrender the city to Rome. This was blasphemy. It was treason. And the Zealot Party knew well the punishment for both.

The Zealot Party took over the Temple's inner courtyard, where only the priests were permitted, and from there unleashed a wave of terror against those they deemed insufficiently loyal to the rebellion: the wealthy aristocracy and upper-class Jews; the old Herodian nobles and the Temple's former leadership; the chief priests and all those who followed the moderate camp. The leaders of the Zealot Party set up their own shadow government and drew lots to determine which of them would be the next high priest. The lot fell to an illiterate country peasant named Phanni son of Samuel, who was dressed up in the high priest's gaudy vestments, placed before the entrance of the Holy of Holies, and taught how to perform the sacrifices while the remnants of the priestly nobility watched from a distance, weeping at what they perceived to be the desecration of their holy lineage.

As the bloodshed and internecine battles between rival groups continued, even more refugees began to flood into the city, adding fuel to the fires of factionalism and discord that threatened to engulf all of Jerusalem. With the moderates silenced, there were now three principal camps vying with one another for control over the city. While the Zealot Party, which consisted of about twenty-five hundred men, held the inner court of the Temple, the outer courts fell into the hands of the former leader of the rebellion in Gischala, a well-to-do urbanite named John, who had barely escaped the Roman destruction of his city.

At first, John of Gischala threw in his lot with the Zealot Party, with whom he shared a devotion to the religious principles of the revolution. Whether John himself could be called a zealot is difficult to say. He was undoubtedly a fierce nationalist with a deep hatred of Rome at a time in which national sentiment and messianic expectation were inextricably linked. He even melted down the sacred vessels of the Temple and turned them into implements of war with which to fight the armies of Rome. But a fight over control of the Temple ultimately forced John to break with the Zealot Party and form his own coalition, which consisted of some six thousand fighting men.

The third and largest rebel camp in Jerusalem was led by Simon son of Giora, one of the bandit leaders who fought off the initial assault on Jerusalem by Cestius Gallus. Simon had spent the first year of the Jewish Revolt scouring the Judean countryside, plundering the lands of the wealthy, setting slaves free, and earning a reputation as the champion of the poor. After a brief stay with the Sicarii in Masada, Simon came to Jerusalem with a massive personal army of ten thousand men. At first, the city welcomed him, hoping he could rein in the excesses of the Zealot Party and clip the wings of John of Gischala, who was becoming increasingly authoritarian in his conduct. Although Simon was unable to wrest the Temple from either of his rivals, he did manage to seize control over most of the upper and lower city.

Yet what truly set Simon apart from the rest of the rebel leaders in Jerusalem is that, from the very beginning, he unabashedly presented himself as messiah and king. Like Menahem before him, Simon dressed himself in kingly robes and paraded about the city as its savior. He declared himself "Master of Jerusalem" and used his divinely anointed position to begin rounding up and executing the upper-class Jews whom he suspected of treason. As a result, Simon son of Giora ultimately came to be recognized as the supreme commander of the fractured rebellion—and just in time. For no sooner had Simon consolidated his authority over the rest of the rebel groups than Titus appeared at the city gates, with four Roman legions in tow, demanding Jerusalem's immediate surrender.

All at once, the factionalism and feuding amongst the Jews gave way to frantic preparations for the impending Roman assault. But Titus was in no hurry to attack. Instead, he ordered his men to build a stone wall around Jerusalem, trapping everyone inside and cutting off all access to food and water. He then set up camp on the Mount of Olives, from which he had an unobstructed view of the city's population as they slowly starved to death.

The famine that ensued was horrible. Entire families perished in their homes. The alleys were filled with the bodies of the dead; there was no room, and no strength, to bury them properly. The inhabitants of Jerusalem crawled through the sewers searching for food. People ate cow dung and tufts of dry grass. They stripped off and chewed the leather from their belts and shoes. There were scattered reports of Jews who succumbed to eating the dead. Those who attempted to escape the city were easily captured and crucified on the Mount of Olives for all to see.

It would have been sufficient for Titus to simply wait for the population to perish on their own. He would not have needed to unsheathe his sword to defeat Jerusalem and end the rebellion. But that is not what his father had sent him there to do. His task was not to starve the Jews into submission; it was to eradicate them from the land they claimed as their own. Thus, in late April of 70 C.E., as death stalked the city and the population perished by the hundreds from hunger and thirst, Titus rallied his legions and stormed Jerusalem.

The Romans threw up ramparts along the walls of the upper city and began bombarding the rebels with heavy artillery. They constructed a massive battering ram that easily breached the first wall surrounding Jerusalem. When the rebels retreated to a second interior wall, that, too, was breached and the gates set on fire. As the flames slowly died down, the city was laid bare for Titus's troops.

The soldiers set upon everyone—man, woman, child, the rich, the poor, those who had joined in the rebellion, those who had remained faithful to Rome, the aristocrats, the priests. It made no difference. They burned everything. The whole city was ablaze. The roar of the flames mixed with screams of agony as the Roman swarm swept through the upper and lower city, littering the ground with corpses, sloshing through streams of blood, literally clambering over heaps of dead bodies in pursuit of the rebels, until finally the Temple was in their sights. With the last of the rebel fighters trapped inside the inner courtyard, the Romans set the entire foundation aflame, making it seem as though the Temple Mount was boiling over at its base with blood and fire. The flames enveloped the Holy of Holies, the dwelling place of the God of Israel, and brought it crashing to the ground in a pile of ash and dust. When the fires finally subsided, Titus gave orders to raze what was left of the city so that no future generation would even remember the name Jerusalem.

Thousands perished, though Simon son of Giora—Simon the failed messiah—was taken alive so that he could be dragged back to Rome in chains for the Triumph that Vespasian had promised his people. Along with Simon came the sacred treasures of the Temple: the golden table and the shewbread offered to the Lord; the lampstand and the seven-branched Menorah; the incense burners and cups; the trumpets and holy vessels. All of these were carried in triumphal procession through the streets of Rome as Vespasian and Titus, crowned with laurels and clad in purple robes, watched in silent resolution. Finally, at the end of the procession, the last of the spoils was carried out for all to see: a copy of the Torah, the supreme symbol of the Jewish religion.

Vespasian's point was hard to miss: This was a victory not over a people, but over their god. It was not Judea but Judaism that had been defeated. Titus publicly presented the destruction of Jerusalem as an act of piety and an offering to the Roman gods. It was not he who had accomplished the task, Titus claimed. He had merely given his arms to his god, who had shown his anger against the god of the Jews.

Remarkably, Vespasian chose to waive the customary practice of *evocatio,* whereby a vanquished enemy had the option of worshipping its god in Rome. Not only would the Jews be forbidden to rebuild their temple, a right offered to nearly every other subject people in the empire; they would now be forced to pay a tax of two drachmas a year—the exact amount Jewish men once paid in shekels to the Temple in Jerusalem—in order to help rebuild the Temple of Jupiter, which was accidentally burned down during the Roman civil war. All Jews, no matter where in the empire they lived, no matter how loyal they had remained to Rome, no matter if they had taken part in the rebellion or not—every Jew, including women and children, was now forced to pay for the upkeep of the central pagan cult of Rome.

Henceforth, Judaism would no longer be deemed a worthy cult. The Jews were now the eternal enemy of Rome. Although mass population transfer had never been a Roman policy, Rome expelled every surviving Jew from Jerusalem and its surrounding environs, ultimately renamed the city Aelia Capitolina, and placed the entire region under direct imperial control. All of Palestine became Vespasian's personal property as the Romans strove to create the impression that there had never been any Jews in Jerusalem. By the year 135 C.E., the name Jerusalem ceased to exist in all official Roman documents.

For those Jews who survived the bloodbath—those huddled naked and starved beyond the collapsed city walls, watching in horror as the Roman soldiers urinated on the smoldering ashes of the House of God—it was perfectly clear who was to blame for the death and devastation. Surely it was not the Lord of Hosts who had brought such destruction upon the sacred city. No. It was the *lestai,* the bandits and the rebels, the Zealots and the Sicarii, the nationalist revolutionaries who had preached independence from Rome, the so-called prophets and false messiahs who had promised salvation from God in return for their fealty and zeal. They were the ones responsible for the Roman onslaught. They were the ones whom God had abandoned.

In the years to come, the Jews would begin to distance themselves as much as possible from the revolutionary idealism that had led to the war with Rome. They would not altogether abandon their apocalyptic expectations. On the contrary, a flourish of apocalyptic writings would emerge over the next century reflecting the continued longing for divine deliverance from Roman rule. The lingering effects of this messianic fervor would even lead to the outbreak of a brief second Jewish war against Rome in 132 C.E., this one led by the messiah known as Simon son of Kochba. For the most part, however, the rabbis of the second century would be compelled by circumstance and by fear of Roman reprisal to develop an interpretation of Judaism that eschewed nationalism. They would come to view the Holy Land in more transcendental terms, fostering a messianic theology that rejected overt political ambitions, as acts of piety and the study of the law took the place of Temple sacrifices in the life of the observant Jew.

But that was all many years away. On this day—the day in which the beaten and bloodied remnants of the ancient Jewish nation were wrenched from their homes, their Temple, their God, and forcibly marched out of the Promised Land to the land of the heathens and idolaters—all that seemed certain was that the world as they knew it had come to an end.

Meanwhile, in triumphant Rome, a short while after the Temple of the Lord had been desecrated, the Jewish nation scattered to the winds, and the religion made a pariah, tradition says a Jew named John Mark took up his quill and composed the first words to the first gospel written about the messiah known as Jesus of Nazareth—not in Hebrew, the language of God, nor in Aramaic, the language of Jesus, but in Greek, the language of the heathens. The language of the impure. The language of the victors.

This is the beginning of the good news of Jesus the Christ.

PART II

The spirit of the Lord God is upon me
because the Lord has anointed me
to bring good news to the meek;
he has sent me to bind up the brokenhearted,
to proclaim liberty to the captives,
and release to the prisoners who are bound;
to proclaim the year of the Lord's favor,
and the day of vengeance for our God.

ISAIAH 61:1–2

Zeal for Your House

O f all the stories told about the life of Jesus of Nazareth, there is one—depicted in countless plays, films, paintings, and Sunday sermons—that, more than any other word or deed, helps reveal who Jesus was and what Jesus meant. It is one of only a handful of events in Jesus's ministry attested to by all four canonized gospels—Matthew, Mark, Luke, and John—adding some measure of weight to its historicity. Yet all four evangelists present this monumental moment in a casual, almost fleeting manner, as though they were either oblivious to its meaning or, more likely, deliberately downplaying an episode whose radical implications would have been immediately recognized by all who witnessed it. So revelatory is this single moment in Jesus's brief life that it alone can be used to clarify his mission, his theology, his politics, his relationship to the Jewish authorities, his relationship to Judaism in general, and his attitude toward the Roman occupation. Above all, this singular event explains why a simple peasant from the low hills of Galilee was seen as such a threat to the established system that he was hunted down, arrested, tortured, and executed.

The year is approximately 30 C.E. Jesus has just entered Jerusalem, riding a donkey and flanked by a frenzied multitude shouting,

"*Hosanna!* Blessed is he who comes in the name of the Lord! Blessed be the coming kingdom of our father David!" The ecstatic crowd sings hymns of praise to God. Some spread cloaks on the road for Jesus to ride over, just as the Israelites did for Jehu when he was declared king (2 Kings 9:12–13). Others saw off palm branches and wave them in the air, in remembrance of the heroic Maccabees who liberated Israel from foreign rule two centuries earlier (1 Maccabees 13:49–53). The entire pageant has been meticulously orchestrated by Jesus and his followers in fulfillment of Zechariah's prophecy: "Rejoice greatly, daughter of Zion! Cry out, daughter of Jerusalem! Behold, your king is coming to you; righteous and victorious is he, humble and riding upon an ass, upon a colt, the son of a donkey" (Zechariah 9:9).

The message conveyed to the city's inhabitants is unmistakable: the long-awaited messiah—the *true* King of the Jews—has come to free Israel from its bondage.

As provocative as his entrance into Jerusalem may be, it pales in comparison to what Jesus does the following day. With his disciples and, one assumes, the praiseful multitude in tow, Jesus enters the Temple's public courtyard—the Court of Gentiles—and sets about "cleansing" it. In a rage, he overturns the tables of the money changers and drives out the vendors hawking cheap food and souvenirs. He releases the sheep and cattle ready to be sold for sacrifice and breaks open the cages of the doves and pigeons, setting the birds to flight. "Take these things out of here!" he shouts.

With the help of his disciples he blocks the entrance to the courtyard, forbidding anyone carrying goods for sale or trade from entering the Temple. Then, as the crowd of vendors, worshippers, priests, and curious onlookers scramble over the scattered detritus, as a stampede of frightened animals, chased by their panicked owners, rushes headlong out of the Temple gates and into the choked streets of Jerusalem, as a corps of Roman guards and heavily armed Temple police blitz through the courtyard looking to arrest whoever is responsible for the mayhem, there stands Jesus, according to the gospels, aloof, seemingly unperturbed, crying out over the din: "It is written: My house shall be called a house of prayer for all nations. But you have made it a den of thieves."

The authorities are irate, and with good reason. There is no law that forbids the presence of vendors in the Court of Gentiles. Other parts of the Temple may have been sacrosanct and off-limits to the lame, the sick, the impure, and, most especially, to the gentile masses. But the outer court was a free-for-all arena that served both as a bustling bazaar and as the administrative headquarters of the Sanhedrin, the supreme Jewish council. The merchants and money changers, those selling beasts for sacrifice, the impure, the heathen, and the heretic, all had a right to enter the Court of Gentiles as they pleased and do business there. It is not surprising, therefore, that the Temple priests demand to know just who this rabble-rouser thinks he is. By what authority does he presume to cleanse the Temple? What sign can he provide to justify such a blatantly criminal act?

Jesus, as is his wont, ignores these questions altogether and instead answers with his own enigmatic prophecy. "Destroy this Temple," he says, "and in three days I will raise it up."

The crowd is dumbstruck, so much so that they apparently do not notice Jesus and his disciples calmly exiting the Temple and walking out of the city, having just taken part in what the Roman authorities would have deemed a capital offense: sedition, punishable by crucifixion. After all, an attack on the business of the Temple is akin to an attack on the priestly nobility, which, considering the Temple's tangled relationship with Rome, is tantamount to an attack on Rome itself.

Put aside for a moment the centuries of exegetical acrobatics that have been thrust upon this bewildering episode in Jesus's ministry; examine the event from a purely historical perspective, and the scene simply boggles the mind. It is not the accuracy of Jesus's prediction about the Temple that concerns us. The gospels were all written after the Temple's destruction in 70 C.E.; Jesus's warning to

Jerusalem that "the days will come upon you, when your enemies will set up ramparts around you and surround you and crush you to the ground—you and your children—and they will not leave within you one stone upon another" (Luke 19:43–44) was put into his mouth by the evangelists after the fact. Rather, what is significant about this episode—what is impossible to ignore—is how blatant and inescapably *zealous* Jesus's actions at the Temple appear.

The disciples certainly recognize this. Watching Jesus break open the cages and kick over tables on a rampage, the gospel of John says the disciples were reminded of the words of King David, who cried, "Zeal for your house has consumed me" (John 2:17; Psalms 69:9).

The Temple authorities also recognize Jesus's zeal and hatch a clever plot to trap him into implicating himself as a zealot revolutionary. Striding up to Jesus in full view of everyone present, they ask, "Teacher, we know that you are true, that you teach the way of God in truth, and that you show deference for no man. Tell us: Is it lawful to pay the tribute to Caesar or not?"

This is no simple question, of course. It is the essential test of zealotry. Ever since the uprising of Judas the Galilean, the question of whether the Law of Moses permitted paying tribute to Rome had become the distinguishing characteristic of those who adhered to zealot principles. The argument was simple and understood by all: Rome's demand for tribute signaled nothing less than a claim of ownership over the land and its inhabitants. But the land did not belong to Rome. The land belonged to God. Caesar had no right to receive tribute, because he had no right to the land. In asking Jesus about the legality of paying tribute to Rome, the religious authorities were asking him an altogether different question: Are you or are you not a zealot?

"Show me a denarius," Jesus says, referring to the Roman coin used to pay the tribute. "Whose image is this and whose inscription?"

"It is Caesar's," the authorities reply.

"Well, then, give back to Caesar the property that belongs to Caesar, and give back to God the property that belongs to God."

It is astonishing that centuries of biblical scholarship have miscast these words as an appeal by Jesus to put aside "the things of this world"—taxes and tributes—and focus one's heart instead on the only things that matter: worship and obedience to God. Such an interpretation perfectly accommodates the perception of Jesus as a detached, celestial spirit wholly unconcerned with material matters, a curious assertion about a man who not only lived in one of the most politically charged periods in Israel's history, but who claimed to be the promised messiah sent to liberate the Jews from Roman occupation. At best, Jesus's response has been viewed as a milquetoast compromise between the priestly and zealot positions—between those who thought it lawful to pay the tribute to Rome and those who did not.

The truth is that Jesus's answer is as clear a statement as one can find in the gospels on where exactly he fell in the debate between the priests and the zealots—not over the issue of the tribute, but over the far more significant question of God's sovereignty over the land. Jesus's words speak for themselves: "Give back (*apodidomi*) to Caesar the property that belongs to Caesar . . ." The verb *apodidomi*, often translated as "render unto," is actually a compound word: *apo* is a preposition that in this case means "back again"; *didomi* is a verb meaning "to give." *Apodidomi* is used specifically when paying someone back property to which he is entitled; the word implies that the person receiving payment is the rightful owner of the thing being paid. In other words, according to Jesus, Caesar is entitled to be "given back" the denarius coin, not because he deserves tribute, but because it is *his* coin: his name and picture are stamped on it. God has nothing to do with it. By extension, God is entitled to be "given back" the land the Romans have seized for themselves because it is *God's* land: "The Land is mine," says the Lord (Leviticus 25:23). Caesar has nothing to do with it.

So then, give back to Caesar what is his, and give back to God what belongs to God. That is the zealot argument in its simplest, most concise form. And it seems to be enough for the authorities in Jerusalem to immediately label Jesus as *lestes*. A bandit. A zealot.

A couple of days later, after sharing a secret Passover meal, Jesus and his disciples head out in the dark of night to the Garden of Gethsemane to hide out among the gnarled olive trees and the quickset shrubs. It is here, on the western slope of the Mount of Olives, not far from where, some years later, the Roman general Titus would launch his siege of Jerusalem, that the authorities find him.

"Have you come out here with swords and clubs to arrest me like a bandit [*lestes*]?" Jesus asks.

That is precisely how they've come for him. John's gospel claims a "cohort" (*speira*) of soldiers marched to Gethsemane—a unit that would comprise between three hundred and six hundred Roman guards—along with the Temple police, all of them carrying "torches and weapons" (John 18:3). John is obviously exaggerating. But the gospels all agree it was a large and heavily armed arresting party that came for Jesus in the night. Such a show of force may explain why, before heading off to Gethsemane, Jesus made sure his followers were armed as well.

"If you do not have a sword," Jesus instructs his disciples immediately after the Passover meal, "go sell your cloak and buy one."

"Master," the disciples respond, "here are two swords."

"It is enough," Jesus says (Luke 22:36–38).

It would not be. After a brief but bloody tussle with his disciples, the guards arrest Jesus and bring him to the authorities in Jerusalem, where he is charged with sedition for, among other things, "forbidding the paying of tribute to Rome," a charge that Jesus does not deny (Luke 23:2).

Declared guilty, Jesus is sent to Golgotha to be crucified alongside two other men who are specifically called *lestai*, bandits (Matthew 27:38–44; Mark 15:27). As with every criminal who hangs on a cross, Jesus is given a plaque, or *titulus*, detailing the crime for which he is being crucified. Jesus's *titulus* reads KING OF THE JEWS. His crime: striving for kingly rule; *sedition*. And so, like every bandit and revolutionary, every rabble-rousing zealot and apocalyptic prophet who came before or after him—like Hezekiah and Judas, Theudas and Athronges, the Egyptian and the Samaritan, Simon son of Giora and Simon son of Kochba—Jesus of Nazareth is killed for daring to claim the mantle of king and messiah.

To be clear, Jesus was not a member of the Zealot Party that launched the war with Rome, because no such party could be said to exist for another thirty years after his death. Nor can Jesus be labeled a violent revolutionary bent on armed rebellion, though his views on the use of violence were far more complex than it is often assumed.

But look closely at Jesus's words and actions at the Temple in Jerusalem—the episode that undoubtedly precipitated his arrest and execution—and this one fact becomes difficult to deny: Jesus was crucified by Rome because his messianic aspirations threatened the occupation of Palestine, and his zealotry endangered the Temple authorities. That singular fact should color everything we read in the gospels about the messiah known as Jesus of Nazareth— from the details of his death on a cross in Golgotha to the launch of his public ministry on the banks of the Jordan River.

Chapter Seven

The Voice Crying Out
in the Wilderness

John the Baptist came out of the desert like an apparition—a wild man clothed in camel hair, a leather belt tied around his waist, feeding on locusts and wild honey. He traveled the length of the Jordan River—through Judea and Peraea, in Bethany and Aenon—preaching a simple and dire message: The end was near. The Kingdom of God was at hand. And woe to those Jews who assumed their descent from Abraham would save them from the coming judgment.

"Already, the ax is laid at the root of the tree," John warned, "and every tree that does not bear good fruit will be cut down and cast into the fire."

To the wealthy who came to him seeking counsel, John said, "The one with two tunics must share with he who has none; the one with food must do the same."

To the tribute collectors who asked him the path to salvation, he said, "Do not exact more than that which has been prescribed to you."

To the soldiers who begged for guidance, he said, "Do not intimidate, do not blackmail, and be content with your wages."

Word of the Baptist spread quickly throughout the land. People came from as far as Galilee, some traveling for days through the stark Judean wilderness to hear him preach at the lip of the Jordan River. Once there, they would strip off their outer garments and cross over to the eastern shore, where John waited to take them by the hand. One by one, he would immerse them in the living waters. When they emerged, they would cross back to the western shore of the Jordan River—as their ancestors had done a thousand years earlier—back to the land promised them by God. In this way, the baptized became the *new* nation of Israel: repentant, redeemed, and ready to receive the Kingdom of God.

As the crowds who flocked to the Jordan grew larger, the Baptist's activities caught the attention of Herod the Great's son, Antipas ("the Fox"), whose tetrarchy included the region of Peraea, on the eastern bank of the river. If the gospel account is to be believed, Antipas imprisoned John because he criticized his marriage to Herodias, who was the wife of Antipas's half brother (also named Herod). Not satisfied with merely locking John up, the wily Herodias hatched a plot to put him to death. On the occasion of Antipas's birthday, Herodias obliged her daughter, the sultry temptress Salome, to perform a lascivious dance for her uncle and stepfather. So aroused was the libidinous old tetrarch by Salome's gyrations that he at once made her a fateful promise.

"Ask of me whatever you wish," Antipas huffed, "and I will give it to you, even half my kingdom."

Salome consulted her mother. "What shall I ask for?"

"The head of John the Baptist," Herodias replied.

Alas, the gospel account is not to be believed. As deliciously scandalous as the story of John's execution may be, it is riddled with errors and historical inaccuracies. The evangelists mistakenly identify Herodias's first husband as Philip, and they seem to confuse the place of John's execution, the fortress of Machaerus, with Antipas's court in the city of Tiberias. The entire gospel story reads like a fanciful folktale with deliberate echoes in the biblical account of Elijah's conflict with Jezebel, the wife of King Ahab.

A more prosaic yet reliable account of the death of John the Baptist can be found in Josephus's *Antiquities*. According to Josephus, Antipas feared that John's growing popularity among the people would lead to an insurrection, "for they seemed ready to do anything that he should advise." That may have been true. John's warning of the coming wrath of God might not have been new or unique in first-century Palestine, but the hope he offered those who cleansed themselves, who made themselves anew and pursued the path of righteousness, had enormous appeal. John promised the Jews who came to him a new world order, the Kingdom of God. And while he never developed the concept beyond a vague notion of equality and justice, the promise itself was enough in those dark, turbulent times to draw to him a wave of Jews from all walks of life—the rich and the poor, the mighty and the weak. Antipas was right to fear John; even his own soldiers were flocking to him. He therefore seized John, charged him with sedition, and sent him to the fortress of Machaerus, where the Baptist was quietly put to death sometime between 28 and 30 C.E.

Yet John's fame far outlived him. Indeed, John's fame outlived Antipas, for it was widely believed that the tetrarch's defeat at the hands of the Nabataean king Aretas IV in 36 C.E., his subsequent exile, and the loss of his title and property were all God's divine punishment for executing John. Long after his death, the Jews were still mulling over the meaning of John's words and deeds; John's disciples were still wandering Judea and Galilee, baptizing people in his name. John's life and legend were preserved in independent "Baptist traditions" composed in Hebrew and Aramaic and passed around from town to town. Many assumed he was the messiah. Some thought he would rise from the dead.

Despite his fame, however, no one seems to have known then—

just as no one knows now—who, exactly, John the Baptist was or where he had come from. The gospel of Luke provides a fantastical account of John's lineage and miraculous birth, which most scholars dismiss out of hand. If there is any historical information to be gleaned from Luke's gospel, however, it is that John may have come from a priestly family; his father, Luke says, belonged to the priestly order of Abijah (Luke 1:5). If that is true, John would have been expected to join the priestly line of his father, though the apocalyptic preacher who walked out of the desert "eating no bread and drinking no wine" had quite clearly rejected his family obligations and his duties to the Temple for a life of asceticism in the wilderness. Perhaps this was the source of John's immense popularity among the masses: he had stripped himself of his priestly privileges so as to offer the Jews a new source of salvation, one that had nothing to do with the Temple and the detestable priesthood: *baptism*.

To be sure, baptisms and water rituals were fairly common throughout the ancient Near East. Bands of "baptizing groups" roamed Syria and Palestine initiating congregants into their orders by immersing them in water. Gentile converts to Judaism would often take a ceremonial bath to rid themselves of their former identity and enter into the chosen tribe. The Jews revered water for its liminal qualities, believing it had the power to transport a person or object from one state to another: from unclean to clean, from profane to holy. The Bible is replete with ablutionary practices: objects (a tent, a sword) were sprinkled with water to dedicate them to the Lord; people (lepers, menstruating women) were fully immersed in water as an act of purification. The priests in the Temple of Jerusalem poured water on their hands before approaching the altar to make sacrifices. The high priest underwent one ritual immersion before entering the Holy of Holies on the Day of Atonement, and another immediately after taking upon himself the sins of the nation.

The most famous ablutionary sect of the time was the aforementioned Essene community. The Essenes were not strictly a monastic movement. Some lived in cities and villages throughout Judea, others separated themselves entirely from the rest of the Jews in communes like that at Qumran, where they practiced celibacy and held all property in common (the only items of personal property an Essene at Qumran would be allowed were a cloak, a linen cloth, and a hatchet for digging a latrine in the wilderness when the need arose). Because the Essenes viewed the physical body as base and corrupt, they developed a rigid system of full immersion baths that had to be completed over and over again to maintain a constant state of ritual purity. Yet the Essenes also practiced a one-time, initiatory water ritual—a baptism of sorts—that was used to welcome new recruits into their community.

This could have been the source of John's unusual baptismal rite. John himself may have been an Essene. There are some tantalizing connections between the two. Both John and the Essene community were based in the wilderness region of Judea at approximately the same time: John is presented as going off into the Judean wilderness at a young age, which would be in keeping with the Essene practice of adopting and training the sons of priests. Both John and the Essenes rejected the Temple authorities: the Essenes maintained their own distinct calendar and their own dietary restrictions and refused the concept of animal sacrifice, which was the primary activity of the Temple. Both saw themselves and their followers as the true tribe of Israel, and both were actively preparing for the end times: the Essenes eagerly awaited an apocalyptic war when "the Sons of Light" (the Essenes) would battle "the Sons of Darkness" (the Temple priests) for control over the Temple of Jerusalem, which the Essenes would purify and make holy again under their leadership. And both John and the Essenes seem to have identified themselves as "the voice crying out in the wilderness" spoken of by the Prophet Isaiah: "Prepare the way of the Lord, make straight the paths of our God" (Isaiah 40:3). All four gospels attribute this verse to John, while for the Essenes, the verse served as the most significant passage of scripture in defining their conception of themselves and their community.

Yet there are enough differences between John and the Essenes to make one cautious about drawing too firm a connection. John is presented not as a member of a community but as a loner, a solitary voice calling out in the wilderness. His is by no means an exclusivist message but one open to all Jews willing to abandon their wicked ways and live a life of righteousness. Most crucially, John does not appear to be obsessed with ritual purity; his baptism seems to have been specifically designed as a one-time affair, not something to be repeated again and again. John may have been influenced by the water rituals of other Jewish sects of his time, including the Essenes, but it appears that the baptism he offered in the Jordan River was uniquely his inspiration.

What, then, did John's baptism mean? The gospel of Mark makes the astonishing claim that what John was offering at the Jordan was "a baptism of repentance for the forgiveness of sins" (Mark 1:4). The unmistakably Christian nature of this phrase casts serious doubt on its historicity. It sounds more like a Christian projection upon the Baptist's actions, not something the Baptist would have claimed for himself—though if that is true, it would be an odd statement for the early church to make about John: that he had the power to forgive sins, even before he knew Jesus.

Josephus explicitly states that John's baptism was "not for the remission of sins, but for the purification of the body." That would make John's ritual more like an initiation rite, a means of entering into his order or sect, a thesis borne out in the book of Acts, in which a group of Corinthians proudly claim to have been baptized *into* John's baptism (Acts 19:1–3). But that, too, would have been problematic for the early Christian community. Because if there is one thing about which all four gospels agree when it comes to John the Baptist, it is that sometime around his thirtieth year, and for reasons unknown, Jesus of Nazareth left his tiny hillside village of Nazareth in Galilee, abandoned his home, his family, and his obligations, and trekked down to Judea to be baptized by John in the Jordan River. Indeed, the life of the historical Jesus begins not with his miraculous birth or his obscured youth but at the moment he first meets John the Baptist.

The problem for the early Christians was that any acceptance of the basic facts of John's interaction with Jesus would have been a tacit admission that John was, at least at first, a superior figure. If John's baptism was for the forgiveness of sins, as Mark claims, then Jesus's acceptance of it indicated a need to be cleansed of his sins by John. If John's baptism was an initiation rite, as Josephus suggests, then clearly Jesus was being admitted into John's movement as just another one of his disciples. This was precisely the claim made by John's followers, who, long after both men had been executed, refused to be absorbed into the Jesus movement because they argued that their master, John, was greater than Jesus. After all, who baptized whom?

John the Baptist's historical importance and his role in launching Jesus's ministry created a difficult dilemma for the gospel writers. John was a popular, well-respected, and almost universally acknowledged priest and prophet. His fame was too great to ignore, his baptism of Jesus too well known to conceal. The story had to be told. But it also had to be massaged and made safe. The two men's roles had to be reversed: Jesus had to be made superior, John inferior. Hence the steady regression of John's character from the first gospel, Mark—wherein he is presented as a prophet and mentor to Jesus—to the last gospel, John, in which the Baptist seems to serve no purpose at all except to acknowledge Jesus's divinity.

Mark casts John the Baptist as a wholly independent figure who baptizes Jesus as one among many who come to him seeking repentance. "There went out to him people from all over Judea, and from Jerusalem, to be baptized by him in the River Jordan, and to confess their sins ... and it happened that, in those days, Jesus came

from Galilee, from Nazareth, and he too was baptized by John in
the Jordan" (Mark 1:5, 9). Mark's Baptist admits that he himself is
not the promised messiah—"There is one coming after me who is
stronger than I am," John says, "one whose sandals I am not worthy
to untie" (Mark 1:7–8)—but strangely, John never actually acknowledges Jesus to be the one he is referring to. Even after Jesus's
perfunctory baptism, when the sky opens and the spirit of God
descends upon him in the form of a dove as a heavenly voice says,
"You are my son: the Beloved. In you I am well pleased," John neither notices nor comments on this moment of divine interjection.
To John, Jesus is merely another supplicant, another son of Abraham who journeys to the Jordan to be initiated into the renewed
tribe of Israel. He simply moves on to the next person waiting to
be baptized.

Writing some two decades later, Matthew recounts the narrative of Jesus's baptism almost word for word from Mark, but he
makes certain to address at least one of his predecessor's glaring
omissions: the moment Jesus arrives on the banks of the Jordan,
John immediately recognizes him as the "one coming after me."

"I baptize you with water," the Baptist says. "He will baptize
you with the Holy Spirit and with fire."

At first, Matthew's John refuses to baptize Jesus, suggesting that
it is he who should be baptized by Jesus. Only after Jesus gives him
permission does John presume to baptize the peasant from Nazareth.

Luke goes one step further, repeating the same story presented
in Mark and Matthew but choosing to gloss over Jesus's actual bap-
tism. "Now when all the people had been baptized, and Jesus too
was baptized, the heavens opened . . ." (Luke 3:21). In other words,
Luke omits any agent in Jesus's baptism. It is not John who baptizes
Jesus. Jesus is merely baptized. Luke buttresses his point by giving
John his own infancy narrative alongside the one he invents for
Jesus to prove that even as fetuses, Jesus was the superior figure:
John's birth to a barren woman, Elizabeth, may have been miracu-

lous, but it was not nearly as miraculous as Jesus's birth to a virgin. This is all part of Luke's concerted effort, which the evangelist carries forth into his gospel's sequel, the book of Acts, to persuade John's disciples to abandon their prophet and follow Jesus instead.

By the time the gospel of John recounts Jesus's baptism, three decades after Mark, John the Baptist is no longer a baptist; the title is never used of him. In fact, Jesus is never actually baptized by John. The Baptist's sole purpose in the fourth gospel is to bear witness to Jesus's divinity. Jesus is not just "stronger" than John the Baptist. He is the light, the Lord, the Lamb of God, the Chosen One. He is the preexistent *logos,* who "existed before me," the Baptist says.

"I myself saw the holy spirit descend upon him from heaven like a dove," John claims of Jesus, correcting another of Mark's original omissions, before expressly commanding his disciples to leave him and follow Jesus instead. For John the evangelist, it was not enough simply to reduce the Baptist; the Baptist had to reduce himself, to publicly denigrate himself before the *true* prophet and messiah.

"I am not the messiah," John the Baptist admits in the fourth gospel. "I have been sent before him . . . *He must increase, as I must decrease*" (John 3:28–30).

This frantic attempt to reduce John's significance, to make him inferior to Jesus—to make him little more than Jesus's herald—betrays an urgent need on the part of the early Christian community to counteract what the historical evidence clearly suggests: whoever the Baptist was, wherever he came from, and however he intended his baptismal ritual, Jesus very likely began his ministry as just another of his disciples. Before his encounter with John, Jesus was an unknown peasant and day laborer toiling away in Galilee. John's baptism not only made him part of the new and redeemed nation of Israel, it initiated him into John's inner circle. Not everyone who was baptized by John became his disciple; many simply returned to their homes. But Jesus did not. The gospels make it clear that rather than returning to Galilee after his baptism, he went "out into the wilderness" of Judea; that is, Jesus went directly into the place whence John had just emerged. And he stayed in the wilderness for a while, not to be "tempted by Satan," as the evangelists imagine it, but to learn from John and to commune with his followers.

The first words of Jesus's public ministry echo John's: "The time is fulfilled. The Kingdom of God is near. Repent and believe in the good news" (Mark 1:15). So does Jesus's first public action: "After this Jesus and his disciples went into Judea and there they were baptizing, and John also was baptizing . . ." (John 3:22–23). Of course, Jesus's first disciples—Andrew and Philip—were not his disciples at all; they were John's (John 1:35–37). They only followed Jesus after John was arrested. Jesus even addresses his enemies among the scribes and Pharisees with the same distinct phrase John uses for them: "You brood of vipers!" (Matthew 12:34).

Jesus remained in Judea for some time after his baptism, moving in and out of John's circle, preaching his master's words and baptizing others alongside him, until Antipas, frightened by John's power and popularity, had him seized and thrown into a dungeon. Only then did Jesus leave Judea and return home to his family.

It would be back in Galilee, among his own people, that Jesus would fully take up John's mantle and begin preaching about the Kingdom of God and the judgment that was to come. Yet Jesus would not simply mimic John. Jesus's message would be far more revolutionary, his conception of the Kingdom of God far more radical, and his sense of his own identity and mission far more dangerous than anything John the Baptist could have conceived. John may have baptized by water. But Jesus would baptize by the Holy Spirit. The Holy Spirit and *fire*.

Chapter Eight

Follow Me

The Galilee to which Jesus returned after his stint with John the Baptist was not the Galilee into which he had been born. The Galilee of Jesus's childhood had undergone a profound psychic trauma, having felt the full force of Rome's retribution for the revolts that erupted throughout the land after the death of Herod the Great in 4 B.C.E.

The Roman response to rebellion, no matter where it arose in the realm, was scripted and predictable: burn the villages, raze the cities, enslave the population. That was likely the command given to the legions of troops dispatched by Emperor Augustus after Herod's death to teach the rebellious Jews a lesson. The Romans easily snuffed out the uprisings in Judea and Peraea. But special attention was given to Galilee, the center of the revolt. Thousands were killed as the countryside was set ablaze. The devastation spread to every town and village; few were spared. The villages of Emmaus and Sampho were laid waste. Sepphoris, which had allowed Judas the Galilean to breach the city's armory, was flattened. The whole of Galilee was consumed in fire and blood. Even tiny Nazareth would not have escaped the wrath of Rome.

Rome may have been right to focus so brutally on Galilee. The region had been a hotbed of revolutionary activity for centuries. Long before the Roman invasion, the term "Galilean" had become synonymous with "rebel." Josephus speaks of the people of Galilee as "inured to war from their infancy," and Galilee itself, which benefited from a rugged topography and mountainous terrain, he describes as "always resistant to hostile invasion."

It did not matter whether the invaders were gentiles or Jews, the Galileans would not submit to foreign rule. Not even King Solomon could tame Galilee; the region and its people fiercely resisted the heavy taxes and forced labor he imposed on them to complete construction of the first Temple in Jerusalem. Nor could the Hasmonaeans—the priest-kings who ruled the land from 140 B.C.E. until the Roman invasion in 63 B.C.E.—ever quite manage to induce the Galileans to submit to the Temple-state they created in Judea. And Galilee was a constant thorn in the side of King Herod, who was not named King of the Jews until after he proved he could rid the troublesome region of the bandit menace.

The Galileans seem to have considered themselves a wholly different people from the rest of the Jews in Palestine. Josephus explicitly refers to the people of Galilee as a separate *ethnoi,* or nation; the Mishnah claims the Galileans had different rules and customs than the Judeans when it came to matters such as marriage or weights and measures. These were pastoral people—country folk—easily recognizable by their provincial customs and their distinctly rustic accent (supposedly it was his Galilean accent that gave Simon Peter away as a follower of Jesus after his arrest: "Certainly you are also one of [Jesus's disciples], for your accent betrays you"; Matthew 26:73). The urban elite in Judea referred to the Galileans derisively as "the people of the land," a term meant to convey their dependence on subsistence farming. But the term had a more sinister connotation, meaning those who are uneducated and impious, those who do not properly abide by the law, particularly when it came to making the obligatory tithes and offerings to the Temple. The literature of the era is full of Judean complaints about the laxity of the Galileans in paying their Temple dues in a timely manner, while a bevy of apocryphal scriptures, such as *The Testament of Levi* and the *Enoch* corpus, reflect a distinctly Galilean critique of the lavish lifestyles of the Judean priesthood, their exploitation of the peasantry, and their shameful collaboration with Rome.

No doubt the Galileans felt a meaningful connection to the Temple as the dwelling place of the spirit of God, but they also evinced a deep disdain for the Temple priests who viewed themselves as the sole arbiters of God's will. There is evidence to suggest that the Galileans were both less observant of the Temple rituals and, given the three-day distance between Galilee and Jerusalem, less likely to make frequent visits to it. Those Galilean farmers and peasants who could scrape enough money together to make it to Jerusalem for the sacred festivals would have found themselves in the humiliating position of handing over their meager sacrifices to wealthy Temple priests, some of whom may have owned the very lands these peasants and farmers labored on back home.

The divide between Judea and Galilee grew wider after Rome placed Galilee under the direct rule of Herod the Great's son, Antipas. For the first time in their history the Galileans had a ruler who actually resided in Galilee. Antipas's tetrarchy transformed the province into a separate political jurisdiction no longer subject to the direct authority of the Temple and the priestly aristocracy in Jerusalem. The Galileans still owed their tithes to the ravenous Temple treasury, and Rome still exercised control over every aspect of life in Galilee: Rome had installed Antipas and Rome commanded him. But Antipas's rule allowed for a small yet meaningful measure of Galilean autonomy. There were no longer any Roman troops stationed in the province; they had been replaced by Antipas's own soldiers. And at least Antipas was a Jew who, for the most part, tried not to offend the religious sensibilities of those under his rule—his marriage to his brother's wife and the execution of John the Baptist notwithstanding.

From around 10 C.E., when Antipas established his capital at

Sepphoris, to 36 C.E., when he was deposed by the emperor Caligula and sent into exile, the Galileans enjoyed a period of peace and tranquillity that was surely a welcome respite from the decade of rebellion and war that had preceded it. But the peace was a ruse, the cessation of conflict a pretense for the physical transformation of Galilee. For in the span of those twenty years, Antipas built two new Greek cities—his first capital, Sepphoris, followed by his second, Tiberias, on the coast of the Sea of Galilee—that completely upended traditional Galilean society.

These were the first real cities that Galilee had ever seen, and they were almost wholly populated with non-Galileans: Roman merchants, Greek-speaking gentiles, pursy Judean settlers. The new cities placed enormous pressure on the region's economy, essentially dividing the province between those with wealth and power and those who served them by providing the labor necessary to maintain their lavish lifestyles. Villages in which subsistence farming or fishing were the norm were gradually overwhelmed by the needs of the cities, as agriculture and food production became singularly focused on feeding the new cosmopolitan population. Taxes were raised, land prices doubled, and debts soared, slowly disintegrating the traditional way of life in Galilee.

When Jesus was born, Galilee was aflame. His first decade of life coincided with the plunder and destruction of the Galilean countryside, his second with its refashioning at the hands of Antipas. When Jesus departed Galilee for Judea and John the Baptist, Antipas had already left Sepphoris for his even larger and more ornate royal seat at Tiberias. By the time he returned, the Galilee he knew—of family farms and open fields, of blooming orchards and vast meadows bursting with wildflowers—looked a lot like the province of Judea he had just left behind: urbanized, Hellenized, iniquitous, and strictly stratified between those who had and those who had not.

Jesus's first stop upon returning to Galilee would surely have been Nazareth, where his family still resided, though he did not stay long in his hometown. Jesus had left Nazareth a simple *tekton*. He returned as something else. His transformation created a deep rift among his neighbors. They seem hardly to recognize the itinerant preacher who suddenly reappeared in their village. The gospels say Jesus's mother, brothers, and sisters were scandalized by what people were saying about him; they tried desperately to silence and restrain him (Mark 3:21). Yet when they approached Jesus and urged him to return home and resume the family business, he refused. "Who are my mother and my brothers?" Jesus asked, looking at those around him. "Here are my mother and my brothers. Whoever does the will of God is my brother and sister and mother" (Mark 3:31–34).

This account in the gospel of Mark is often interpreted as suggesting that Jesus's family rejected his teachings and denied his identity as messiah. But there is nothing in Jesus's reply to his family that hints at hostility between him and his brothers and sisters. Nor is there anything in the gospels to indicate that Jesus's family rebuffed his messianic ambitions. On the contrary, Jesus's brothers played fairly significant roles in the movement he founded. His brother James became the leader of the community in Jerusalem after his crucifixion. Perhaps his family was slow in accepting Jesus's teachings and his extraordinary claims. But the historical evidence suggests that they all eventually came to believe in him and his mission.

Jesus's neighbors were a different story, however. The gospel paints his fellow Nazareans as distressed by the return of "Mary's son." Although a few spoke well of him and were amazed by his words, most were deeply disturbed by his presence and his teachings. Jesus quickly became an outcast in the small hilltop community. The gospel of Luke claims the residents of Nazareth finally drove him out to the brow of the hill on which the village was built and tried to push him off a cliff (Luke 4:14–30). The story is suspect; there is no cliff to be pushed off in Nazareth, just a gently sloping hillside. Still, the fact remains that, at least at first, Jesus was unable to find much of a following in Nazareth. "No prophet is accepted in his hometown," he said before abandoning his childhood home for a nearby fishing village called Capernaum on the northern coast of the Sea of Galilee.

Capernaum was the ideal place for Jesus to launch his ministry, as it perfectly reflected the calamitous changes wrought by the new Galilean economy under Antipas's rule. The seaside village of some fifteen hundred mostly farmers and fishermen, known for its temperate climate and its fertile soil, would become Jesus's base of operations throughout the first year of his mission in Galilee. The entire village stretched along a wide expanse of the seacoast, allowing the cool air to nurture all manner of plants and trees. Clumps of lush littoral vegetation thrived along the vast coastline throughout the year, while thickets of walnut and pine, fig and olive trees dotted the low-lying hills inland. The true gift of Capernaum was the magnificent sea itself, which teemed with an array of fish that had nourished and sustained the population for centuries.

By the time Jesus set up his ministry there, however, Capernaum's economy had become almost wholly centered on serving the needs of the new cities that had cropped up around it, especially the new capital, Tiberias, which lay just a few kilometers to the south. Food production had increased exponentially, and with it the standard of living for those farmers and fishermen who had the capacity to purchase more cultivatable land or to buy more boats and nets. But, as in the rest of Galilee, the profits from this increase in the means of production disproportionately benefited the large landowners and moneylenders who resided outside Capernaum: the wealthy priests in Judea and the new urban elite in Sepphoris and Tiberias. The majority of Capernaum's residents had been left behind by the new Galilean economy. It would be these people whom Jesus would specifically target—those who found themselves cast to the fringes of society, whose lives had been disrupted by the rapid social and economic shifts taking place throughout Galilee.

This is not to say that Jesus was interested solely in the poor, or that only the poor would follow him. A number of fairly prosperous benefactors—the toll collectors Levi (Mark 2:13–15) and Zacchaeus (Luke 19:1–10) and the wealthy patron Jairus (Mark 5:21–43), to name a few—would come to fund Jesus's mission by providing food and lodging to him and his followers. But Jesus's message was designed to be a direct challenge to the wealthy and the powerful, be they the occupiers in Rome, the collaborators in the Temple, or the new moneyed class in the Greek cities of Galilee. The message was simple: the Lord God had seen the suffering of the poor and dispossessed; he had heard their cries of anguish. And he was finally going to do something about it. This may not have been a new message—John preached much the same thing— but it was a message being delivered to a new Galilee, by a man who, as a tried and true Galilean himself, shared the anti-Judea, anti-Temple sentiments that permeated the province.

Jesus was not in Capernaum for long before he began gathering to himself a small group of like-minded Galileans, mostly culled from the ranks of the fishing village's disaffected youth, who would become his first disciples (actually, Jesus may have arrived with a couple of disciples already in tow, those who had left John the Baptist after his capture and followed Jesus instead). According to the gospel of Mark, Jesus found his first followers while walking along the edge of the Sea of Galilee. Spying two young fishermen, Simon and his brother Andrew, casting nets, he said, "Follow me, and I will make you fishers of men." The brothers, Mark writes, immediately dropped their nets and went with him. Sometime later Jesus came upon another pair of fishermen—James and John, the young sons of Zebedee—and made them the same offer. They, too, left their boat and their nets and followed Jesus (Mark 1:16–20).

What set the disciples apart from the crowds that swelled and shrank whenever Jesus entered one village or another is that they actually traveled with Jesus. Unlike the enthusiastic but fickle masses, the disciples were specifically called by Jesus to leave their homes and their families behind to follow him from town to town, village to village. "If anyone comes to me and does not hate his father and mother and wife and children and brothers and sisters— yes even his life—he cannot be my disciple." (Luke 14:26 | Matthew 10:37).

The gospel of Luke claims that there were seventy-two disciples in all (Luke 10:1–12), and they undoubtedly included women, some of whom, in defiance of tradition, are actually named in the New Testament: Joanna, the wife of Herod's steward, Chuza; Mary, the mother of James and Joseph; Mary, the wife of Clopas; Susanna; Salome; and perhaps most famous of all, Mary from Magdala, whom Jesus had cured of "seven demons" (Luke 8:2). That these women functioned as Jesus's disciples is demonstrated by the fact that all four gospels present them as traveling with Jesus from town to town (Mark 15:40–41; Matthew 27:55–56; Luke 8:2–3; 23:49; John 19:25). The gospels claim "many other women . . . followed [Jesus] and served him," too (Mark 15:40–41), from his first days preaching in Galilee to his last breath on the hill in Golgotha.

But among the seventy-two, there was an inner core of disciples— all of them men—who would serve a special function in Jesus's ministry. These were known simply as "the Twelve." They included the brothers James and John—the sons of Zebedee—who would be called *Boanerges,* "the sons of thunder"; Philip, who was from Bethsaida and who began as one of John the Baptist's disciples before he switched his allegiance to Jesus (John 1:35–44); Andrew, who the gospel of John claims also began as a follower of the Baptist, though the synoptic gospels contradict this assertion by locating him in Capernaum; Andrew's brother Simon, the disciple whom Jesus nicknames Peter; Matthew, who is sometimes erroneously associated with another of Jesus's disciples, Levi, the toll collector; Jude the son of James; James the son of Alphaeus; Thomas, who would become legendary for doubting Jesus's resurrection; Bartholomew, about whom almost nothing is known; another Simon, known as "the Zealot," a designation meant to signal his commitment to the biblical doctrine of zeal, not his association with the Zealot Party, which would not exist for another thirty years; and Judas Iscariot, the man the gospels claim would one day betray Jesus to the high priest Caiaphas.

The Twelve will become the principal bearers of Jesus's message—the *apostoloi,* or "ambassadors"—apostles sent off to neighboring towns and villages to preach independently and without supervision (Luke 9:1–6). They would not be the leaders of Jesus's movement, but rather its chief missionaries. Yet the Twelve had another more symbolic function, one that would manifest itself later in Jesus's ministry. For they will come to represent the restoration of the twelve tribes of Israel, long since destroyed and scattered.

With his home base firmly established and his handpicked group of disciples growing, Jesus began visiting the village synagogue to preach his message to the people of Capernaum. The gospels say that those who heard him were astonished at his teaching, though not so much because of his words. Again, at this point, Jesus was merely echoing his master, John the Baptist: "From that time [when Jesus arrived in Capernaum]," Matthew writes, "Jesus began to proclaim, 'Repent! The Kingdom of Heaven is near'" (Matthew 4:17). Rather, what astonished the crowds at that Capernaum synagogue was the charismatic authority with which Jesus spoke, "for he taught them as one with authority, and not as the scribes" (Matthew 7:28; Mark 1:22; Luke 4:31).

The comparison to the scribes, emphasized in all three synoptic gospels, is conspicuous and telling. Unlike John the Baptist, who was likely raised in a family of Judean priests, Jesus was a peasant. He spoke like a peasant. He taught in Aramaic, the common tongue. His authority was not that of the bookish scholars and the priestly aristocracy. Their authority came from their solemn lucubration and their intimate connection to the Temple. Jesus's authority came directly from God. Indeed, from the moment he entered the synagogue in this small coastal village, Jesus went out of his way to set himself in direct opposition to the guardians of the Temple and the Jewish cult by challenging their authority as God's representatives on earth.

Although the gospels portray Jesus as being in conflict with a whole range of Jewish authorities who are often lumped together into formulaic categories such as "the chief priests and elders," or "the scribes and Pharisees," these were separate and distinct groups in first-century Palestine, and Jesus had different relationships with each of them. While the gospels tend to paint the Pharisees as Jesus's main detractors, the fact is that his relations with the Pharisees, while occasionally testy, were, for the most part, fairly civil and even friendly at times. Legend says it was a Pharisee who warned Jesus that his life was in danger (Luke 13:31), a Pharisee who helped bury him after his execution (John 19:39–40), a Pharisee who saved the lives of his disciples after he ascended into heaven (Acts 5:34). Jesus dined with Pharisees, he debated them, he lived among them; a few Pharisees were even counted among his followers.

In contrast, the handful of encounters Jesus had with the priestly nobility and the learned elite of legal scholars (the scribes) who represent them is always portrayed by the gospels in the most hostile light. To whom else was Jesus referring when he said, "You have turned my house into a den of thieves"? It was not the merchants and money changers he was addressing as he raged through the Temple courtyard, overturning tables and breaking open cages. It was those who profited most heavily from the Temple's commerce, and who did so on the backs of poor Galileans like himself.

Like his zealous predecessors, Jesus was less concerned with the pagan empire occupying Palestine than he was with the Jewish imposter occupying God's Temple. Both would come to view Jesus as a threat, and both would seek his death. But there can be no doubt that Jesus's main antagonist in the gospels is neither the distant emperor in Rome nor his heathen officials in Judea. It is the high priest Caiaphas, who would become the main instigator of the plot to execute Jesus precisely because of the threat he posed to the Temple's authority (Mark 14:1–2; Matthew 26:57–66; John 11:49–50).

As Jesus's ministry expanded, becoming ever more urgent and confrontational, his words and actions would increasingly reflect a deep antagonism toward the high priest and the Judean religious establishment, who, in Jesus's words, loved "to prance around in long robes and be greeted with respect in the marketplaces, and to have the front seats in the synagogues and the places of honor at feasts."

"They devour the homes of widows and make long prayers for the sake of appearance," Jesus says of the scribes. And for that, "their condemnation will be the greater" (Mark 12:38–40). Jesus's parables, especially, were riddled with the same anticlerical sentiments that shaped the politics and piety of Galilee, and that would become the hallmark of his ministry. Consider the famous parable of the Good Samaritan:

A certain man went down from Jerusalem to Jericho. He fell among thieves who stripped him of his clothes, beat him, and left him half dead. By chance, a priest came down that road, and when he saw the man, he passed by on the other side. A Levite (priest) also came by that place and seeing the man, he, too, passed on the other side. But a certain Samaritan on a journey came where the man was, and when he saw him, he had compassion. He went to him and bandaged his wounds and poured oil and wine on them. He placed the man on his own animal, and led him to an inn, and took care of him. The following day he gave the innkeeper two denarii and said, "Take care of him; when I come back I will repay you whatever more you spend" (Luke 10:30–37).

Christians have long interpreted this parable as reflecting the importance of helping those in distress. But for the audience gathered at Jesus's feet, the parable would have had less to do with the goodness of the Samaritan than with the baseness of the two priests.

The Jews considered the Samaritans to be the lowliest, most impure people in Palestine for one chief reason: the Samaritans rejected the primacy of the Temple of Jerusalem as the sole legitimate place of worship. Instead, they worshipped the God of Israel in their own temple on Mount Gerizim, on the western bank of the Jordan River. For those among Jesus's listeners who recognized themselves as the beaten, half-dead man left lying on the road, the lesson of the parable would have been self-evident: the Samaritan, who denies the authority of the Temple, goes out of his way to fulfill the commandment of the Lord to "love your neighbor as yourself" (the parable itself was given in response to the question "Who is my neighbor?"). The priests, who derive their wealth and authority from their connection to the Temple, ignore the commandment altogether for fear of defiling their ritual purity and thus endangering that connection.

The people of Capernaum devoured this brazenly anticlerical message. Almost immediately, large crowds began to gather around Jesus. Some recognized him as the boy born in Nazareth to a family of woodworkers. Others heard of the power of his words and came to listen to him preach out of curiosity. Still, at this point, Jesus's reputation was contained along the shores of Capernaum. Outside this fishing village, no one else had yet heard of the charismatic Galilean preacher—not Antipas in Tiberias, not Caiaphas in Jerusalem.

But then something happened that would change everything.

While standing at the Capernaum synagogue, speaking about the Kingdom of God, Jesus was suddenly interrupted by a man the gospels describe as having "an unclean spirit."

"What have we to do with you, Jesus of Nazareth?" the man cried out. "Have you come to destroy us? I know who you are, oh holy one of God."

Jesus cut him off. "Silence! Come out of him!"

All at once, the man fell to the floor, writhing in convulsions. A great cry came out of his mouth. And he was still.

Everyone in the synagogue was amazed. "What is this?" the people asked one another. "A new teaching? And with such authority that he commands the spirits and they obey him?" (Mark 1:23–28).

After that, Jesus's fame could no longer be confined to Capernaum. News of the itinerant preacher spread throughout the region, into the whole of Galilee. In every town and village the crowds grew larger as people everywhere came out, not so much to hear his message but to see the wondrous deeds they had heard about. For while the disciples would ultimately recognize Jesus as the promised messiah and the heir to the kingdom of David, while the Romans would view him as a false claimant to the office of King of the Jews, and while the scribes and the Temple priests would come to consider him a blasphemous threat to their control of the Jewish religion, for the vast majority of Jews in Palestine—those he claimed to have been sent to free from oppression—Jesus was neither messiah nor king, but just another traveling miracle worker and professional exorcist roaming through Galilee performing deeds.

Chapter Nine

By the Finger of God

It did not take long for the people of Capernaum to realize what they had in their midst. Jesus was surely not the first exorcist to walk the shores of the Sea of Galilee. In first-century Palestine, professional wonder worker was a vocation as well established as that of woodworker or mason, and far better paid. Galilee especially abounded with charismatic fantasts claiming to channel the divine for a nominal fee. Yet from the perspective of the Galileans, what set Jesus apart from his fellow exorcists and healers is that he seemed to be providing his services free of charge. That first exorcism in the Capernaum synagogue may have shocked the rabbis and elders who saw in it a "new kind of teaching"—the gospels say a slew of scribes began descending upon the city immediately afterward to see for themselves the challenge posed to their authority by this simple peasant. But for the people of Capernaum, what mattered was not so much the source of Jesus's healings. What mattered was their cost.

By evening, word had reached all of Capernaum about the free healer in their city. Jesus and his companions had taken shelter in the house of the brothers Simon and Andrew, where Simon's mother-in-law lay in bed with a fever. When the brothers told

Jesus of her illness, he went to her and took her hand, and at once she was healed. Soon after, a great horde gathered at Simon's house, carrying with them the lame, the lepers, and those possessed by demons. The next morning, the crush of sick and infirm had grown even larger.

To escape the crowds Jesus suggested leaving Capernaum for a few days. "Let us go into the next towns so I may proclaim my message there as well" (Mark 1:38). But news of the itinerant miracle worker had already reached the neighboring cities. Everywhere Jesus went—Bethsaida, Gerasa, Jericho—the blind, the deaf, the mute, and the paralytic swarmed to him. And Jesus healed them all. When he finally returned to Capernaum a few days later, so many had huddled at Simon's door that a group of men had to tear a hole in the roof just so they could lower their paralyzed friend down for Jesus to heal.

To the modern mind, the stories of Jesus's healings and exorcisms seem implausible, to say the least. Acceptance of his miracles forms the principal divide between the historian and the worshipper, the scholar and the seeker. It may seem somewhat incongruous, then, to say that there is more accumulated historical material confirming Jesus's miracles than there is regarding either his birth in Nazareth or his death at Golgotha. To be clear, there is no evidence to support any particular miraculous action by Jesus. Attempts by scholars to judge the authenticity of one or another of Jesus's healings or exorcisms have proven a useless exercise. It is senseless to argue that it is *more likely* that Jesus healed a paralytic but *less likely* that he raised Lazarus from the dead. All of Jesus's miracle stories were embellished with the passage of time and convoluted with Christological significance, and thus none of them can be historically validated. It is equally senseless to try to demythologize Jesus's miracles by searching for some rational basis to explain them away: Jesus only *appeared* to walk on water because of the changing tides; Jesus only *seemed* to exorcise a demon from a person who was in reality epileptic. How one in the modern world views Jesus's miraculous actions is irrelevant. All that can be known is how the people of his time viewed them. And therein lies the historical evidence. For while debates raged within the early church over who Jesus was—a rabbi? the messiah? God incarnate?—there was never any debate, either among his followers or his detractors, about his role as an exorcist and miracle worker.

All of the gospels, including the noncanonized scriptures, confirm Jesus's miraculous deeds, as does the earliest source material, Q. Nearly a third of the gospel of Mark consists solely of Jesus's healings and exorcisms. The early church not only maintained a vivid memory of Jesus's miracles, it built its very foundation upon them. Jesus's apostles were marked by their ability to mimic his miraculous powers, to heal and exorcise people in his name. Even those who did not accept him as messiah still viewed Jesus as "a doer of startling deeds." At no point in the gospels do Jesus's enemies ever deny his miracles, though they do question their motive and source. Well into the second and third centuries, the Jewish intellectuals and pagan philosophers who wrote treatises denouncing Christianity took Jesus's status as an exorcist and miracle worker for granted. They may have denounced Jesus as nothing more than a traveling magician, but they did not doubt his magical abilities.

Again, Jesus was not the only miracle worker trolling though Palestine healing the sick and casting out demons. This was a world steeped in magic and Jesus was just one of an untold number of diviners and dream interpreters, magicians and medicine men who wandered Judea and Galilee. There was Honi the Circle-Drawer, so named because during a time of drought he drew a circle in the dirt and stood inside it. "I swear by your great name that I will not move from here until you have mercy on your sons," Honi shouted up to God. And the rains came at once. Honi's grandsons Abba Hilqiah and Hanan the Hidden were also widely credited with miraculous deeds; both lived in Galilee around the same time as Jesus. Another Jewish miracle worker, Rabbi Hanina ben Dosa, who resided in the village of Arab just a few kilometers from Jesus's home in Nazareth, had the power to pray over the sick and even intercede on their behalf to discern who would live and who would die. Perhaps the most famous miracle worker of the time was Apollonius of Tyana. Described as a "holy man" who taught the concept of a "Supreme God," Apollonius performed miraculous deeds everywhere he went. He healed the lame, the blind, the paralytic. He even raised a girl from the dead.

Nor was Jesus the sole exorcist in Palestine. The itinerant Jewish exorcist was a familiar sight, and exorcisms themselves could be a lucrative enterprise. Many exorcists are mentioned in the gospels (Matthew 12:27; Luke 11:19; Mark 9:38–40; see also Acts 19:11–17). Some, like the famed exorcist Eleazar, who may have been an Essene, used amulets and incantations to draw demons out of the afflicted through their noses. Others, such as Rabbi Simon ben Yohai, could cast out demons simply by uttering the demon's name; like Jesus, Yohai would first command the demon to identify itself, which then gave him authority over it. The book of Acts portrays Paul as an exorcist who used Jesus's name as a talisman of power against demonic forces (Acts 16:16–18, 19:12). Exorcism instructions have even been found within the Dead Sea Scrolls.

The reason exorcisms were so commonplace in Jesus's time is that the Jews viewed illness as a manifestation either of divine judgment or of demonic activity. However one wishes to define demon possession—as a medical problem or a mental illness, epilepsy or schizophrenia—the fact remains that the people of Palestine understood these problems to be signs of possession, and they saw Jesus as one of a number of professional exorcists with the power to bring healing to those afflicted.

It may be true that, unlike many of his fellow exorcists and miracle workers, Jesus also maintained messianic ambitions. But so did the failed messiahs Theudas and the Egyptian, both of whom used their miraculous deeds to gain followers and make messianic claims. These men and their fellow wonder workers were known by Jews and gentiles alike as "men of deeds," the same term that was applied to Jesus. What is more, the literary form of the miracle stories found in the Jewish and pagan writings of the first and second centuries is almost identical to that of the gospels; the same basic vocabulary is used to describe both the miracle and the miracle worker. Simply put, Jesus's status as an exorcist and miracle worker may seem unusual, even absurd, to modern skeptics, but it did not deviate greatly from the standard expectation of exorcists and miracle workers in first-century Palestine. Whether Greek, Roman, Jewish, or Christian, all peoples in the ancient Near East viewed magic and miracle as a standard facet of their world.

That said, there was a distinct difference between magic and miracle in the ancient mind, not in their methods or outcome—both were considered ways of disrupting the natural order of the universe—but in the way in which each was perceived. In the Graeco-Roman world, magicians were ubiquitous, but magic was considered a form of charlatanry. There were a handful of Roman laws against "magic-working," and magicians themselves could be expelled or even executed if they were found to practice what was sometimes referred to as "dark magic." In Judaism, too, magicians were fairly prevalent, despite the prohibition against magic in the Law of Moses, where it is punishable by death. "No one shall be found among you," the Bible warns, "who engages in divination, or is a witch, an enchanter, or a sorcerer, or one who casts spells, or who consults spirits, one who is a wizard or a necromancer" (Deuteronomy 18:10–11).

The discrepancy between law and practice when it came to the magical arts can best be explained by the variable ways in which "magic" was defined. The word itself had extreme negative connotations, but only when applied to the practices of other peoples and religions. "Although the nations you are about to dispossess give heed to soothsayers and diviners," God tells the Israelites, "as for you, the Lord your God does not permit you to do so" (Deuteronomy 18:14). And yet God regularly has his servants engage in magical acts in order to prove his might. So, for example, God commands Moses and Aaron to "perform a wonder" in front of Pharaoh by transforming a staff into a snake. But when Pharaoh's "wise men" do the same trick, they are dismissed as "magicians" (Exodus 7:1–13, 9:8–12). In other words, a representative of God—such as Moses, Elijah, or Elisha—performs miracles, whereas a "false prophet"—such as Pharaoh's wise men or the priests of Baal—performs magic.

This explains why the early Christians went to such lengths to argue that Jesus was *not* a magician. Throughout the second and third centuries, the church's Jewish and Roman detractors wrote numerous tracts accusing Jesus of having used magic to captivate people and trick them into following him. "But though they saw such works, they asserted it was magical art," the second-century Christian apologist Justin Martyr wrote of his critics. "For they dared to call [Jesus] a magician, and a deceiver of the people."

Note that these enemies of the church did not deny that Jesus performed wondrous deeds. They merely labeled those deeds "magic." Regardless, church leaders, such as the famed third-century theologian Origen of Alexandria, responded furiously to these accusations, decrying the "slanderous and childish charge [that] Jesus was a magician," or that he performed his miracles by means of magical devices. As the early church father Irenaeus, bishop of Lugdunum, argued, it was precisely the lack of such magical devices that distinguished Jesus's miraculous actions from those of the common magician. Jesus, in the words of Irenaeus, performed his deeds "without any power of incantations, without the juice of herbs and of grasses, without any anxious watching of sacrifices, of libations, or of seasons."

Despite Irenaeus's protestations, however, Jesus's miraculous actions in the gospels, especially in the earliest gospel, Mark, do bear a striking resemblance to the actions of similar magicians and wonder workers of the time, which is why more than a few contemporary biblical scholars have openly labeled Jesus a magician. No doubt Jesus uses a magician's techniques—incantations, rehearsed formulae, spitting, repeated supplications—in some of his miracles. Once, in the region of the Decapolis, a group of villagers brought a deaf-mute man to Jesus and begged him for help. Jesus took the man aside, away from the crowd. Then, in a bizarre set of ritualized actions that could have come directly from an ancient magician's manual, Jesus placed his fingers in the deaf man's ears, spat, touched his tongue, and, looking up to the heavens, chanted the word *ephphatha,* which means "be opened" in Aramaic. Immediately the man's ears were opened and his tongue released (Mark 7:31–35).

In Bethsaida, Jesus performed a similar action on a blind man. He led the man away from the crowds, spat directly into his eyes, placed his hands on him, and asked, "Do you see anything?"

"I can see people," the man said. "But they look like walking trees."

Jesus repeated the ritual formula once more. This time the miracle took; the man regained his sight (Mark 8:22–26).

The gospel of Mark narrates an even more curious story about a woman who had been suffering from hemorrhages for twelve years. She had seen numerous doctors and spent all the money she possessed, but had found no relief from her condition. Having heard about Jesus, she came up behind him in a crowd, reached out, and touched his cloak. At once, her hemorrhaging ceased and she felt in her body that she had been healed.

What is remarkable about this story is that, according to Mark, Jesus "felt power drained from him." He stopped in his tracks and shouted, "Who touched my cloak?" The woman fell down before him and confessed the truth. "Daughter," Jesus replied. "Your faith has healed you" (Mark 5:24–34).

Mark's narrative seems to suggest that Jesus was a passive conduit through which healing power coursed like an electrical current. That is in keeping with the way in which magical processes are described in the texts of the time. It is certainly noteworthy that Matthew's retelling of the hemorrhaging-woman story twenty years later omits the magical quality of Mark's version. In Matthew, Jesus turns around when the woman touches him, acknowledges and addresses her, and only then does he actively heal her illness (Matthew 9:20–22).

Despite the magical elements that can be traced in some of his miracles, the fact is that nowhere in the gospels does anyone actually charge Jesus with performing magic. It would have been an easy accusation for his enemies to make, one that would have carried an immediate death sentence. Yet when Jesus stood before the Roman and Jewish authorities to answer the charges against him, he was accused of many misdeeds—sedition, blasphemy, rejecting the Law of Moses, refusing to pay the tribute, threatening the Temple—but being a magician was not one of them.

It is also worth noting that Jesus never exacted a fee for his services. Magicians, healers, miracle workers, exorcists—these were skilled and fairly well-paid professions in first-century Palestine. Eleazar the Exorcist was once asked to perform his feats for no less a personage than Emperor Vespasian. In the book of Acts, a professional magician popularly known as Simon Magus offers the apostles money to be trained in the art of manipulating the Holy Spirit to heal the sick. "Give me this power also," Simon asks Peter and John, "so that anyone I lay my hands upon may receive the Holy Spirit."

"May your money perish with you," Peter replies, "for you thought you could purchase with money what God gives as a free gift" (Acts 8:9–24).

Peter's answer may seem extreme. But he is merely following the command of his messiah, who told his disciples to "heal the sick, cleanse the lepers, raise the dead, and cast out the demons. You received [these gifts] without payment. *Give them out without payment*" (Matthew 10:8 | Luke 9:1–2).

In the end, it may be futile to argue about whether Jesus was a magician or a miracle worker. Magic and miracle are perhaps best thought of as two sides of the same coin in ancient Palestine. The church fathers were right about one thing, however. There is clearly something unique and distinctive about Jesus's miraculous actions in the gospels. It is not simply that Jesus's work is free of charge, or that his healings do not always employ a magician's methods. It is that Jesus's miracles are not intended as an end in themselves. Rather, his actions serve a pedagogical purpose. They are a means of conveying a very specific message to the Jews.

A clue to what that message might be surfaces in an intriguing passage in Q. As recounted in the gospels of Matthew and Luke, John the Baptist is languishing in a prison cell atop the fortress of Machaerus, awaiting his execution, when he hears of the wondrous deeds being performed in Galilee by one of his former disciples. Curious about the reports, John sends a messenger to ask Jesus whether he is "the one who is to come."

"Go tell John what you hear and see," Jesus tells the messenger. "The blind see, the lame walk, the lepers are cleansed, the deaf hear, the dead are raised up, and the poor are brought good news" (Matthew 11:1–6 | Luke 7:18–23).

Jesus's words are a deliberate reference to the prophet Isaiah, who long ago foretold a day when Israel would be redeemed and Jerusalem renewed, a day when God's kingdom would be established on earth. "Then the eyes of the blind shall be opened, and the ears of the deaf shall be unstopped, the lame shall leap like deer, and the tongue of the mute shall sing for joy," Isaiah promised. "The dead shall live, and the corpses shall rise" (Isaiah 35:5–6, 26:19).

By connecting his miracles with Isaiah's prophecy, Jesus is stating in no uncertain terms that the year of the Lord's favor, the day of God's vengeance, which the prophets predicted, has finally arrived. God's reign has begun. "If by the finger of God I cast out demons, then surely the Kingdom of God has come upon you" (Matthew 12:28 | Luke 11:20). Jesus's miracles are thus the manifestation of God's kingdom on earth. It is the finger of God that heals the blind, the deaf, the mute—the finger of God that exorcises the demons. Jesus's task is simply to wield that finger as God's agent on earth.

Except that God already had agents on earth. They were the ones clothed in fine white robes milling about the Temple, hovering over the mountains of incense and the ceaseless sacrifices. The chief function of the priestly nobility was not only to preside over the Temple rituals, but to control access to the Temple itself. The very purpose of designing the Temple of Jerusalem as a series of ever more restrictive ingressions was to maintain the priestly monopoly over who can and cannot come into the presence of God and to what degree. The sick, the lame, the leper, the "demon-possessed," menstruating women, those with bodily discharges, those who had recently given birth—none of these were permitted to enter the Temple and take part in the rituals unless first purified according to the priestly code. With every leper cleansed, every paralytic healed, every demon cast out, Jesus was not only challenging that priestly code, he was invalidating the very purpose of the priesthood.

Thus, in the gospel of Matthew, when a leper comes to him begging to be healed, Jesus reaches out and touches him, healing his affliction. But he does not stop there. "Go show yourself to the priest," he tells the man. "Offer him as a testimony the things that the Law of Moses commanded for your cleansing."

Jesus is joking. His command to the leper is a jest—a calculated swipe at the priestly code. The leper is not just ill, after all. He is impure. He is ceremonially unclean and unworthy of entering the Temple of God. His illness contaminates the entire community. According to the Law of Moses to which Jesus refers, the only way for a leper to be cleansed is to complete the most laborious and costly ritual, one that could be conducted solely by a priest. First the leper must bring the priest two clean birds, along with some cedarwood, crimson yarn, and hyssop. One of the birds must be sacrificed immediately and the living bird, the cedarwood, the yarn, and the hyssop dipped in its blood. The blood must then be sprinkled upon the leper and the living bird released. Seven days later, the leper must shave off all his hair and bathe himself in water. On the eighth day, the leper must take two male lambs, free of blemish, and one ewe lamb, also without blemish, as well as a grain offering of choice flour mixed with oil, back to the priest, who will make of them a burnt offering to the Lord. The priest must smear the blood from the offering on the leper's right earlobe, on his right thumb, and on the big toe of his right foot. He must then sprinkle the leper with the oil seven times. Only after all of this is complete shall the leper be considered free of the sin and guilt that led to his leprosy in the first place; only then shall he be allowed to rejoin the community of God (Leviticus 14).

Obviously, Jesus is not telling the leper he has just healed to buy two birds, two lambs, a ewe, a strip of cedarwood, a spool of crimson yarn, a sprig of hyssop, a bushel of flour, and a jar of oil and to give them all to the priest as an offering to God. He is telling him to present himself to the priest, *having already been cleansed*. This is a direct challenge not only to the priest's authority, but to the Temple itself. Jesus did not only heal the leper, he purified him, making him eligible to appear at the Temple as a true Israelite. And he did so for free, as a gift from God—without tithe, without sacrifice—thus seizing for himself the powers granted solely to the priesthood to deem a man worthy of entering the presence of God.

Such a blatant attack on the legitimacy of the Temple could be scorned and discounted so long as Jesus remains ensconced in the backwoods of Galilee. But once he and his disciples leave their base in Capernaum and begin slowly making their way to Jerusalem, healing the sick and casting out demons along the way, Jesus's collision with the priestly authorities, and the Roman Empire that supports them, becomes inevitable. Soon, the authorities in Jerusalem will no longer be able to ignore this itinerant exorcist and miracle worker. The closer he draws to the Holy City, the more urgent the need to silence him will become. For it is not just Jesus's miraculous actions that they fear; it is the simple yet incredibly dangerous message conveyed through them.

The Kingdom of God is at hand.

Chapter Ten

May Your Kingdom Come

"To what shall I compare the Kingdom of God?" Jesus asked. It is like a mighty king who, having prepared a grand wedding banquet for his son, sends forth his servants to the four corners of the kingdom to invite his honored guests to the joyous occasion.

"Tell my guests I have readied the banquet," the king instructs his servants. "The oxen and cattle have been fattened and butchered. Everything is prepared. Come to the wedding festivities."

The servants go out to spread the king's tidings. Yet one by one the honored guests decline the invitation. "I have recently purchased a piece of land," one says. "I must tend to it. Please accept my regrets."

"I have bought five yoke of oxen and I must test them out," says another. "Please accept my regrets."

"I myself just got married," says a third. "I cannot come."

When the servants return, they inform the king that none of his guests have accepted the invitation, that some of those invited not only refused to attend the celebration, they seized the king's servants, mistreated them, even killed them.

In a rage the king orders the servants to search the streets and back alleys of the kingdom, to gather everyone they can find—young and old, poor and weak, the lame, the crippled, the blind, the outcast—and to bring them all to the banquet.

The servants do so, and the feast commences. But in the midst of the celebrations the king notices a guest who was not invited; he is not wearing the wedding clothes.

"How did you get in here?" the king asks the stranger.

The man has no answer.

"Tie him hand and foot!" the king commands. "Throw him out into the darkness, where there will be weeping and gnashing of teeth. For many will be invited, but few are chosen."

As for those guests who refused to come to the wedding, the ones who seized and killed his servants—the king unleashes his army to drive them out of their homes, to slaughter them like sheep, and burn their cities to the ground.

"He who has ears to hear, let him hear" (Matthew 22:1–4 | Luke 14:16–24).

Of this there can be no doubt: the central theme and unifying message of Jesus's brief ministry was the promise of the Kingdom of God. Practically everything Jesus said or did in the gospels served the function of publicly proclaiming the Kingdom's coming. It was the very first thing he preached about after separating from John the Baptist: "Repent, the Kingdom of God is near" (Mark 1:15). It was the core of the Lord's prayer, which John taught to Jesus and Jesus in turn taught to his disciples: "Our Father, who is in heaven, holy is your name. May your Kingdom come . . ." (Matthew 6:9–13 | Luke 11:1–2). It was what Jesus's followers were told to strive for above all else—"Seek first the Kingdom of God, and God's justice, then all these things shall be added unto you" (Matthew 6:33 | Luke 12:31)—for only by forsaking everything and everyone for the Kingdom of God would they have any hope of entering it (Matthew 10:37–39 | Luke 14:25–27).

Jesus spoke so often, and so abstractly, about the Kingdom of God that it is difficult to know whether he himself had a unified conception of it. The phrase, along with its Matthaean equivalent "Kingdom of Heaven," hardly appears in the New Testament outside of the gospels. Although numerous passages in the Hebrew Scriptures describe God as king and sole sovereign, the exact phrase "Kingdom of God" appears only in the apocryphal text *The Wisdom of Solomon* (10:10), in which God's kingdom is envisioned as physically situated in heaven, the place where God's throne sits, where the angelic court sees to his every demand, and where his will is done always and without fail.

Yet the Kingdom of God in Jesus's teachings is not a celestial kingdom existing on a cosmic plane. Those who claim otherwise often point to a single unreliable passage in the gospel of John in which Jesus allegedly tells Pilate, "My kingdom is not of this world" (John 18:36). Not only is this the sole passage in the gospels where Jesus makes such a claim, it is an imprecise translation of the original Greek. The phrase *ouk estin ek tou kosmou* is perhaps better translated as "not part of this order/system [of government]." Even if one accepts the historicity of the passage (and very few scholars do), Jesus was not claiming that the Kingdom of God is unearthly; he was saying it is unlike any kingdom or government on earth.

Neither did Jesus present the Kingdom of God as some distant future kingdom to be established at the end of time. When Jesus said, "the Kingdom of God has drawn near" (Mark 1:15) or "the Kingdom of God is in your midst" (Luke 17:21), he was pointing to God's saving action in his present age, at his present time. True, Jesus spoke of wars and uprisings, earthquakes and famine, false messiahs and prophets who would presage the establishment of the Kingdom of God on earth (Mark 13:5–37). But far from auguring some future apocalypse, Jesus's words were in reality a perfectly apt description of the era in which he lived: an era of wars, famines, and false messiahs. In fact, Jesus seemed to expect the Kingdom of God to be established at any moment: "I tell you, there are those here who will not taste death until they have seen the Kingdom of God come with power" (Mark 9:1).

If the Kingdom of God is neither purely celestial nor wholly eschatological, then what Jesus was proposing must have been a physical and present kingdom: a *real* kingdom, with an *actual* king that was about to be established on earth. That is certainly how the Jews would have understood it. Jesus's particular conception of the Kingdom of God may have been distinctive and somewhat unique, but its connotations would not have been unfamiliar to his audience. Jesus was merely reiterating what the zealots had been preaching for years. Simply put, the Kingdom of God was shorthand for belief in God as the sole sovereign, the one and only king, not just over Israel, but over all the world. "Everything in heaven and earth belongs to you," the Bible states of God. "Yours is the kingdom . . . You rule over everything" (1 Chronicles 29:11–12; see also Numbers 23:21; Deuteronomy 33:5). In fact, the concept of the sole sovereignty of God lay behind the message of all the great prophets of old. Elijah, Elisha, Micah, Amos, Isaiah, Jeremiah—these men vowed that God would deliver the Jews from bondage and liberate Israel from foreign rule if only they refused to serve any earthly master or bow to any king save the one and only king of the universe. The same belief formed the foundation of nearly every Jewish resistance movement, from the Maccabees who threw off the yoke of Seleucid rule in 164 B.C.E., after the mad Greek king Antiochus Epiphanes demanded that the Jews worship him like a god, to the radicals and revolutionaries who resisted the Roman occupation—the bandits, the Sicarii, the zealots, and the martyrs at Masada—all the way to the last of the great failed messiahs, Simon son of Kochba, whose rebellion in 132 C.E. invoked the exact phrase "Kingdom of God" as a call for freedom from foreign rule.

Jesus's view of the sole sovereignty of God was not all that different from the view of the prophets, bandits, zealots, and messiahs who came before and after him, as evidenced by his answer to the question about paying tribute to Caesar. Actually, his view of God's reign was not so different from that of his master, John the Baptist, from whom he likely picked up the phrase "Kingdom of God."

What made Jesus's interpretation of the Kingdom of God different from John's, however, was his agreement with the zealots that God's reign required not just an internal transformation toward justice and righteousness, but a complete reversal of the present political, religious, and economic system. "Blessed are you who are poor, for the Kingdom of God is yours. Blessed are you who are hungry, for you shall be fed. Blessed are you who mourn, for you shall soon be laughing" (Luke 6:20–21).

These abiding words of the Beatitudes are, more than anything else, a promise of impending deliverance from subservience and foreign rule. They predict a radically new world order wherein the meek inherit the earth, the sick are healed, the weak become strong, the hungry are fed, and the poor are made rich. In the Kingdom of God, wealth will be redistributed and debts canceled. "The first shall be last and the last shall be first" (Matthew 5:3–12 | Luke 6:20–24).

But that also means that when the Kingdom of God is established on earth, the rich will be made poor, the strong will become weak, and the powerful will be displaced by the powerless. "How hard it will be for the wealthy to enter the Kingdom of God!" (Mark 10:23). The Kingdom of God is not some utopian fantasy wherein God vindicates the poor and the dispossessed. It is a chilling new reality in which God's wrath rains down upon the rich, the strong, and the powerful. "Woe to you who are rich, for you have received your consolation. Woe to you who are full, for you shall hunger. Woe to you laughing now, for soon you will mourn" (Luke 6:24–25).

The implications of Jesus's words are clear: The Kingdom of God is about to be established on earth; God is on the verge of restoring Israel to glory. But God's restoration cannot happen without the destruction of the present order. God's rule cannot be established without the annihilation of the present leaders. Saying "the Kingdom of God is at hand," therefore, is akin to saying the end of the Roman Empire is at hand. It means God is going to replace Caesar as ruler of the land. The Temple priests, the wealthy Jewish aristocracy, the Herodian elite, and the heathen usurper in distant Rome—all of these were about to feel the wrath of God.

The Kingdom of God is a call to revolution, plain and simple. And what revolution, especially one fought against an empire whose armies had ravaged the land set aside by God for his chosen people, could be free of violence and bloodshed? If the Kingdom of God is not an ethereal fantasy, how else could it be established upon a land occupied by a massive imperial presence except through the use of force? The prophets, bandits, zealots, and messiahs of Jesus's time all knew this, which is why they did not hesitate to employ violence in trying to establish God's rule on earth. The question is, did Jesus feel the same? Did he agree with his fellow messiahs Hezekiah the bandit chief, Judas the Galilean, Menahem, Simon son of Giora, Simon son of Kochba, and the rest, that violence was necessary to bring about the rule of God on earth? Did he follow the zealot doctrine that the land had to be forcibly cleansed of all foreign elements just as God had demanded in the scriptures?

There may be no more important question than this for those trying to pry the historical Jesus away from the Christian Christ. The common depiction of Jesus as an inveterate peacemaker who "loved his enemies" and "turned the other cheek" has been built mostly on his portrayal as an apolitical preacher with no interest in or, for that matter, knowledge of the politically turbulent world in which he lived. That picture of Jesus has already been shown to be a complete fabrication. The Jesus of history had a far more complex attitude toward violence. There is no evidence that Jesus himself openly advocated violent actions. But he was certainly no pacifist. "Do not think that I have come to bring peace on earth. I have not come to bring peace, but the sword" (Matthew 10:34 | Luke 12:51).

After the Jewish Revolt and the destruction of Jerusalem, the early Christian church tried desperately to distance Jesus from the zealous nationalism that had led to that awful war. As a result, statements such as "love your enemies" and "turn the other cheek" were deliberately cleansed of their Jewish context and transformed into abstract ethical principles that all peoples could abide regardless of their ethnic, cultural, or religious persuasions.

Yet if one wants to uncover what Jesus himself truly believed, one must never lose sight of this fundamental fact: *Jesus was not a Christian.* Jesus was a Jew preaching Judaism to other Jews. His was a Jewish mission, one concerned exclusively with the fate of his fellow Jews. Israel was all that mattered to Jesus. He insisted that his mission was "solely to the lost sheep of the house of Israel" (Matthew 15:24) and commanded his disciples to share the good news with none but their fellow Jews: "Go nowhere near the gentiles and do not enter the city of the Samaritans" (Matthew 10:5–6). Obviously, the disciples took this command to heart. As the book of Acts indicates, they did not begin preaching to gentiles until at least two decades after Jesus's death. Whenever Jesus himself encountered gentiles, he always kept them at a distance and often healed them reluctantly. As he explained to the Syrophoenician woman who came to him seeking help for her daughter, "Let the children [by which Jesus means Israel] be fed first, for it is not right to take the children's bread and throw it to the dogs [by which he means gentiles like her]" (Mark 7:27).

When it came to the heart and soul of the Jewish faith—the Law of Moses—Jesus was adamant that his mission was not to abolish the law but to fulfill it (Matthew 5:17). That law made a clear distinction between relations *among* Jews and relations *between* Jews and foreigners. The oft-repeated commandment to "love your neighbor as yourself" was not Jesus's invention. It comes directly from the Torah and is meant to be applied strictly in the context of internal relations within Israel. The verse in question reads: "You shall not take vengeance or bear a grudge *against any of your people,* but you shall love your neighbor as yourself" (Leviticus 19:18). To the Israelites, as well as to Jesus's community in first-century Palestine, "neighbor" meant one's fellow Jews, whether friend or foe. With regard to the treatment of foreigners and outsiders, oppressors and occupiers, however, the Torah could not be clearer: "You shall drive them out before you. You shall make no covenant with them and their gods. *They shall not live in your land*" (Exodus 23:31–33).

For those who view Jesus as the literally begotten son of God, Jesus's Jewishness is immaterial. If Christ is divine, then he stands above any particular law or custom. But for those seeking the simple Jewish peasant and charismatic preacher who lived in Palestine two thousand years ago, there is nothing more important than this one undeniable truth: the same God whom the Bible calls "a man of war" (Exodus 15:3), the God who repeatedly commands the wholesale slaughter of every foreign man, woman, and child who occupies the land of the Jews, the "blood-spattered God" of Abraham, and Moses, and Jacob, and Joshua (Isaiah 63:3), the God who "shatters the heads of his enemies," bids his warriors to bathe their feet in their blood and leave their corpses to be eaten by dogs (Psalms 68:21–23)—that is the *only* God that Jesus knew and the *sole* God he worshipped.

There is no reason to consider Jesus's conception of his neighbors and enemies to have been any more or less expansive than that of any other Jew of his time. His commands to "love your enemies" and "turn the other cheek" must be read as being directed exclusively at his fellow Jews and meant as a model of peaceful relations exclusively within the Jewish community. The commands have nothing to do with how to treat foreigners and outsiders, especially those savage "plunderers of the world" who occupied God's land in direct violation of the Law of Moses, which Jesus viewed himself as fulfilling. *They shall not live in your land.*

In any case, neither the commandment to love one's enemies nor the plea to turn the other cheek is equivalent to a call for nonviolence or nonresistance. Jesus was not a fool. He understood what every other claimant to the mantle of the messiah understood: God's sovereignty could not be established except through force. "From the days of John the Baptist until now the Kingdom of God has been coming violently, and the violent ones try to snatch it away" (Matthew 11:12 | Luke 16:16).

That is not to say that Jesus thought his rag-tag band of disciples was going to defeat Rome. On the contrary, he assumed God would do it for them. That is, after all, what God had always done for the Jews. It was God who drowned Pharaoh's army, not the Israelites (Exodus 14). It was God who brought down the walls of Jericho, not Joshua's trumpet (Joshua 6). God destroyed the Amalekites and the Jebusites. He hurled stones from heaven upon the Amorites, killing every last one of them (Joshua 10). He exterminated the Canaanites so the Jews could have this land in the first place. God had defeated Israel's enemies in the past and he would do so again, but only if his followers remained faithful and zealous for the Lord.

It was precisely to prepare for the unavoidable consequences of establishing the Kingdom of God on earth that Jesus handpicked his twelve apostles. The Jews of Jesus's time believed that a day would come when the twelve tribes of Israel would be reconstituted to once again form a single, united nation. The prophets had predicted it: "I shall restore the fortunes of my people, Israel and Judah, says the Lord, and I shall bring them back to the land that I gave their ancestors and they shall take possession of it" (Jeremiah 30:3). By designating the Twelve and promising that they would "sit on twelve thrones judging the twelve tribes of Israel" (Matthew 19:28 | Luke 22:28–30), Jesus was signaling that the day they had been waiting for, when the Lord of Hosts would "break the yoke from off the neck" of the Jews and "burst their bonds" (Jeremiah 30:8), had arrived. The restoration and renewal of the *true* nation of Israel, which John the Baptist had preached, was finally at hand. The Kingdom of God was here.

This was a daring and provocative message. For as the prophet Isaiah warned, God would "gather the scattered people of Israel and the dispersed people of Judah" for a single purpose: *war*. The new, reconstituted Israel will, in the words of the prophet, "raise a signal-banner to the nations," it will "swoop down on the backs of the Philistines in the west" and "plunder the people of the east." It will repossess the land God gave the Jews and wipe from it forever the foul stench of foreign occupation (Isaiah 11:11–16).

The designation of the Twelve is, if not a call to war, an admission of its inevitability, which is why Jesus expressly warned them of what was to come: "If anyone wishes to follow me, let him deny himself and take up his cross and follow me" (Mark 8:34). This is not the statement of self-denial it has so often been interpreted as being. The cross is the punishment for sedition, not a symbol of self-abnegation. Jesus was warning the Twelve that their status as the embodiment of the twelve tribes that will reconstitute the nation of Israel and throw off the yoke of occupation would rightly be understood by Rome as treason and thus inevitably lead to crucifixion. It was an admission that Jesus frequently made for himself. Over and over again, Jesus reminded his disciples of what lay ahead for him: rejection, arrest, torture, and execution (Matthew 16:21, 17:22–23, 20:18–19; Mark 8:31, 9:31, 10:33; Luke 9:22, 44, 18:32–33). It could be argued that the evangelists, who were writing decades after the events they described, knew that Jesus's story would end on a cross in Golgotha, and so they put these predictions into Jesus's mouth to prove his prowess as a prophet. But the sheer volume of Jesus's statements about his inevitable capture and crucifixion indicates that his frequent self-prophecies may be historical. Then again, it does not take a prophet to predict what happens to someone who challenges either the priestly control of the Temple or the Roman occupation of Palestine. The road ahead for Jesus and the Twelve had been made manifest by the many messianic aspirants who came before him. The destination was clear.

That explains why Jesus went to such lengths to hide the truth about the Kingdom of God from all but his disciples. Jesus recognized that the new world order he envisioned was so radical, so dangerous, so revolutionary, that Rome's only conceivable response to it would be to arrest and execute them all for sedition. He therefore consciously chose to veil the Kingdom of God in abstruse and enigmatic parables that are nearly impossible to understand. "The secret of the Kingdom of God has been given to you to know," Jesus tells his disciples. "But to outsiders, everything is said in parables so that they may see and not perceive, they may hear and not understand" (Mark 4:11–12).

What, then, is the Kingdom of God in Jesus's teachings? It is at once the joyous wedding feast within the king's royal hall, and the blood-soaked streets outside its walls. It is a treasure hidden in a field; sell all you have and buy that field (Matthew 13:44). It is a pearl tucked inside a shell; sacrifice everything to seek out that shell (Matthew 13:45). It is a mustard seed—the smallest of seeds—buried in soil. One day soon it will bloom into a majestic tree, and birds shall nest in its branches (Matthew 13:31–32). It is a net drawn from the sea, bursting with fish both good and bad; the good shall be kept, the bad discarded (Matthew 13:47). It is a meadow choking with both weeds and wheat. When the reaper comes, he will harvest the wheat. But the weeds he will bundle together and toss into the fire (Matthew 13:24–30). And the reaper is nearly here. God's will is about to be done on earth, just as it is in heaven. So then, take your hand off the plow and do not look back, let the dead bury the dead, leave behind your husband and your wife, your brothers and sisters and children, and prepare yourself to receive the Kingdom of God. "Already, the ax is laid at the root of the tree."

Of course, none of Jesus's obfuscations about the meaning and implications of the Kingdom of God would keep him from being seized and crucified. Jesus's assertion that the present order was about to be reversed, that the rich and the powerful were going to be made poor and weak, that the twelve tribes of Israel would soon be reconstituted into a single nation and God made once again the sole ruler in Jerusalem—none of these provocative statements would have been well received in the Temple, where the high priest reigned, or the Antonia Fortress, where Rome governed. After all, if the Kingdom of God, as Jesus presented it, was in fact a real, physical kingdom, then did it not require a real, physical king? Was not Jesus claiming for himself that royal title? He promised a throne for each of his twelve apostles. Did he not have in mind a throne for himself?

Granted, Jesus provided no specifics about the new world order he envisioned (though neither did any other royal claimant of his time). There are no practical programs, no detailed agendas, no specific political or economic recommendations in Jesus's teachings about the Kingdom of God. He seems to have had no interest at all in laying out how God's reign on earth would actually function. That was for God alone to determine. But there is no question that Jesus had a clear vision for his own role in the Kingdom of God: "If by the finger of God I cast out demons, then surely the Kingdom of God has come upon you."

The presence of the Kingdom of God may have empowered Jesus to heal the sick and the demon-possessed. But at the same time, it was Jesus's healings and exorcisms that were bringing the Kingdom of God to fruition. It was, in other words, a symbiotic relationship. As God's agent on earth—the one who wielded God's finger—Jesus himself was ushering in the Kingdom of God and establishing God's dominion through his miraculous actions. He was, in effect, the Kingdom of God personified. Who else should sit on God's throne?

No wonder, then, that at the end of his life, when he stood beaten and bruised before Pontius Pilate to answer the charges made against him, Jesus was asked but a single question. It was the only question that mattered, the only question he would have been brought before the Roman governor to answer before being sent off to the cross to receive the standard punishment for all rebels and insurrectionists.

"Are you the King of the Jews?"

Chapter Eleven

Who Do You Say I Am?

Two years have passed, more or less, since Jesus of Nazareth first met John the Baptist at the lip of the Jordan River and followed him into the Judean desert. In that time, Jesus has not only carried on his master's message about the Kingdom of God; he has expanded it into a movement of national liberation for the afflicted and oppressed—a movement founded upon the promise that God would soon intervene on behalf of the meek and the poor, that he would smite the imperial Roman power just as he smote Pharaoh's army so long ago and free his Temple from the hands of the hypocrites who controlled it. Jesus's movement has drawn to him a corps of zealous disciples, twelve of whom have been given the authority to preach his message on their own. In every town and city they enter, in the villages and the countryside, great crowds gather to hear Jesus and his disciples preach, and to take part in the free healings and exorcisms they offer to those who seek their help.

Despite their relative success, however, Jesus and his disciples have for the most part restricted their activities to the northern provinces of Galilee, Phoenicia, and Gaulanitis, wisely keeping a safe distance from Judea and the seat of the Roman occupation in Jerusalem. They have cut a circuitous route through the Galilean countryside, altogether bypassing the royal cities of Sepphoris and Tiberias, lest they confront the tetrarch's forces. Although they've approached the prosperous ports of Tyre and Sidon, they have refrained from entering either. They have rambled along the edge of the Decapolis, yet strictly avoided the Greek cities themselves and the heathen populations therein. In place of the region's wealthy *cosmopoleis,* Jesus has focused his attention on poorer villages such as Nazareth, Capernaum, Bethsaida, and Nain, where his promise of a new world order has been eagerly received, as well as on the coastal towns that rim the Sea of Galilee, save for Tiberias, of course, where Herod Antipas stews on his throne.

But now word of Jesus and his band of followers has finally reached Antipas's court. Certainly, Jesus has not been shy in condemning "that Fox" who claims the tetrarchy of Galilee and Peraea, nor has he ceased pouring contempt upon the hypocrite priests and scribes—the "brood of vipers"—who he claims will be displaced in the coming Kingdom of God by harlots and toll collectors. Not only has he healed those whom the Temple cast out as sinners beyond salvation, he has cleansed them of their sins, thus rendering irrelevant the entire priestly establishment and their costly, exclusivist rituals. His healings and exorcisms have drawn crowds too large for the tetrarch in Tiberias to ignore, though, at least for now, the fickle masses seem less interested in Jesus's teachings than in his "tricks," so much so that when they keep asking for a sign so that they may believe his message, Jesus seems finally to have had enough. "It is an evil and adulterous generation that seeks a sign; no sign shall be given to it" (Matthew 12:38).

All of this activity has the sycophants at Antipas's court chattering about who this Galilean preacher may be. Some think he is Elijah reborn, or perhaps one of the other "prophets of old." That is not a wholly unreasonable conclusion. Elijah, who lived in the northern kingdom of Israel in the ninth century B.C.E., was the paradigm of the wonder-working prophet. A fearsome and uncompromising warrior for Yahweh, Elijah strove to root out the worship of the Canaanite god Baal among the Israelites. "How long will you continue limping along with two opinions?" Elijah asked the people. "If Yahweh is god, then follow him; if Baal is god, then follow him" (1 Kings 18:21).

To prove Yahweh's superiority, Elijah challenged four hundred and fifty priests of Baal to a contest. They would prepare two altars, each with a bull placed on a pillar of wood. The priests would pray to Baal for fire to consume the offering, while Elijah prayed to Yahweh.

Day and night the priests of Baal prayed. They shouted aloud and cut themselves with swords and lances until they were awash in blood. They cried and begged and pleaded with Baal to bring down fire, but nothing happened.

Elijah then poured twelve jars of water on his pyre, took a step back, and called upon the god of Abraham, Isaac, and Israel to show his might. At once a great ball of fire fell down from heaven and consumed the bull, the wood, the stones, the dust on the ground, and the pools of water surrounding the sacrifice. When the Israelites saw the work of Yahweh, they fell down on their knees and worshipped him as God. But Elijah was not finished. He seized the four hundred and fifty priests of Baal, forced them down into the valley of Wadi Kishon, and, according to the scriptures, slaughtered every last one of them with his own hands, for he was "zealous for the Lord God Almighty" (1 Kings 18:20–40, 19:10).

So great was Elijah's zeal that he was not allowed to die but was taken up to heaven in a whirlwind to sit beside God's throne (2 Kings 2:11). His return at the end of time, when he would gather together the twelve tribes of Israel and sweep in the messianic age, was predicted by the prophet Malachi: "Behold, I am sending the prophet Elijah to you before the great and terrible day of the Lord comes. He will turn the hearts of fathers to their sons, and the hearts of sons to their fathers, lest I come and smite the land with a curse" (Malachi 4:5–6).

Malachi's prophecy explains why the courtiers at Tiberias see in

Jesus the reincarnation of Israel's quintessential end-times prophet. Jesus has done little to discourage such comparisons, consciously taking upon himself the symbols of the prophet Elijah—the itinerant ministry, the peremptory calling of disciples, the mission to reconstitute the twelve tribes, the strict focus on the northern regions of Israel, and the signs and wonders he performs everywhere he goes.

Antipas, however, is unconvinced by the mutterings of his courtiers. He believes that the preacher from Nazareth is not Elijah but John the Baptist, whom he killed, risen from the dead. Blinded by guilt over John's execution, he is incapable of conceiving Jesus's true identity (Matthew 14:1–2; Mark 6:14–16; Luke 9:7–9).

Meanwhile, Jesus and his disciples continue their slow journey toward Judea and Jerusalem. Leaving behind the village of Bethsaida, where, according to the Gospel of Mark, Jesus fed five thousand people with only five loaves of bread and two fish (Mark 6:30–44), the disciples begin traveling along the outskirts of Caesarea Philippi, a Roman city north of the Sea of Galilee that serves as the seat of the tetrarchy of Herod the Great's other son, Philip. As they walk, Jesus casually asks his followers, "Who do the people say I am?"

The disciples' response reflects the speculations at Tiberias: "Some say you are John the Baptist. Others say Elijah. Still others say you are Jeremiah or one of the other prophets risen from the dead."

Jesus stops and turns to his disciples. "But who do *you* say I am?"

It falls upon Simon Peter, the nominal leader of the Twelve, to answer for the rest: "You are messiah," Peter says, inferring at this fateful juncture in the gospel story the mystery that the tetrarch in Tiberias could not possibly comprehend (Matthew 16:13–16; Mark 8:27–29; Luke 9:18–20).

Six days later, Jesus takes Peter and the brothers James and John—the sons of Zebedee—to a high mountain, where he is miraculously transformed before their eyes. "His clothes became dazzling white, like snow," Mark writes, "whiter than any fuller on earth could whiten them." Suddenly Elijah, the prophet and precursor to the messiah, appears on the mountain. With him is Moses, the great liberator and lawgiver of Israel, the man who broke the bonds of the Israelites and shepherded the people of God back to the Promised Land.

Elijah's presence on the mountain has already been primed by the speculations in Tiberias and by the ruminations of the disciples at Caesarea Philippi. But Moses's appearance is something else entirely. The parallels between the so-called transfiguration story and the Exodus account of Moses receiving the law on Mount Sinai are hard to miss. Moses also took three companions with him up the mountain—Aaron, Nadab and Abihu—and he, too, was physically transformed by the experience. Yet whereas Moses's transformation was the result of his coming into contact with God's glory, Jesus is transformed by his own glory. Indeed, the scene is written in such a way so that Moses and Elijah—the Law and the Prophets—are clearly made subordinate to Jesus.

The disciples are terrified by the vision, and rightly so. Peter tries to ease the disquiet by offering to build three tabernacles at the site: one for Jesus, one for Elijah, and one for Moses. As he speaks, a cloud consumes the mountain—just as it did centuries ago on Mount Sinai—and a voice from within echoes the words that were uttered from on high the day that Jesus began his ministry at the Jordan River: "This is my son. The Beloved. Listen to him," God says, bestowing upon Jesus the same sobriquet (*ho Agapitos,* "the Beloved") that God had given to King David. Thus, what Antipas's court could not conceive, and Simon Peter could only surmise, is now divinely confirmed in a voice from a cloud atop a mountain: Jesus of Nazareth is the anointed messiah, the King of the Jews (Matthew 17:1–8; Mark 9:2–8; Luke 9:28–36).

What makes these three clearly interconnected scenes so significant is that up to this point in Jesus's ministry, particularly as it has been presented in the earliest gospel, Mark, Jesus has made no statement whatsoever about his messianic identity. In fact, he has repeatedly tried to conceal whatever messianic aspirations he may or may not have had. He silences the demons that recognize him (Mark 1:23–25, 34, 3:11–12). He swears those he heals to secrecy (Mark 1:43–45, 5:40–43, 7:32–36, 8:22–26). He veils himself in incomprehensible parables and goes out of his way to obscure his identity and mission from the crowds that gather around him (Mark 7:24). Over and over again Jesus rebuffs, avoids, eludes, and sometimes downright rejects the title of messiah bestowed upon him by others.

There is a term for this strange phenomenon, which has its origins in the gospel of Mark but which can be traced throughout the gospels. It is called the "messianic secret."

Some believe that the messianic secret is the evangelist's own invention, that it is either a literary device to slowly reveal Jesus's true identity or a clever ploy to emphasize just how wondrous and compelling Jesus's messianic presence was; despite his many attempts to hide his identity from the crowds, it simply could not be concealed. "The more he ordered them [not to tell anyone about him]," Mark writes, "the more excessively they proclaimed it" (Mark 7:36).

Yet that assumes a level of literary skill in the gospel of Mark for which no evidence exists (Mark's gospel is written in a coarse, elementary Greek that betrays the author's limited education). The notion that the messianic secret may have been Mark's way of slowly revealing Jesus's identity belies the fundamental theological assertion that launches the gospel in the first place: "This is the beginning of the good news of Jesus *the Christ*" (Mark 1:1). Regardless, even at the moment in which Jesus's messianic identity is first surmised by Simon Peter in his dramatic confession outside Caesarea Philippi—indeed, even when his identity is spectacularly revealed by God upon the mountaintop—Jesus still commands his disciples to secrecy, sternly ordering them not to tell anyone what

Peter confessed (Mark 8:30), and forbidding the three witnesses to his transfiguration to utter a word about what they saw (Mark 9:9).

It is more likely that the messianic secret can be traced to the historical Jesus, though it may have been embellished and reconstructed in Mark's gospel before being adopted haphazardly and with obvious reservations by Matthew and Luke. That the messianic secret may be historical helps explain why Mark's redactors went to such lengths to compensate for their predecessor's portrayal of a messiah who seems to want nothing to do with the title. For example, while Mark's account of Simon Peter's confession ends with Jesus neither accepting nor rejecting the title but simply ordering the disciples "not to tell anyone about him," Matthew's account of the same story, which took shape twenty years later, has Jesus responding to Peter with a resounding confirmation of his messianic identity: "Blessed are you, Simon son of Jonah!" Jesus exclaims. "Flesh and blood did not reveal this to you; it was my father in heaven who did so" (Matthew 16:17).

In Mark, the miraculous moment on the mountaintop ends without comment from Jesus, only a firm reminder not to tell anyone what had happened. But in Matthew, the transfiguration ends with a lengthy discourse by Jesus in which he identifies John the Baptist as Elijah reborn, thereby explicitly claiming for himself, as the successor to John/Elijah, the mantle of the messiah (Matthew 17:9–13). And yet, despite these apologetic elaborations, even Matthew and Luke conclude both Peter's confession and the transfiguration with strict commands by Jesus to, in Matthew's words, "not tell anyone that *he was the messiah*" (Matthew 16:20).

If it is true that the messianic secret can be traced to the historical Jesus, then it could very well be the key to unlocking, not who the early church thought Jesus was, but who Jesus himself thought he was. Admittedly, this is no easy task. It is extremely difficult, if not impossible, to rely on the gospels to access Jesus's self-consciousness. As has been repeatedly noted, the gospels are not about a man known as Jesus of Nazareth who lived two thousand years ago; they are about a messiah whom the gospel writers viewed as an eternal being sitting at the right hand of God. The first-century Jews who wrote about Jesus had already made up their minds about who he was. They were constructing a theological argument about the nature and function of Jesus *as Christ,* not composing a historical biography about a human being.

Still, there is no mistaking the tension that exists in the gospels between how the early church viewed Jesus and how Jesus seems to view himself. Obviously, the disciples who followed Jesus recognized him as messiah, either during his lifetime or immediately after his death. But one should not forget that messianic expectations were by no means uniformly defined in first-century Palestine. Even those Jews who agreed that Jesus was the messiah did not agree about what being the messiah actually meant. When they scoured the smattering of prophecies in the scriptures, they discovered a confusing, often contradictory, array of views and opinions about the messiah's mission and identity. He would be an eschatological prophet who will usher in the End of Days (Daniel 7:13–14; Jeremiah 31:31–34). He would be a liberator who will release the Jews from bondage (Deuteronomy 18:15–19; Isaiah 49:1–7). He would be a royal claimant who will recreate the Kingdom of David (Micah 5:1–5; Zechariah 9:1–10).

In first-century Palestine, nearly every claimant to the mantle of the messiah neatly fit one of these messianic paradigms. Hezekiah the bandit chief, Judas the Galilean, Simon of Peraea, and Athronges the shepherd all modeled themselves after the Davidic ideal, as did Menahem and Simon son of Giora during the Jewish War. These were king-messiahs whose royal aspirations were clearly defined in their revolutionary actions against Rome and its clients in Jerusalem. Others, such as Theudas the wonder worker, the Egyptian, and the Samaritan cast themselves as liberator-messiahs in the mold of Moses, each would-be messiah promising to free his followers from the yoke of Roman occupation through some miraculous deed. Oracular prophets such as John the Baptist and the holy man Jesus ben Ananias may not have overtly assumed any messianic ambitions, but their prophecies about the End Times and the coming judgment of God clearly conformed to the prophet-messiah archetype one finds both in the Hebrew Scripture and in the rabbinic traditions and commentaries known as the Targum.

The problem for the early church is that Jesus did not fit any of the messianic paradigms offered in the Hebrew Bible, nor did he fulfill a single requirement expected of the messiah. Jesus spoke about the end of days, but it did not come to pass, not even after the Romans destroyed Jerusalem and defiled God's Temple. He promised that God would liberate the Jews from bondage, but God did no such thing. He vowed that the twelve tribes of Israel would be reconstituted and the nation restored; instead, the Romans expropriated the Promised Land, slaughtered its inhabitants, and exiled the survivors. The Kingdom of God that Jesus predicted never arrived; the new world order he described never took shape. According to the standards of the Jewish religion and the Hebrew Scriptures, Jesus was as successful in his messianic aspirations as any of the other would-be messiahs.

The early church obviously recognized this dilemma and, as will become apparent, made a conscious decision to change those messianic standards. They mixed and matched the different depictions of the messiah found in the Hebrew Bible to create a candidate that transcended any particular messianic model or expectation. Jesus may not have been prophet, liberator, or king. But that is because he rose above such simple messianic paradigms. As the transfiguration proved, Jesus was greater than Elijah (the prophet), greater than Moses (the liberator), even greater than David (the king).

That may have been how the early church understood Jesus's identity. But it does not appear to be how Jesus himself understood it. After all, in the entire first gospel there exists not a single definitive messianic statement from Jesus himself, not even at the very end when he stands before the high priest Caiaphas and somewhat passively accepts the title that others keep foisting upon him (Mark 14:62). The same is true for the early Q source material, which also contains not a single messianic statement by Jesus.

Perhaps Jesus was loath to take on the multiple expectations the Jews had of the messiah. Perhaps he rejected the designation outright. Either way, the fact remains that, especially in Mark, every time someone tries to ascribe the title of messiah to him—whether a demon, or a supplicant, or one of the disciples, or even God himself—Jesus brushes it off or, at best, accepts it reluctantly and always with a caveat.

However Jesus understood his mission and identity—whether he himself believed he was the messiah—what the evidence from the earliest gospel suggests is that, for whatever reason, Jesus of Nazareth did not openly refer to himself as messiah. Nor, by the way, did Jesus call himself "Son of God," another title that others seem to have ascribed to him. (Contrary to Christian conceptions, the title "Son of God" was not a description of Jesus's filial connection to God but rather the traditional designation for Israel's kings. Numerous figures are called "Son of God" in the Bible, none more often than David, the greatest king—2 Samuel 7:14; Psalms 2:7, 89:26; Isaiah 42:1). Rather, when it came to referring to himself, Jesus used an altogether different title, one so enigmatic and unique that for centuries scholars have been desperately trying to figure out what he could have possibly meant by it. Jesus called himself "the Son of Man."

The phrase "the Son of Man" (*ho huios tou anthropou* in Greek) appears some eighty times in the New Testament, and only once, in a positively operatic passage from the book of Acts, does it occur on the lips of anyone other than Jesus. In that passage from Acts, a follower of Jesus named Stephen is about to be stoned to death for proclaiming Jesus to be the promised messiah. As an angry crowd of Jews encircles him, Stephen has a sudden, rapturous vision in which he looks up to the heavens and sees Jesus wrapped in the glory of God. "Look!" Stephen shouts, his arms thrust into the air. "I can see the heavens opening, and the Son of Man standing at the right hand of God" (7:56). These are the last words he utters before the stones begin to fly.

Stephen's distinctly formulaic use of the title is proof that Christians did in fact refer to Jesus as the Son of Man after his death. But the extreme rarity of the term outside of the gospels, and the fact that it never occurs in the letters of Paul, make it unlikely that the Son of Man was a Christological expression made up by the early church to describe Jesus. On the contrary, this title, which is so ambiguous, and so infrequently found in the Hebrew Scriptures that to this day no one is certain what it actually means, is almost certainly one that Jesus gave himself.

It should be mentioned, of course, that Jesus spoke Aramaic, not Greek, meaning that if the expression "the Son of Man" can indeed be traced back to him, he would have used the phrase *bar enash(a),* or perhaps its Hebrew equivalent, *ben adam,* both of which mean "son of a human being." In other words, saying "son of man" in Hebrew or Aramaic is equivalent to saying "man," which is exactly how the Hebrew Bible most often uses the term: "God is not a man that he should lie; nor is he a son of man [*ben adam*] that he should repent" (Numbers 23:19).

A case could be made that this is also how Jesus used the term—as a common Hebrew/Aramaic idiom for "man." The idiomatic sense is certainly present in some of the earliest Son of Man sayings in Q and the gospel of Mark:

"Foxes have holes and birds of the air have nests but the Son of Man [i.e., 'a man such as I'] has no place to lay his head" (Matthew 8:20 | Luke 9:58).

"Whoever speaks a word against the Son of Man [i.e., 'any man'] it shall be forgiven of him; but whoever speaks against the Holy Spirit shall not be forgiven, neither in this age nor the one to come" (Matthew 12:32 | Luke 12:10).

Some have even argued that Jesus deliberately used the expression to emphasize his humanity, that it was a way for him to say, "I am a human being [*bar enash*]." However, such an explanation is predicated on the assumption that the people of Jesus's time needed to be reminded that he was in fact "a human being," as though that were somehow in doubt. It most certainly was not. Modern Christians may consider Jesus to be God incarnate, but such a conception of the messiah is anathema to five thousand years of Jewish scripture, thought, and theology. The idea that Jesus's audience would have needed constant reminding that he was "just a man" makes no sense at all.

In any case, while it is true that the Aramaic phrase in its indefinite form (*bar enash* rather than the definite *bar enasha*) can be translated as "*a* son of man," or just "man," the Greek version *ho huios tou anthropou* can only mean "*the* son of man." The difference between the Aramaic and Greek is significant and not likely the result of a poor translation by the evangelists. In employing the definite form of the phrase, Jesus was using it in a wholly new and unprecedented way: as a *title*, not as an idiom. Simply put, Jesus was not calling himself "a son of man." He was calling himself *the* Son of Man.

Jesus's idiosyncratic use of this cryptic phrase would have been completely new to his audience. It is often assumed that when Jesus spoke of himself as the Son of Man, the Jews knew what he was talking about. They did not. In fact, the Jews of Jesus's time had no unified conception of "son of man." It is not that the Jews were unfamiliar with the phrase, which would have instantly triggered an array of imagery from the books of Ezekiel, Daniel, or the Psalms. It is that they would not have recognized it as a title, the way they would have with, say, the Son of God.

Jesus, too, would have looked to the Hebrew Scriptures to draw his imagery for the Son of Man as a distinct individual rather than as just a byword for "man." He could have used the book of Ezekiel, wherein the prophet is referred to as "son of man" nearly ninety times: "[God] said to me, 'Oh, son of man [*ben adam*], stand on your feet and I will speak to you'" (Ezekiel 2:1). Yet if there is one thing scholars agree on, it is that the primary source for Jesus's particular interpretation of the phrase likely came from the book of Daniel.

Written during the reign of the Seleucid king Antiochus Epiphanes (175 B.C.E.–164 B.C.E.)—the king who thought he was a god—the book of Daniel records a series of apocalyptic visions the prophet claims to have had while serving as seer for the Babylonian court. In one of these visions, Daniel sees four monstrous beasts rise out of a great sea—each beast representing one of four great kingdoms: Babylon, Persia, Medea, and the Greek kingdom of Antiochus. The four beasts are let loose upon the earth to plunder and trample upon the cities of men. In the midst of the death and destruction, Daniel sees what he describes as "the Ancient of Days" (God) sitting upon a throne made of flames, his clothes white as snow, the hair on his head like pure wool. "A thousand thousands served him," Daniel writes, "and ten thousand times ten thousand stood attending him." The Ancient of Days passes judgment on the beasts, killing and burning some with fire, taking dominion and authority away from the rest. Then, as Daniel stands in awe of the spectacle, he sees "one like a son of man [*bar enash*] coming with the clouds of heaven."

"He came to the Ancient of Days and was presented before him," Daniel writes of this mysterious figure. "And to him was given dominion and glory and a kingdom, so that all peoples, nations, and languages should serve him. His dominion shall be everlasting; it shall never be destroyed" (Daniel 7:1–14). Thus, the "one like a son of man," by which Daniel appears to be referring to a distinct individual, is given sovereignty over the earth and accorded power and authority to rule over all nations and all peoples *as king*.

Daniel and Ezekiel are not the only books that use "son of man" to refer to a singular and specific person. The phrase appears in much the same way in the apocryphal books 4 Ezra and 1 Enoch, more specifically in the parables section of Enoch popularly called the *Similitudes* (1 Enoch 37–72). In the *Similitudes,* Enoch has a vision in which he looks up to heaven and sees a person he describes as "the son of man to whom belongs righteousness." He calls this figure "the Chosen One" and suggests that he was appointed by God before creation to come down to earth and judge humanity on God's behalf. He will be granted eternal power and kingship over the earth and will pass fiery judgment on the kings of this world. The wealthy and the powerful will plead for his mercy, but no mercy shall be shown them. At the end of the passage, the reader discovers that this son of man is actually Enoch himself.

In 4 Ezra, the son-of-man figure bursts out of the sea, flying on "the clouds of heaven." As in Daniel and Enoch, Ezra's son of man also comes to judge the wicked. Tasked with reconstituting the twelve tribes of Israel, he will gather his forces on Mount Zion and destroy the armies of men. But while Ezra's apocalyptic judge appears as "something like the figure of a man," he is no mere mortal. He is a preexistent being with supernatural powers who shoots fire out his mouth to consume God's enemies.

Both 4 Ezra and the *Similitudes* of Enoch were written near the end of the first century C.E., after the destruction of Jerusalem and long after Jesus's death. No doubt these two apocryphal texts influenced the early Christians, who may have latched on to the more spiritual, preexistent son of man ideal described in them to reinterpret Jesus's mission and identity and help explain why he failed to accomplish any of his messianic functions on earth. The gospel of Matthew in particular, which was written around the same time as the *Similitudes* and 4 Ezra, seems to have borrowed a great deal of imagery from them, including the "throne of glory" upon which the Son of Man will sit at the end of time (Matthew 19:28; 1 Enoch 62:5) and the "furnace of fire" into which he will throw all evildoers (Matthew 13:41–42; 1 Enoch 54:3–6)—neither of these phrases appears anywhere else in the New Testament. But there is no way that Jesus of Nazareth, who died more than sixty years before either the *Similitudes* or 4 Ezra was composed, could have been influenced by either. So while the Enoch/Ezra image of an eternal son of man chosen by God from the beginning of time to judge mankind and rule on earth on God's behalf does eventually get transposed upon Jesus (so much so that by the time John writes his gospel, the Son of Man is a purely divine figure—the *logos*— very much like the primal man in 4 Ezra), Jesus himself could not have understood the Son of Man in the same way.

If one accepts the consensus view that Jesus's main, if not sole, reference for the Son of Man was the book of Daniel, then one should look to that passage in the gospels in which Jesus's use of the title most closely echoes Daniel's in order to uncover what Jesus may have meant by it. As it happens, this particular son-of-man saying, which takes place near the end of Jesus's life, is one that most scholars agree is authentic and traceable to the historical Jesus.

According to the gospels, Jesus has been dragged before the Sanhedrin to answer the charges made against him. As one after another, the chief priests, the elders, and the scribes fling accusations his way, Jesus sits impassively, silent, and unresponsive. Finally, the high priest Caiaphas stands and asks Jesus directly, "Are you the messiah?"

It is here, at the end of the journey that began on the sacred shores of the Jordan River, that the messianic secret is finally peeled away and Jesus's true nature seemingly revealed.

"I am," Jesus answers.

But then immediately this clearest and most concise statement yet by Jesus of his messianic identity is muddied with an ecstatic exhortation, borrowed directly from the book of Daniel, that once again throws everything into confusion: "And you will see the Son of Man seated at the right hand of the Power, and coming with the clouds of heaven" (Mark 14:62).

The first half of Jesus's response to the high priest is an allusion to the Psalms, in which God promises King David that he shall sit at his right hand, "until I make your enemies a footstool for your feet" (Psalm 110:1). But the phrase "coming with the clouds of heaven" is a direct reference to the son of man of Daniel's vision (Daniel 7:13).

This is not the first time that Jesus has diverted someone's declaration of him as messiah into a diatribe about the Son of Man. After Peter's confession near Caesarea Philippi, Jesus first silences him, then goes on to describe how the Son of Man must suffer and be rejected before being killed and rising again three days later (Mark 8:31). After the transfiguration, Jesus swears the disciples to secrecy, but only until "after the Son of Man is raised from the dead" (Mark 9:9). In both cases, it is clear that Jesus's conception of the Son of Man is to take precedence over other people's assertion of his messianic identity. Even at the end of his life, when he stands in the presence of his accusers, he is willing to accept the generic title of messiah only if it can be made to fit his specific interpretation, à la the book of Daniel, of the Son of Man.

What this suggests is that the key to uncovering the messianic secret, and therefore Jesus's own sense of self, lies in deciphering his unique interpretation of the "one like a son of man" in Daniel. And here is where one can come closest to discovering who Jesus thought he was. For while the curious son-of-man figure in Daniel is never explicitly identified as messiah, he is clearly and unambiguously called *king*—one who will rule on behalf of God over all peoples on earth. Could that be what Jesus means when he gives himself the strange title "the Son of Man"? Is he calling himself king?

To be sure, Jesus speaks at length about the Son of Man, and often in contradictory terms. He is powerful (Mark 14:62) yet suffering (Mark 13:26). He is present on earth (Mark 2:10) yet coming in the future (Mark 8:38). He will be rejected by men (Mark 10:33), yet he will judge over them (Mark 14:62). He is both ruler (Mark 8:38) and servant (Mark 10:45). But what appears on the surface as a set of contradictory statements is in fact fairly consistent with how Jesus describes the Kingdom of God. Indeed, the two ideas—the Son of Man and the Kingdom of God—are often linked together in the gospels, as though they represent one and the same concept. Both are described in startlingly similar terms, and occasionally the two are presented as interchangeable, as when the gospel of Matthew changes the famous verse in Mark 9:1—"I tell you, there are those here who will not taste death until they have seen the Kingdom of God come with power"—to "I tell you there are those standing here who will not taste death until they see the Son of Man *coming in his kingdom*" (Matthew 16:28).

By replacing one term with the other, Matthew implies that the kingdom belonging to the Son of Man is one and the same as the Kingdom of God. And since the Kingdom of God is built upon a complete reversal of the present order, wherein the poor become powerful and the meek are made mighty, what better king to rule over it on God's behalf than one who himself embodies the new social order flipped on its head? A peasant king. A king with no place to lay his head. A king who came to serve, not to be served. A king riding on a donkey.

When Jesus calls himself the Son of Man, using the description from Daniel as a title, he is making a clear statement about how he views his identity and his mission. He is associating himself with the paradigm of the Davidic messiah, the king who will rule the earth on God's behalf, who will gather the twelve tribes of Israel (in Jesus's case, through his twelve apostles, who will "sit on twelve thrones") and restore the nation of Israel to its former glory. He is claiming the same position as King David, "at the right hand of the Power." In short, he is calling himself king. He is stating, albeit in a deliberately cryptic way, that his role is not merely to usher in the Kingdom of God through his miraculous actions; it is to rule that kingdom on God's behalf.

Recognizing the obvious danger of his kingly ambitions and wanting to avoid, if at all possible, the fate of the others who dared claim the title, Jesus attempts to restrain all declarations of him as messiah, opting instead for the more ambiguous, less openly

charged title "the Son of Man." The messianic secret was born precisely from the tension that arises between Jesus's desire to promote
his son-of-man identity over the messianic title given to him by his
followers.

Regardless of how Jesus viewed himself, the fact remains that he
was never able to establish the Kingdom of God. The choice for
the early church was clear: either Jesus was just another failed messiah, or what the Jews of Jesus's time expected of the messiah was
wrong and had to be adjusted. For those who fell into the latter
camp, the apocalyptic imagery of 1 Enoch and 4 Ezra, both written
long after Jesus's death, paved a way forward, allowing the early
church to replace Jesus's understanding of himself as king and messiah with a new, post–Jewish Revolt paradigm of the messiah as a
preexistent, predetermined, heavenly, even divine Son of Man, one
whose "kingdom" was not of this world.

But Jesus's kingdom—the Kingdom of God—was very much
of this world. And while the idea of a poor Galilean peasant claiming kingship for himself may seem laughable, it is no more absurd
than the kingly ambitions of Jesus's fellow messiahs Judas the Galilean, Menahem, Simon son of Giora, Simon son of Kochba, and
the rest. Like them, Jesus's royal claims were based not on his power
or wealth. Like them, Jesus had no great army with which to over-
turn the kingdoms of men, no fleet to sweep the Roman seas. The
sole weapon he had with which to build the Kingdom of God was
the one used by all the messiahs who came before or after him, the
same weapon used by the rebels and bandits who would eventually
push the Roman empire out of the city of God: *zeal*.

Now, with the festival of Passover at hand—the commemora-
tion of Israel's liberation from heathen rule—Jesus will finally take
this message to Jerusalem. Armed with zeal as his weapon, he will
directly challenge the Temple authorities and their Roman over-
seers over who truly rules this holy land. But though it may be
Passover, Jesus will not be entering the sacred city as a lowly pilgrim. He is Jerusalem's rightful king; he is coming to stake his

claim to God's throne. And the only way a king would enter Jerusalem is with a praiseful multitude waving palm branches, declaring his victory over God's enemies, laying their cloaks on the road before him, shouting: "Hosanna! Hosanna to the *Son of David*! Blessed is the King who comes in the name of the Lord" (Matthew 21:9; Mark 11:9–10; Luke 19:38).

Chapter Twelve

No King but Caesar

He is praying when they finally come for him: an unruly crowd wielding swords, torches, and wooden clubs, sent by the chief priests and elders to seize Jesus from his hideout in the Garden of Gethsemane. The crowd is not unexpected. Jesus had warned his disciples they would come for him. That is why they are hiding in Gethsemane, shrouded in darkness, and armed with swords—just as Jesus had commanded. They are ready for a confrontation. But the arresting party knows precisely where to find them. They have been tipped off by one of the Twelve, Judas Iscariot, who knows their location and can easily identify Jesus. Still, Jesus and his disciples will not be taken easily. One of them draws his sword and a brief melee ensues in which a servant of the high priest is injured. Resistance is useless, however, and the disciples are forced to abandon their master and flee into the night as Jesus is seized, bound, and dragged back to the city to face his accusers.

They bring him to the courtyard of the high priest Caiaphas, where the chief priests, the scribes, and elders—the whole of the Sanhedrin—have gathered. There, they question him about the threats he's made to the Temple, using his own words against him: "We heard him say 'I will bring down this Temple made with human hands, and in three days I will build another made not with hands.'"

This is a grave accusation. The Temple is the chief civic and religious institution of the Jews. It is the primary source of the Jewish faith and the principal symbol of Rome's hegemony over Judea. Even the slightest threat to the Temple would instantly arouse the attention of the priestly and Roman authorities. A few years earlier, when two zealous rabbis, Judas son of Sepphoraeus and Matthias son of Margalus, shared with their students their plans to remove the golden eagle that Herod the Great had placed above the Temple's main gate, both rabbis and forty of their students were rounded up and burned alive.

Yet Jesus refuses to answer the charges leveled against him, probably because there is no answer to be made. After all, he has publicly and repeatedly threatened the Temple of Jerusalem, vowing that "not one stone would be left upon another; all will be thrown down" (Mark 13:2). He has been in Jerusalem only a few days but already he has caused a riot at the Court of Gentiles, violently disrupting the Temple's financial transactions. He has replaced the costly blood and flesh sacrifice mandated by the Temple with his free healings and exorcisms. For years he has raged against the Temple priesthood, threatening their primacy and power. He has condemned the scribes and the elders as "a brood of vipers" and promised that the Kingdom of God would sweep away the entire priestly class. His very ministry is founded upon the destruction of the present order and the removal from power of every single person who now stands in judgment of him. What else is there to say?

When morning comes, Jesus is bound again and escorted through the rough stone ramparts of the Antonia Fortress to appear before Pontius Pilate. As governor, Pilate's chief responsibility in Jerusalem is to maintain order on behalf of the emperor. The only reason a poor Jewish peasant and day laborer would be brought before him is if he had jeopardized that order. Otherwise there would be no hearing, no questions asked, no need for a defense. Pilate, as the histories reveal, was not one for trials. In his ten years as governor of Jerusalem, he had sent thousands upon thousands to the cross with a simple scratch of his reed pen on a slip of papyrus. The notion that he would even be in the same room as Jesus, let alone deign to grant him a "trial," beggars the imagination. Either the threat posed by Jesus to the stability of Jerusalem is so great that he is one of only a handful of Jews to have the opportunity to stand before Pilate and answer for his alleged crimes, or else the so-called trial before Pilate is pure legend.

There is reason to suspect the latter. The scene does have an unmistakable air of theater to it. This is the final moment in Jesus's ministry, the end of a journey that began some years earlier on the banks of the Jordan River. In the gospel of Mark, Jesus speaks only one other time after his interview with Pilate—when he is writhing on the cross. "My God, my God, why have you forsaken me?" (Mark 15:34).

Yet in Mark's telling of the story, something happens between Jesus's trial before Pilate and his death on a cross that is so incredible, so obviously contrived, that it casts suspicion over the entire episode leading up to Jesus's crucifixion. Pilate, having interviewed Jesus and found him innocent of all charges, presents him to the Jews along with a bandit (*lestes*) named bar Abbas who has been accused of murdering Roman guards during an insurrection at the Temple. According to Mark, it was a custom of the Roman governor during the feast of Passover to release one prisoner to the Jews, anyone for whom they asked. When Pilate asks the crowd which prisoner they would like to have released—Jesus, the preacher and traitor to Rome, or bar Abbas, the insurrectionist and murderer— the crowd demands the release of the insurrectionist and the crucifixion of the preacher.

"Why?" Pilate asks, pained at the thought of having to put an innocent Jewish peasant to death. "What evil has he done?"

But the crowd shouts all the louder for Jesus's death. "Crucify him! Crucify him!" (Mark 15:1–20).

The scene is absolutely nonsensical. Never mind that outside the gospels there exists not a shred of historical evidence for any such Passover custom on the part of any Roman governor. What is truly beyond belief is the portrayal of Pontius Pilate—a man renowned for his loathing of the Jews, his total disregard for Jewish rituals and customs, and his penchant for absentmindedly signing so many execution orders that a formal complaint was lodged against him in Rome—spending even a moment of his time pondering the fate of yet another Jewish rabble-rouser.

Why would Mark have concocted such a patently fictitious scene, one that his Jewish audience would immediately have recognized as false? The answer is simple: Mark was not writing for a Jewish audience. Mark's audience was in Rome, where he himself resided. His account of the life and death of Jesus of Nazareth was written mere months after the Jewish Revolt had been crushed and Jerusalem destroyed.

Like the Jews, the early Christians struggled to make sense of the trauma of the Jewish Revolt and its aftermath. More to the point, they had to reinterpret Jesus's revolutionary message and his self-identity as the kingly Son of Man in light of the fact that the Kingdom of God they were awaiting never materialized. Scattered across the Roman Empire, it was only natural for the gospel writers to distance themselves from the Jewish independence movement by erasing, as much as possible, any hint of radicalism or violence, revolution or zealotry, from the story of Jesus, and to adapt Jesus's words and actions to the new political situation in which they found themselves. That task was made somewhat easier by the fact that many among Jerusalem's Christian community seem to have sat out the war with Rome, viewing it as a welcomed sign of the end times promised by their messiah. According to the third-century historian Eusebius of Caesarea, a large number of

Christians in Jerusalem fled to the other side of the Jordan River. "The people of the church at Jerusalem," Eusebius wrote, "in accordance with a certain oracle that was vouchsafed by way of revelation to approved men there, had been commanded to depart from the city before the war, and to inhabit a certain city of Peraea they called Pella." By most accounts, the church they left behind was demolished in 70 C.E. and all signs of the first Christian community in Jerusalem were buried in a mound of rubble and ash.

With the Temple in ruins and the Jewish religion made pariah, the Jews who followed Jesus as messiah had an easy decision to make: they could either maintain their cultic connections to their parent religion and thus share in Rome's enmity (Rome's enmity toward Christians would peak much later), or they could divorce themselves from Judaism and transform their messiah from a fierce Jewish nationalist into a pacifistic preacher of good works whose kingdom was not of this world.

It was not only fear of Roman reprisal that drove these early Christians. With Jerusalem despoiled, Christianity was no longer a tiny Jewish sect centered in a predominantly Jewish land surrounded by hundreds of thousands of Jews. After 70 C.E., the center of the Christian movement shifted from Jewish Jerusalem to the Graeco-Roman cities of the Mediterranean: Alexandria, Corinth, Ephesus, Damascus, Antioch, Rome. A generation after Jesus's crucifixion, his non-Jewish followers outnumbered and overshadowed the Jewish ones. By the end of the first century, when the bulk of the gospels were being written, Rome—in particular the Roman intellectual elite—had become the primary target of Christian evangelism.

Reaching out to this particular audience required a bit of creativity on the part of the evangelists. Not only did all traces of revolutionary zeal have to be removed from the life of Jesus, the Romans had to be completely absolved of any responsibility for Jesus's death. *It was the Jews who killed the messiah.* The Romans were unwitting pawns of the high priest Caiaphas, who desperately wanted to murder Jesus but who did not have the legal means to do so. The high priest duped the Roman governor Pontius Pilate into carrying out a tragic miscarriage of justice. Poor Pilate tried everything he could to save Jesus. But the Jews cried out for blood, leaving Pilate no choice but to give in to them, to hand Jesus over to be crucified. Indeed, the farther each gospel gets from 70 C.E. and the destruction of Jerusalem, the more detached and outlandish Pilate's role in Jesus's death becomes.

The gospel of Matthew, written in Damascus some twenty years after the Jewish Revolt, paints a picture of Pontius Pilate at great pains to set Jesus free. Having been warned by his wife not to have anything to do with "that innocent man," and recognizing that the religious authorities are handing Jesus over to him solely "out of jealousy," Matthew's Pilate literally washes his hands of any blame for Jesus's death. "I am innocent of this man's blood," he tells the Jews. "See to it yourselves."

In Matthew's retelling of Mark, the Jews respond to Pilate "as a whole"—that is, as an entire nation (*pas ho laos*)—that they themselves will accept the blame for Jesus's death from this day until the end of time: "May his blood be on our heads, and on our children!" (Matthew 27:1–26).

Luke, writing in the Greek city of Antioch at around the same time as Matthew, not only confirms Pilate's guiltlessness for Jesus's death; he unexpectedly extends that amnesty to Herod Antipas as well. Luke's copy of Mark presents Pilate excoriating the chief priests, the religious leaders, and the people for the accusations they have dared to level against Jesus. "You brought this person to me as one who was turning the people away [from the Law]. I have examined him in your presence and found him guilty of none of the charges you have brought against him. Neither has Herod, when I sent [Jesus] to him. He has done nothing worthy of death" (Luke 23:13–15). After trying *three separate times* to dissuade the Jews from their bloodlust, Pilate reluctantly consents to their demands and hands Jesus over to be crucified.

Not surprisingly, it is the last of the canonized gospels that pushes the conceit of Pilate's innocence—and the Jews' guilt—to the extreme. In the gospel of John, written in Ephesus sometime after 100 C.E., Pilate does everything he can to save the life of this poor Jewish peasant, not because he thinks Jesus is guiltless, but because he seems to believe that Jesus may in fact be the "Son of God." Nevertheless, after struggling in vain against the Jewish authorities to set Jesus free, the ruthless prefect who commands legions of troops and who regularly sends them into the streets to slaughter the Jews whenever they protest any of his decisions (as he did when the Jews objected to his pilfering of the Temple treasury to pay for Jerusalem's aqueducts) is *forced* by the demands of the unruly crowd to give Jesus up.

As Pilate hands him over to be crucified, Jesus himself removes all doubt as to who is truly responsible for his death: "The one who handed me over to you is guilty of a greater sin," Jesus tells Pilate, personally absolving him of all guilt by laying the blame squarely on the Jewish religious authorities. John then adds one final, unforgivable insult to a Jewish nation that, at the time, was on the verge of a full-scale insurrection, by attributing to them the most foul, the most blasphemous piece of pure heresy that any Jew in first-century Palestine could conceivably utter. When asked by Pilate what he should do with "their king," the Jews reply, "We have no king but Caesar!" (John 19:1–16).

Thus, a story concocted by Mark strictly for evangelistic purposes to shift the blame for Jesus's death away from Rome is stretched with the passage of time to the point of absurdity, becoming in the process the basis for two thousand years of Christian anti-Semitism.

It is, of course, not inconceivable that Jesus would have received a brief audience with the Roman governor, but, again, only if the magnitude of his crime warranted special attention. Jesus was no simple troublemaker, after all. His provocative entry into Jerusalem trailed by a multitude of devotees declaring him king, his act of public disturbance at the Temple, the size of the force that marched into Gethsemane to arrest him—all of these indicate that the authorities viewed Jesus of Nazareth as a serious threat to the stability and order of Judea. Such a "criminal" would very likely have been deemed worthy of Pilate's attention. But any trial Jesus received would have been brief and perfunctory, its sole purpose to officially record the charges for which he was being executed. Hence, the one question that Pilate asks Jesus in all four gospel accounts: "Are you the King of the Jews?"

If the gospel story were a drama (and it is), Jesus's answer to Pilate's question would serve as the climax that unfurls the story's denouement: the crucifixion. This is the moment when the price must be paid for all that Jesus has said and done over the years: the attacks against the priestly authorities, the condemnation of the Roman occupation, the claims of kingly authority. It has all led to this inevitable moment of judgment, just as Jesus said it would. From here it will be the cross and the tomb.

And yet perhaps no other moment in Jesus's brief life is more opaque and inaccessible to scholars than this one. That has partly to do with the multiple traditions upon which the story of Jesus's trial and crucifixion rely. Recall that while Mark was the first written gospel, it was preceded by blocks of oral and written traditions about Jesus that were transmitted by his earliest followers. One of these "blocks" has already been introduced: the material unique to the gospels of Matthew and Luke that scholars term Q. But there is reason to believe that other blocks of traditions existed before the gospel of Mark that dealt exclusively with Jesus's death and resurrection. These so-called passion narratives set up a basic sequence of events that the earliest Christians believed occurred at the end of Jesus's life. The Last Supper. The betrayal by Judas Iscariot. The arrest at Gethsemane. The appearance before the high priest and Pilate. The crucifixion and the burial. The resurrection three days later.

This sequence of events did not actually contain a narrative, but was designed strictly for liturgical purposes. It was a means for the early Christians to relive the last days of their messiah through ritual by, for instance, sharing the same meal he shared with his disciples, praying the same prayers he offered in Gethsemane, and so on. Mark's contribution to the passion narratives was his transformation of this ritualized sequence of events into a cohesive story about the death of Jesus, which his redactors, Matthew and Luke, integrated into their gospels along with their own unique flourishes (John may have relied on a separate set of passion narratives for his gospel, since almost none of the details he provides about the last days of Jesus match what is found in the Synoptics).

As with everything else in the gospels, the story of Jesus's arrest, trial, and execution was written for one reason and one reason only: to prove that he was the promised messiah. Factual accuracy was irrelevant. What mattered was Christology, not history. The gospel writers obviously recognized how integral Jesus's death was to the nascent community, but the story of that death needed elaborating. It needed to be slowed down and refocused. It required certain details and embellishments on the part of the evangelists. As a result, this final, most significant episode in the story of Jesus of Nazareth is also the one most clouded by theological enhancements and flat-out fabrications. The only means the modern reader has at his or her disposal to try to retrieve some semblance of historical accuracy in the passion narratives is to slowly strip away the theological overlay imposed by the evangelists on Jesus's final days and return to the most primitive version of the story that can be excavated from the gospels. And the only way to do that is to start at the end of the story, with Jesus nailed to a cross.

Crucifixion was a widespread and exceedingly common form of execution in antiquity, one used by Persians, Indians, Assyrians, Scythians, Romans, and Greeks. Even the Jews practiced crucifixion; the punishment is mentioned numerous times in rabbinic sources. The reason crucifixion was so common is because it was so cheap. It could be carried out almost anywhere; all one needed

was a tree. The torture could last for days without the need for a
torturer. The procedure of the crucifixion—how the victim was
hanged—was left completely to the executioner. Some were nailed
with their heads downward. Some had their private parts impaled.
Some were hooded. Most were stripped naked.

It was Rome that conventionalized crucifixion as a form of
state punishment, creating a sense of uniformity in the process,
particularly when it came to the nailing of the hands and feet to a
crossbeam. So commonplace was crucifixion in the Roman Empire that Cicero referred to it as "that plague." Among the citizenry,
the word "cross" (*crux*) became a popular and particularly vulgar
taunt, akin to "go hang yourself."

Yet it would be inaccurate to refer to crucifixion as a death
penalty, for it was often the case that the victim was first executed,
then nailed to a cross. The purpose of crucifixion was not so much
to kill the criminal as it was to serve as a deterrent to others who
might defy the state. For that reason, crucifixions were always carried out in public—at crossroads, in theaters, on hills, or on high
ground—anywhere where the population had no choice but to
bear witness to the gruesome scene. The criminal was always left
hanging long after he had died; the crucified were almost never
buried. Because the entire point of the crucifixion was to humili-
ate the victim and frighten the witnesses, the corpse would be left
where it hung to be eaten by dogs and picked clean by the birds of
prey. The bones would then be thrown onto a heap of trash, which
is how Golgotha, the place of Jesus's crucifixion, earned its name:
the place of skulls. Simply put, crucifixion was more than a capital
punishment for Rome; it was a public reminder of what happens
when one challenges the empire. That is why it was reserved solely
for the most extreme political crimes: treason, rebellion, sedition,
banditry.

If one knew nothing else about Jesus of Nazareth save that he
was crucified by Rome, one would know practically all that was
needed to uncover who he was, what he was, and why he ended

up nailed to a cross. His offense, in the eyes of Rome, is self-evident. It was etched upon a plaque and placed above his head for all to see: *Jesus of Nazareth, King of the Jews*. His crime was daring to assume kingly ambitions.

The gospels testify that Jesus was crucified alongside other *lestai,* or bandits: revolutionaries, just like him. Luke, obviously uncomfortable with the implications of the term, changes *lestai* to *kakourgoi,* or "evildoers." But try as he might, Luke cannot avoid the most basic fact about his messiah: Jesus was executed by the Roman state for the crime of sedition. Everything else about the last days of Jesus of Nazareth must be interpreted through this singular, stubborn fact.

So, then, one can dismiss the theatrical trial before Pilate as pure fiction for all the reasons stated above. If Jesus did in fact appear before Pilate, it would have been brief and, for Pilate, utterly forgettable. The governor may not have bothered to look up from his logbook long enough to register Jesus's face, let alone engage in a lengthy conversation with him about the meaning of truth.

He would have asked his one question: "Are you the King of the Jews?" He would have registered Jesus's answer. He would have logged the crime. And he would have sent Jesus on his way to join the countless others dying or already dead up on Golgotha.

Even the earlier trial before the Sanhedrin must be reexamined in the light of the cross. The story of that trial, as it is presented in the gospels, is full of contradictions and inconsistencies, but the general outline is as follows: Jesus is arrested at night, on the eve of the Sabbath, during the festival of Passover. He is brought under cover of darkness to the courtyard of the high priest, where the members of the Sanhedrin await him. At once, a group of witnesses appear and testify that Jesus has made threats against the Temple of Jerusalem. When Jesus refuses to answer these accusations, the high priest asks him directly whether he is the messiah. Jesus's answer varies in all four gospels, but it always includes a declaration of himself as the Son of Man. The declaration infuriates the high priest, who immediately charges Jesus with blasphemy, the punishment for which is death. The next morning, the Sanhedrin hands Jesus over to Pilate to be crucified.

The problems with this scene are too numerous to count. The trial before the Sanhedrin violates nearly every requirement laid down by Jewish law for a legal proceeding. The Mishnah is adamant on this subject. The Sanhedrin is not permitted to meet at night. It is not permitted to meet during Passover. It is not permitted to meet on the eve of the Sabbath. It is certainly not permitted to meet so casually in the courtyard (*aule*) of the high priest, as Matthew and Mark claim. And it must begin with a detailed list of why the accused is innocent before any witnesses are allowed to come forth. The argument that the trial rules laid down by the rabbis in the Mishnah did not apply in the thirties, when Jesus was tried, falls flat when one remembers that the gospels were also not written in the thirties. The social, religious, and political context for the narrative of Jesus's trial before the Sanhedrin was post–70 C.E. rabbinic Judaism: the era of the Mishnah. At the very least, what these flagrant inaccuracies demonstrate is the evangelists' extremely poor grasp of Jewish law and Sanhedrin practice. That alone should cast doubt on the historicity of the trial before Caiaphas.

Even if one excuses all of the above violations, the most troublesome aspect of the Sanhedrin trial is its verdict. If the high priest did in fact question Jesus about his messianic ambitions, and if Jesus's answer did signify blasphemy, then the Torah could not be clearer about the punishment:"The one who blasphemes the name of the Lord shall surely be put to death: *the congregation shall stone him to death*" (Leviticus 24:16). That is the punishment inflicted upon Stephen for his blasphemy when he calls Jesus the Son of Man (Acts 7:1–60). Stephen is not transferred to Roman authorities to answer for his crime; he is stoned to death on the spot. It may be true that under the Roman imperium, the Jews did not have the authority to execute criminals (though that did not stop them from killing Stephen). But one cannot lose sight of the fundamental fact with which we began: Jesus is not stoned to death by the Jews for blasphemy; he is crucified by Rome for sedition.

Just as there may be a kernel of truth in the story of Jesus's trial before Pilate, there may also be a kernel of truth in the story of the Sanhedrin trial. The Jewish authorities arrested Jesus because they viewed him both as a threat to their control of the Temple and as a menace to the social order of Jerusalem, which under their agreement with Rome they were responsible for maintaining. Because the Jewish authorities technically had no jurisdiction in capital cases, they handed Jesus over to the Romans to answer for his seditious teachings. The personal relationship between Pilate and Caiaphas may have facilitated the transfer, but the Roman authorities surely needed little convincing to put yet another Jewish insurrectionist to death. Pilate dealt with Jesus the way he dealt with all threats to the social order: he sent him to the cross. No trial was held. No trial was necessary. It was Passover, after all, always a time of heightened tensions in Jerusalem. The city was bursting at its seams with pilgrims. Any hint of trouble had to be immediately addressed. And whatever else Jesus may have been, he was certainly trouble.

With his crime recorded in Pilate's logbook, Jesus would have been led out of the Antonia Fortress and taken to the courtyard, where he would be stripped naked, tied to a stake, and savagely scourged, as was the custom for all those sentenced to the cross. The Romans would then have placed a crossbeam behind the nape of his neck and hooked his arms back over it—again, as was the custom—so that the messiah who had promised to remove the yoke of occupation from the necks of the Jews would himself be yoked like an animal led to slaughter.

As with all those condemned to crucifixion, Jesus would have been forced to carry the crossbeam himself to a hill situated outside the walls of Jerusalem, directly on the road leading into the city gates—perhaps the same road he had used a few days earlier to enter the city as its rightful king. This way, every pilgrim entering Jerusalem for the holy festivities would have no choice but to bear witness to his suffering, to be reminded of what happens to those who defy the rule of Rome. The crossbeam would be attached to a scaffold or post, and Jesus's wrists and ankles would be nailed to the structure with three iron spikes. A heave, and the cross would be lifted to the vertical. Death would not have taken long. In a few short hours, Jesus's lungs would have tired, and breathing become impossible to sustain.

Thus, on a bald hill covered in crosses, beset by the moans of agony from hundreds of dying criminals, as a murder of crows circled eagerly over his head waiting for him to breathe his last, the messiah known as Jesus of Nazareth would have met the same ignominious end as every other messiah who came before or after him.

Except that unlike those other messiahs, this one would not be forgotten.

PART III

Blow a trumpet in Zion;
raise a shout on my holy mountain!
Let all the inhabitants of the land tremble,
for the day of the Lord is coming,
it is near;
a day of darkness and gloom,
a day of clouds and thick darkness.

JOEL 2:1–2

God Made Flesh

Stephen—he who was stoned to death by an angry mob of Jews for blasphemy—was the first of Jesus's followers to be killed after the crucifixion, though he would not be the last. It is curious that the first man martyred for calling Jesus "Christ" did not himself know Jesus of Nazareth. Stephen was not a disciple, after all. He never met the Galilean peasant and day laborer who claimed the throne of the Kingdom of God. He did not walk with Jesus or talk to him. He was not part of the ecstatic crowd that welcomed Jesus into Jerusalem as its rightful ruler. He took no part in the disturbance at the Temple. He was not there when Jesus was arrested and charged with sedition. He did not watch Jesus die.

Stephen did not hear about Jesus of Nazareth until after his crucifixion. A Greek-speaking Jew who lived in one of the many Hellenistic provinces outside the Holy Land, Stephen had come to Jerusalem on pilgrimage, along with thousands of other Diaspora Jews just like him. He was probably presenting his sacrifice to the Temple priests when he spied a band of mostly Galilean farmers and fishermen wandering about the Court of Gentiles, preaching about a simple Nazarean whom they called messiah.

By itself, such a spectacle would not have been unusual in Jerusalem, certainly not during the festivals and feast days, when Jews from all over the Roman Empire flocked to the sacred city to make their Temple offerings. Jerusalem was the center of spiritual activity for the Jews, the cultic heart of the Jewish nation. Every sectarian, every fanatic, every zealot, messiah, and self-proclaimed prophet, eventually made his way to Jerusalem to missionize or admonish, to offer God's mercy or warn of God's wrath. The festivals in particular were an ideal time for these schismatics to reach as wide and international an audience as possible.

So when Stephen saw the gaggle of hirsute men and ragged women huddled beneath a portico in the Temple's outer court—simple provincials who had sold their possessions and given the proceeds to the poor; who held all things in common and owned nothing themselves save their tunics and sandals—he probably did not pay much attention at first. He may have pricked up his ears at the suggestion that these particular schismatics followed a messiah who had already been killed (crucified, no less!). He may have been astonished to learn that, despite the fact that Jesus's death *by definition* disqualified him as liberator of Israel, his followers still called him messiah. But even that would not have been completely unheard of in Jerusalem. Were not John the Baptist's followers still preaching about their late master, still baptizing Jews in his name?

What truly would have caught Stephen's attention was the staggering claim by these Jews that, unlike every other criminal crucified by Rome, their messiah was not left on the cross for his bones to be picked clean by the greedy birds Stephen had seen circling above Golgotha when he passed through the gates of Jerusalem. No, the corpse of this particular peasant—this Jesus of Nazareth—had been brought down from the cross and placed in an extravagant rock-hewn tomb fit for the wealthiest of men in Judea. More remarkable still, his followers claimed that three days after their messiah had been placed in the rich man's tomb, he came back to life. God raised him up again, freed him from death's grip. The spokesman of the group, a fisherman from Capernaum called Simon Peter, swore that he witnessed this resurrection with his own eyes, as did many others among them.

To be clear, this was not the resurrection of the dead that the Pharisees expected at the end of days and the Sadducees denied. This was not the gravestones cracking open and the earth coughing up the buried masses, as the prophet Isaiah had envisioned (Isaiah 26:19). This had nothing to do with the rebirth of the "House of Israel" foretold by the prophet Ezekiel, wherein God breathes new life into the dry bones of the nation (Ezekiel 37). This was a lone individual, dead and buried in rock for days, suddenly rising up and walking out of his tomb of his own accord, not as a spirit or ghost, but as flesh and blood.

Nothing quite like what these followers of Jesus were contending existed at the time. Belief in the resurrection of the dead could be found among the ancient Egyptians and Persians, of course. The Greeks believed in the immortality of the soul, though not of the body. Some gods—for instance, Osiris—were thought to have died and risen again. Some men—Julius Caesar, Caesar Augustus—became gods after they died. But the concept of an individual dying and rising again, in the flesh, into a life everlasting was extremely rare in the ancient world and practically nonexistent in Judaism.

And yet what the followers of Jesus were arguing was not only that he rose from the dead, but that his resurrection confirmed his status as messiah, an extraordinary claim without precedent in Jewish history. Despite two millennia of Christian apologetics, the fact is that belief in a dying and rising messiah simply did not exist in Judaism. In the entirety of the Hebrew Bible there is not a single passage of scripture or prophecy about the promised messiah that even hints of his ignominious death, let alone his bodily resurrection. The prophet Isaiah speaks of an exalted "suffering servant" who would be "stricken for the transgressions of [God's] people"

(Isaiah 52:13–53:12). But Isaiah never identifies this nameless servant as the messiah, nor does he claim that the stricken servant rose from the dead. The prophet Daniel mentions "an anointed one" (i.e., messiah) who "shall be cut off and shall have nothing" (Daniel 9:26). But Daniel's anointed is not killed; he is merely deposed by a "prince who is to come." It may be true that, centuries after Jesus's death, Christians would interpret these verses in such a way as to help make sense of their messiah's failure to accomplish any of the messianic tasks expected of him. But the Jews of Jesus's time had no conception of a messiah who suffers and dies. They were awaiting a messiah who triumphs and lives.

What Jesus's followers were proposing was a breathtakingly bold redefinition, not just of the messianic prophecies but of the very nature and function of the Jewish messiah. The fisherman, Simon Peter, displaying the reckless confidence of one uninitiated in the scriptures, even went so far as to argue that King David himself had prophesied Jesus's crucifixion and resurrection in one of his Psalms. "Being a prophet, and knowing God had sworn an oath to him that the fruit of his loins, of his flesh, would be raised as the messiah to be seated on his throne," Peter told the pilgrims gathered at the Temple, "David, foreseeing [Jesus], spoke of the resurrection of the messiah, saying that 'his soul was not left in Hades, nor did his flesh see corruption'" (Acts 2:30–31).

Had Stephen been knowledgeable about the sacred texts, had he been a scribe or a scholar saturated in the scriptures, had he simply been an inhabitant of Jerusalem, for whom the sound of the Psalms cascading from the Temple walls would have been as familiar as the sound of his own voice, he would have known immediately that King David never said any such thing about the messiah. The "prophecy" Peter speaks of was a Psalm David sang about *himself*:

Therefore my heart is glad, and my honor rejoices;
my body also dwells secure.

For you did not forsake my soul to Sheol [the underworld or
   "Hades"],
or allow your godly one to see the Pit.
[Rather] you taught me the way of life;
in your presence there is an abundance of joy,
in your right hand there is eternal pleasure.

PSALMS 16:9–11

But—and here lies the key to understanding the dramatic transformation that took place in Jesus's message after his death—Stephen
was not a scribe or scholar. He was not an expert in the scriptures.
He did not live in Jerusalem. As such, he was the perfect audience
for this new, innovative, and thoroughly unorthodox interpretation
of the messiah being peddled by a group of unschooled ecstatics
whose certainty in their message was matched only by the passion
with which they preached it.

Stephen converted to the Jesus movement shortly after Jesus's
death. As with most converts from the distant Diaspora, he would
have abandoned his hometown, sold his possessions, pooled his
resources into the community, and made a home for himself in Jerusalem, under the shadow of the Temple walls. Although he would
spend only a brief time as a member of the new community—
perhaps a year or two—his violent death soon after his conversion
would forever enshrine his name in the annals of Christian history.

The story of that celebrated death can be found in the book of
Acts, which chronicles the first few decades of the Jesus movement
after the crucifixion. The evangelist Luke, who allegedly composed the book as a sequel to his gospel, presents Stephen's stoning
as a watershed movement in the early history of the church. Stephen is called a man "full of grace and power [who] did great
wonders and signs among the people" (Acts 6:8). His speech and
wisdom, Luke claims, were so powerful that few could stand against
him. In fact, Stephen's spectacular death in the book of Acts be-

comes, for Luke, a coda to Jesus's passion narrative; Luke's gospel, alone among the Synoptics, transfers to Stephen's "trial" the accusation made against Jesus that he had threatened to destroy the Temple.

"This man [Stephen] never ceases blaspheming against this holy place [the Temple] and the law," a gang of stone-wielding vigilantes cries out. "We have heard him say that Jesus of Nazareth will demolish this place and will change the customs that Moses handed down to us" (Acts 6:13–14).

Luke also provides Stephen with the self-defense that Jesus never received in his gospel. In a long and rambling diatribe before the mob, Stephen summarizes nearly all of Jewish history, starting with Abraham and ending with Jesus. The speech, which is obviously Luke's creation, is riddled with the most basic errors: it misidentifies the burial site of the great patriarch Jacob, and it inexplicably claims that an angel gave the law to Moses when even the most uneducated Jew in Palestine would have known it was God himself who gave Moses the law. However, the speech's true significance comes near the end, when in a fit of ecstasy, Stephen looks up to the heavens and sees "the Son of Man standing at the right hand of God" (Acts 7:56).

The image seems to have been a favorite of the early Christian community. Mark, yet another Greek-speaking Jew from the Diaspora, has Jesus say something similar to the high priest in his gospel: "And you will see the Son of Man seated at the right hand of the Power" (Mark 14:62), which is then picked up by Matthew and Luke—two more Greek-speaking Diaspora Jews—in their own accounts. But whereas Jesus in the Synoptics is directly quoting Psalm 110 so as to draw a connection between himself and King David, Stephen's speech in Acts consciously replaces the phrase "the right hand of the Power" with "the right hand of God." There is a reason for the change. In ancient Israel, the right hand was a symbol of power and authority; it signified a position of exaltation. Sitting "at the right hand of God" means sharing in God's glory, being one with God in honor and essence. As Thomas Aquinas wrote, "to sit on the right hand of the Father is nothing else than to share in the glory of the Godhead ... [Jesus] sits at the right hand of the Father, because He has the same Nature as the Father."

In other words, Stephen's Son of Man is not the kingly figure of Daniel who comes "with the clouds of heaven." He does not establish his kingdom on earth "so that all peoples, nations, and languages should serve him" (Daniel 7:1–14). He is not even the messiah any longer. The Son of Man, in Stephen's vision, is a pre-existent, heavenly being whose kingdom is not of this world; who stands at the right hand of God, equal in glory and honor; who is, in form and substance, *God made flesh.*

That is all it takes for the stones to start flying.

Understand that there can be no greater blasphemy for a Jew than what Stephen suggests. The claim that an individual died and rose again into eternal life may have been unprecedented in Judaism. But the presumption of a "god–man" was simply anathema. What Stephen cries out in the midst of his death throes is nothing less than the launch of a wholly new religion, one radically and irreconcilably divorced from everything Stephen's own religion had ever posited about the nature of God and man and the relationship of the one to the other. One can say that it was not only Stephen who died that day outside the gates of Jerusalem. Buried with him under the rubble of stones is the last trace of the historical person known as Jesus of Nazareth. The story of the zealous Galilean peasant and Jewish nationalist who donned the mantle of messiah and launched a foolhardy rebellion against the corrupt Temple priesthood and the vicious Roman occupation comes to an abrupt end, not with his death on the cross, nor with the empty tomb, but at the first moment one of his followers dares suggest he is God.

Stephen was martyred sometime between 33 and 35 C.E. Among those in the crowd who countenanced his stoning was a pious young Pharisee from a wealthy Roman city on the Mediter-

ranean Sea called Tarsus. His name was Saul, and he was a true
zealot: a fervent follower of the Law of Moses who had burnished
a reputation for violently suppressing blasphemies such as Stephen's. Around 49 C.E., a mere fifteen years after he gladly watched
Stephen die, this same fanatical Pharisee, now an ardent Christian
convert renamed Paul, would write a letter to his friends in the
Greek city of Philippi in which he unambiguously, and without
reservation, calls Jesus of Nazareth God. "He was in the form of
God," Paul wrote, though he was "born in the likeness of man"
(Philippians 2:6–7).

How could this have happened? How could a failed messiah
who died a shameful death as a state criminal be transformed, in
the span of a few years, into the creator of the heavens and the
earth: God incarnate?

The answer to that question relies on recognizing this one
rather remarkable fact: practically every word ever written about
Jesus of Nazareth, including every gospel story in Matthew, Mark,
Luke, and John, was written by people who, like Stephen and Paul,
never actually knew Jesus when he was alive (recall that, with the
possible exception of Luke, the gospels were not written by those
after whom they were named). Those who did know Jesus—those
who followed him into Jerusalem as its king and helped him cleanse
the Temple in God's name, who were there when he was arrested
and who watched him die a lonely death—played a surprisingly
small role in defining the movement Jesus left behind. The members of Jesus's family, and especially his brother James, who would
lead the community in Jesus's absence, were certainly influential in
the decades after the crucifixion. But they were hampered by their
decision to remain more or less ensconced in Jerusalem waiting for
Jesus to return, until they and their community, like nearly everyone else in the holy city, were annihilated by Titus's army in 70 C.E.
The apostles who were tasked by Jesus to spread his message did
leave Jerusalem and fan out across the land bearing the good news.
But they were severely limited by their inability to theologically

expound on the new faith or compose instructive narratives about the life and death of Jesus. These were farmers and fishermen, after all; they could neither read nor write.

The task of defining Jesus's message fell instead to a new crop of educated, urbanized, Greek-speaking Diaspora Jews who would become the primary vehicles for the expansion of the new faith. As these extraordinary men and women, many of them immersed in Greek philosophy and Hellenistic thought, began to reinterpret Jesus's message so as to make it more palatable both to their fellow Greek-speaking Jews and to their gentile neighbors in the Diaspora, they gradually transformed Jesus from a revolutionary zealot to a Romanized demigod, from a man who tried and failed to free the Jews from Roman oppression to a celestial being wholly uninterested in any earthly matter.

This transformation did not occur without conflict or difficulty. The original Aramaic-speaking followers of Jesus, including the members of his family and the remnants of the Twelve, openly clashed with the Greek-speaking Diaspora Jews when it came to the correct understanding of Jesus's message. The discord between the two groups resulted in the emergence of two distinct and competing camps of Christian interpretation in the decades after the crucifixion: one championed by Jesus's brother, James; the other promoted by the former Pharisee, Paul. As we shall see, it would be the contest between these two bitter and openly hostile adversaries that, more than anything else, would shape Christianity as the global religion we know today.

Chapter Thirteen

If Christ Has Not Been Risen

It was at the sixth hour of the day—the day before the Sabbath—when, according to the gospel, a crowning darkness came over the whole of the earth, as though all creation had paused to bear witness to the death of this simple Nazarean, scourged and executed for calling himself King of the Jews. At the ninth hour, Jesus suddenly cried out, "My God, my God, why have you forsaken me?" Someone soaked a sponge in sour wine and raised it to his lips to ease his suffering. Finally, no longer able to bear the heaving pressure on his lungs, Jesus lifted his head to the sky and, with a loud, agonized cry, gave up his spirit.

Jesus's end would have been swift and unnoticed by all, save, perhaps, for the handful of female disciples who stood weeping at the bottom of the hill, gazing up at their maimed and mutilated master: most of the men had scattered into the night at the first sign of trouble in Gethsemane. The death of a state criminal hanging on a cross atop Golgotha was a tragically banal event. Dozens died with Jesus that day, their broken bodies hanging limp for days afterward to serve the ravenous birds that circled above and the dogs that came out under cover of night to finish what the birds left behind.

Yet Jesus was no common criminal, not for the evangelists who composed the narrative of his final moments. He was God's agent on earth. His death could not have conceivably gone unnoticed, either by the Roman governor who sent him to the cross or by the high priest who handed him over to die. And so, when Jesus yielded his soul to heaven, at the precise moment of his final breath, the gospels say that the veil in the Temple, which separated the altar from the Holy of Holies—the blood-spattered veil sprinkled with the sacrifice of a thousand thousand offerings, the veil that the high priest, and only the high priest, would draw back as he entered the private presence of God—was violently rent in two, from top to bottom.

"Surely this was a son of God," a bewildered centurion at the foot of the cross declares, before running off to Pilate to report what had happened.

The tearing of the Temple's veil is a fitting end to the passion narratives, the perfect symbol of what the death of Jesus meant for the men and women who reflected upon it many decades later. Jesus's sacrifice, they argued, removed the barrier between humanity and God. The veil that separated the divine presence from the rest of the world had been torn away. Through Jesus's death, everyone could now access God's spirit, without ritual or priestly mediation. The high priest's high-priced prerogative, the very Temple itself, was suddenly made irrelevant. The body of Christ had replaced the Temple rituals, just as the words of Jesus had supplanted the Torah.

Of course, these are theological reflections rendered years after the Temple had already been destroyed; it is not difficult to consider Jesus's death to have displaced a Temple that no longer existed. For the disciples who remained in Jerusalem after the crucifixion, however, the Temple and the priesthood were still very much a reality. The veil that hung before the Holy of Holies was still apparent to all. The high priest and his cohort still controlled the Temple Mount. Pilate's soldiers still roamed the stone streets of

Jerusalem. Not much had changed at all. The world remained essentially as it was before their messiah had been taken from them.

The disciples faced a profound test of their faith after Jesus's death. The crucifixion marked the end of their dream of overturning the existing system, of reconstituting the twelve tribes of Israel and ruling over them in God's name. The Kingdom of God would not be established on earth, as Jesus had promised. The meek and the poor would not exchange places with the rich and the powerful. The Roman occupation would not be overthrown. As with the followers of every other messiah the empire had killed, there was nothing left for Jesus's disciples to do but abandon their cause, renounce their revolutionary activities, and return to their farms and villages.

Then something extraordinary happened. What exactly that something was is impossible to know. Jesus's resurrection is an exceedingly difficult topic for the historian to discuss, not least because it falls beyond the scope of any examination of the historical Jesus. Obviously, the notion of a man dying a gruesome death and returning to life three days later defies all logic, reason, and sense. One could simply stop the argument there, dismiss the resurrection as a lie, and declare belief in the risen Jesus to be the product of a deludable mind.

However, there is this nagging fact to consider: one after another of those who claimed to have witnessed the risen Jesus went to their own gruesome deaths refusing to recant their testimony. That is not, in itself, unusual. Many zealous Jews died horribly for refusing to deny their beliefs. But these first followers of Jesus were not being asked to reject matters of faith based on events that took place centuries, if not millennia, before. They were being asked to deny something they themselves personally, directly encountered.

The disciples were themselves fugitives in Jerusalem, complicit in the sedition that led to Jesus's crucifixion. They were repeatedly arrested and abused for their preaching; more than once their leaders had been brought before the Sanhedrin to answer charges of blasphemy. They were beaten, whipped, stoned, and crucified, yet they would not cease proclaiming the risen Jesus. And it worked! Perhaps the most obvious reason not to dismiss the disciples' resurrection experiences out of hand is that, among all the other failed messiahs who came before and after him, Jesus alone is still called messiah. It was precisely the fervor with which the followers of Jesus believed in his resurrection that transformed this tiny Jewish sect into the largest religion in the world.

Although the first resurrection stories were not written until the mid- to late nineties (there is no resurrection appearance in either the Q source materials, compiled in around 50 C.E., or in the gospel of Mark, written after 70 C.E.), belief in the resurrection seems to have been part of the earliest liturgical formula of the nascent Christian community. Paul—the former Pharisee who would become the most influential interpreter of Jesus's message— writes about the resurrection in a letter addressed to the Christian community in the Greek city of Corinth, sometime around 50 C.E. "For I give over to you the first things which I myself accepted," Paul writes, "that Christ died for the sake of our sins, *according to the scriptures;* that he was buried and that he rose again on the third day, *according to the scriptures;* that he was seen by Cephas [Simon Peter], then by the Twelve. After that, he was seen by over five hundred brothers at once, many of whom are still alive, though some have died. After that, he was seen by [his brother] James; then by all the apostles. And, last of all, he was seen by me as well . . ." (1 Corinthians 15:3–8).

Paul may have written those words in 50 C.E., but he is repeating what is likely a much older formula, one that may be traced to the early forties. That means belief in the resurrection of Jesus was among the community's first attestations of faith—earlier than the passion narratives, earlier even than the story of the virgin birth.

Nevertheless, the fact remains that the resurrection is not a historical event. It may have had historical ripples, but the event itself falls outside the scope of history and into the realm of faith. It is, in fact, the ultimate test of faith for Christians, as Paul wrote in that same letter to the Corinthians: "If Christ has not been risen, then our preaching is empty and your faith is in vain" (1 Corinthians 15:17).

Paul makes a key point. Without the resurrection, the whole edifice of Jesus's claim to the mantle of the messiah comes crashing down. The resurrection solves an insurmountable problem, one that would have been impossible for the disciples to ignore: Jesus's crucifixion invalidates his claim to be the messiah and successor to David. According to the Law of Moses, Jesus's crucifixion actually marks him as the accursed of God: "Anyone hung on a tree [that is, crucified] is under God's curse" (Deuteronomy 21:23). But if Jesus did not actually die—if his death were merely the prelude to his spiritual evolution—then the cross would no longer be a curse or a symbol of failure. It would be transformed into a symbol of victory.

Precisely because the resurrection claim was so preposterous and unique, an entirely new edifice needed to be constructed to replace the one that had crumbled in the shadow of the cross. The resurrection stories in the gospels were created to do just that: to put flesh and bones upon an already accepted creed; to create narrative out of established belief; and, most of all, to counter the charges of critics who denied the claim, who argued that Jesus's followers saw nothing more than a ghost or a spirit, who thought it was the disciples themselves who stole Jesus's body to make it appear as though he rose again. By the time these stories were written, six decades had passed since the crucifixion. In that time, the evangelists had heard just about every conceivable objection to the resurrection, and they were able to create narratives to counter each and every one of them.

The disciples saw a ghost? Could a ghost eat fish and bread, as the risen Jesus does in Luke 24:42–43?

Jesus was merely an incorporeal spirit? "Does a spirit have flesh and bones?" the risen Jesus asks his incredulous disciples as he offers his hands and feet to touch as proof (Luke 24:36–39).

Jesus's body was stolen? How so, when Matthew has conveniently placed armed guards at his tomb—guards who saw for themselves the risen Jesus, but who were bribed by the priests to say the disciples had stolen the body from under their noses? "And this story has been spread among the Jews to this day" (Matthew 28:1–15).

Again, these stories are not meant to be accounts of historical events; they are carefully crafted rebuttals to an argument that is taking place offscreen. Still, it is one thing to argue that Jesus of Nazareth rose from the dead. That is, in the end, purely a matter of faith. It is something else entirely to say that he did so *according to the scriptures*. Luke portrays the risen Jesus as addressing this issue himself by patiently explaining to his disciples, who "had hoped he was the one to redeem Israel" (Luke 24:21), how his death and resurrection were in reality the fulfillment of the messianic prophecies, how everything written about the messiah "in the Law of Moses, the prophets, and the Psalms" led to the cross and the empty tomb. "Thus it is written that the messiah would suffer and rise again on the third day," Jesus instructs his disciples (Luke 24:44–46).

Except that nowhere is any such thing written: not in the Law of Moses, not in the prophets, not in the Psalms. In the entire history of Jewish thought there is not a single line of scripture that says the messiah is to suffer, die, and rise again on the third day, which may explain why Jesus does not bother to cite any scripture to back up his incredible claim.

No wonder Jesus's followers had such a difficult time convincing their fellow Jews in Jerusalem to accept their message. When

Paul writes in his letter to the Corinthians that the crucifixion is "a stumbling block to the Jews," he is grossly understating the disciples' dilemma (1 Corinthians 1:23). To the Jews, a crucified messiah was nothing less than a contradiction in terms. The very fact of Jesus's crucifixion annulled his messianic claims. Even the disciples recognized this problem. That is why they so desperately tried to deflect their dashed hopes by arguing that the Kingdom of God they had hoped to establish was in actuality a celestial kingdom, not an earthly one; that the messianic prophecies had been misconstrued; that the scriptures, properly interpreted, said the opposite of what everyone thought they did; that embedded deep in the texts was a secret truth about the dying and rising messiah that only they could uncover. The problem was that in a city as steeped in the scriptures as Jerusalem, such an argument would have fallen on deaf ears, especially when it came from a group of illiterate peasants from the backwoods of Galilee whose only experience with the scriptures was what little they heard of them in their synagogues back home. Try as they might, the disciples simply could not persuade a significant number of Jerusalemites to accept Jesus as the long-awaited liberator of Israel.

The disciples could have left Jerusalem, fanned out across Galilee with their message, returned to their villages to preach among their friends and neighbors. But Jerusalem was the place of Jesus's death and resurrection, the place to which they believed he would soon return. It was the center of Judaism, and despite their peculiar interpretation of the scriptures, the disciples were, above all else, Jews. Theirs was an altogether Jewish movement intended, in those first few years after Jesus's crucifixion, for an exclusively Jewish audience. They had no intention of abandoning the sacred city or divorcing themselves from Judaism, regardless of the persecution they faced from the priestly authorities. The movement's principal leaders—the apostles Peter and John, and Jesus's brother, James—maintained their fealty to Jewish customs and Mosaic Law to the end. Under their leadership, the Jerusalem church became known as the "mother assembly." No matter how far and wide the movement spread, no matter how many other "assemblies" were established in cities such as Philippi, Corinth, or even Rome, no matter how many new converts—Jew or gentile—the movement attracted, every assembly, every convert, and every missionary would fall under the authority of the "mother assembly" in Jerusalem, until the day it was burned to the ground.

There was another, more practical advantage to centering the movement in Jerusalem. The yearly cycle of festivals and feasts brought thousands of Jews from across the empire directly to them. And unlike the Jews living in Jerusalem, who seem to have easily dismissed Jesus's followers as uninformed at best, heretical at worst, the Diaspora Jews, who lived far from the sacred city and beyond the reach of the Temple, proved far more susceptible to the disciples' message.

As small minorities living in large cosmopolitan centers like Antioch and Alexandria, these Diaspora Jews had become deeply acculturated to both Roman society and Greek ideas. Surrounded by a host of different races and religions, they tended to be more open to questioning Jewish beliefs and practices, even when it came to such basic matters as circumcision and dietary restrictions. Unlike their brethren in the Holy Land, Diaspora Jews spoke Greek, not Aramaic: Greek was the language of their thought processes, the language of their worship. They experienced the scriptures not in the original Hebrew but in a Greek translation (the Septuagint), which offered new and originative ways of expressing their faith, allowing them to more easily harmonize traditional biblical cosmology with Greek philosophy. Consider the Jewish scriptures that came out of the Diaspora. Books such as *The Wisdom of Solomon,* which anthropomorphizes Wisdom as a woman to be sought above all else, and *Jesus Son of Sirach* (commonly referred to as *The Book of Ecclesiasticus*) read more like Greek philosophical tracts than like Semitic scriptures.

It is not surprising, therefore, that Diaspora Jews were more receptive to the innovative interpretation of the scriptures being offered by Jesus's followers. In fact, it did not take long for these Greek-speaking Jews to outnumber the original Aramaic-speaking followers of Jesus in Jerusalem. According to the book of Acts, the community was divided into two separate and distinct camps: the "Hebrews," the term used by Acts to refer to the Jerusalem-based believers under the leadership of James and the apostles, and the "Hellenists," those Jews who came from the Diaspora and who spoke Greek as their primary language (Acts 6:1).

It was not just language that separated the Hebrews from the Hellenists. The Hebrews were primarily peasants, farmers, and fishermen—transplants in Jerusalem from the Judean and Galilean countryside. The Hellenists were more sophisticated and urbane, better educated, and certainly wealthier, as evidenced by their ability to travel hundreds of kilometers to make pilgrimage at the Temple. It was, however, the division in language that would ultimately prove decisive in differentiating the two communities. The Hellenists, who worshipped Jesus in Greek, relied on a language that provided a vastly different set of symbols and metaphors than did either Aramaic or Hebrew. The difference in language gradually led to differences in doctrine, as the Hellenists began to meld their Greek-inspired worldviews with the Hebrews' already idiosyncratic reading of the Jewish scriptures.

When conflict broke out between the two communities over the equal distribution of communal resources, the apostles designated seven leaders among the Hellenists to see to their own needs. Known as "the Seven," these leaders are listed in the book of Acts as Philip, Prochorus, Nicanor, Timon, Parmenas, Nicolaus (a Gentile convert from Antioch), and, of course, Stephen, whose death at the hands of an angry mob would make permanent the division between the Hebrews and Hellenists.

A wave of persecution followed Stephen's death. The religious authorities, who until then seemed to have grudgingly tolerated the presence of Jesus's followers in Jerusalem, were incensed by

Stephen's shockingly heretical words. It was bad enough to call a crucified peasant messiah; it was unforgivably blasphemous to call him God. In response, the authorities systematically expelled the Hellenists from Jerusalem, an act that, interestingly, did not seem to have been greatly opposed by the Hebrews. Indeed, the fact that the Jerusalem assembly continued to thrive under the shadow of the Temple for decades after Stephen's death indicates that the Hebrews remained somewhat unaffected by the persecutions of the Hellenists. It was as though the priestly authorities did not consider the two groups to be related.

Meanwhile, the expelled Hellenists flooded back into the Diaspora. Armed with the message they had adopted from the Hebrews in Jerusalem, they began transmitting it, *in Greek,* to their fellow Diaspora Jews, those living in the Gentile cities of Ashdod and Caesarea, in the coastal regions of Syria-Palestine, in Cyprus and Phoenicia and Antioch, the city in which they were, for the first time, referred to as Christians (Acts 11:27). Little by little over the following decade, the Jewish sect founded by a group of rural Galileans morphed into a religion of urbanized Greek speakers. No longer bound by the confines of the Temple and the Jewish religion, the Hellenist preachers began to gradually shed Jesus's message of its nationalistic concerns, transforming it into a universal calling that would be more appealing to those living in a Graeco-Roman milieu. In doing so, they unchained themselves from the strictures of Jewish law, until it ceased to have any primacy. Jesus did not come to fulfill the law, the Hellenists argued. He came to abolish it. Jesus's condemnation was not of the priests who defiled the Temple with their wealth and hypocrisy. His condemnation was of the Temple itself.

Still, at this point, the Hellenists reserved their preaching solely for their fellow Jews, as Luke writes in the book of Acts: "They spoke the word to no one but the Jews" (Acts 11:19). This was still a primarily Jewish movement, one that blossomed through the theological experimentation that marked the Diaspora experience in the Roman Empire. But then a few among the Hellenists began sharing the message of Jesus with gentiles, "so that a great number of them became believers." The gentile mission was not paramount—not yet. But the farther the Hellenists spread from Jerusalem and the heart of the Jesus movement, the more their focus shifted from an exclusively Jewish audience to a primarily gentile one. The more their focus shifted to converting gentiles, the more they allowed certain syncretistic elements borrowed from Greek gnosticism and Roman religions to creep into the movement. And the more the movement was shaped by these new "pagan" converts, the more forcefully it discarded its Jewish past for a Graeco-Roman future.

All of this was still many years away. It would not be until after the destruction of Jerusalem in 70 c.e. that the mission to the Jews would be abandoned and Christianity transformed into a Romanized religion. Yet even at this early stage in the Jesus movement, the path toward gentile dominance was being set, though the tipping point would not come until a young Pharisee and Hellenistic Jew from Tarsus named Saul—the same Saul who had countenanced Stephen's stoning for blasphemy—met the risen Jesus on the road to Damascus and became known forevermore as Paul.

Chapter Fourteen

Am I Not an Apostle?

Saul of Tarsus was still breathing threats against the disciples when he left Jerusalem to find and punish the Hellenists who had fled to Damascus after Stephen's stoning. Saul was not asked by the high priest to hunt down these followers of Jesus; he went of his own accord. An educated, Greek-speaking, Diaspora Jew and citizen of one of the wealthiest port cities in the Roman Empire, Saul was zealously devoted to the Temple and Torah. "Circumcised on the eighth day, of the stock of Israel, of the tribe of Benjamin, a Hebrew born of Hebrews," he writes of himself in a letter to the Philippians, "as to [knowledge of] the law, a Pharisee; as to zeal, a persecutor of the church; as to righteousness under the law, blameless" (Philippians 3:5–6).

It was while en route to Damascus that the young Pharisee had an ecstatic experience that would change everything for him, and for the faith he would adopt as his own. As he approached the city gates with his traveling companions, he was suddenly struck by a light from heaven flashing all around him. He fell to the ground in a heap. A voice said to him, "Saul, Saul, why are you persecuting me?"

"Who are you, Lord?" Saul asked.

The reply broke through the blinding white light, "I am Jesus."
Struck blind by the vision, Saul made his way to Damascus, where he met a follower of Jesus named Ananias, who laid hands upon him and restored his sight. Immediately, something like scales dropped from Saul's eyes and he was filled with the Holy Spirit. Right then and there, Saul was baptized into the Jesus movement. He changed his name to Paul and immediately began preaching the risen Jesus, not to his fellow Jews, but to the gentiles who had, up to this point, been more or less ignored by the movement's chief missionaries.

The story of Paul's dramatic conversion on the road to Damascus is a bit of propagandistic legend created by the evangelist Luke; Paul himself never recounts the story of being blinded by the sight of Jesus. If the traditions can be believed, Luke was a young devotee of Paul: he is mentioned in two letters, Colossians and Timothy, commonly attributed to Paul but written long after his death. Luke wrote the book of Acts as a kind of eulogy to his former master some thirty to forty years after Paul had died. In fact, Acts is less an account of the apostles than it is a reverential biography of Paul; the apostles disappear from the book early on, serving as little more than the bridge between Jesus and Paul. In Luke's reimagining, it is Paul—not James, nor Peter, nor John, nor any of the Twelve—who is the true successor to Jesus. The activity of the apostles in Jerusalem serves only as prelude to Paul's preaching in the Diaspora.

Although Paul does not divulge any details about his conversion, he does repeatedly insist that he has witnessed the risen Jesus for himself, and that this experience has endowed him with the same apostolic authority as the Twelve. "Am I not an apostle?" Paul writes in defense of his credentials, which were frequently challenged by the mother assembly in Jerusalem. "Have I not seen Jesus our Lord?" (1 Corinthians 9:1).

Paul may have considered himself an apostle, but it seems that few if any of the other movement leaders agreed. Not even Luke,

Paul's sycophant, whose writings betray a deliberate, if ahistorical, attempt to elevate his mentor's status in the founding of the church, seems to consider Paul an apostle. Luke makes it clear there are only twelve apostles, one for each tribe of Israel, just as Jesus had intended. In recounting the story of how the remaining eleven apostles replaced Judas Iscariot with Matthias after Jesus's death, Luke notes that the new recruit needed to be someone who "accompanied [the disciples] all the time that the Lord Jesus went in and out among us, starting with John's baptism, right up to the day [Jesus] was taken from us" (Acts 1:21). Such a requirement would clearly have ruled out Paul, who converted to the movement around 37 C.E., nearly a decade after Jesus had died. But that does not deter Paul, who not only demands to be called an apostle—"even if I am not an apostle to others, at least I am to you," he tells his beloved community in Corinth (1 Corinthians 9:2)—he insists he is far superior to all the other apostles.

"Are they Hebrews?" Paul writes of the apostles. "So am I! Are they Israelites? So am I! Are they the seed of Abraham? So am I! Are they servants of Christ? *I am a better one* (though it may be foolish to say so), with greater labors, more floggings, more imprisonments, and more often near death" (2 Corinthians 11:22–23). Paul holds particular contempt for the Jerusalem-based triumvirate of James, Peter, and John, whom he derides as the "so-called pillars of the church" (Galatians 2:9). "Whatever they are makes no difference to me," he writes. "Those leaders contributed nothing to me" (Galatians 2:6). The apostles may have walked and talked with the living Jesus (or, as Paul dismissively calls him, "Jesus-in-the-flesh"). But Paul walks and talks with the divine Jesus: they have, according to Paul, conversations in which Jesus imparts secret instructions intended solely for his ears. The apostles may have been hand-picked by Jesus as they toiled away on their fields or brought up their fishing nets. But Jesus chose Paul before he was born: he was, he tells the Galatians, called by Jesus into apostleship while still in his mother's womb (Galatians 1:15). Simply put, Paul does not consider himself the thirteenth apostle. He thinks he is the *first* apostle.

The claim of apostleship is an urgent one for Paul, as it was the only way to justify his entirely self-ascribed mission to the gentiles, which the leaders of the Jesus movement in Jerusalem appear not to have initially supported. Although there was a great deal of discussion among the apostles over how strictly the new community should adhere to the Law of Moses, with some advocating rigorous compliance and others taking a more moderate stance, there was little argument about whom the community was meant to serve: this was a Jewish movement intended for a Jewish audience. Even the Hellenists reserved their preaching mostly for the Jews. If a handful of gentiles decided to accept Jesus as messiah, so be it, as long as they submitted to circumcision and the law.

Yet, for Paul, there is no room whatsoever for debating the role of the Law of Moses in the new community. Not only does Paul reject the primacy of Jewish law, he refers to it as a "ministry of death, chiseled in letters on a stone tablet" that must be superseded by "a ministry of the Spirit come in glory" (2 Corinthians 3:7–8). He calls his fellow believers who continue to practice circumcision— the quintessential mark of the nation of Israel—"dogs and evildoers" who "mutilate the flesh" (Philippians 3:2). These are startling statements for a former Pharisee to make. But for Paul they reflect the truth about Jesus that he feels he alone recognizes, which is that "Christ is the end of the Torah" (Romans 10:4).

Paul's breezy dismissal of the very foundation of Judaism was as shocking to the leaders of the Jesus movement in Jerusalem as it would have been to Jesus himself. After all, Jesus claimed to have come to fulfill the Law of Moses, not to abolish it. Far from rejecting the law, Jesus continually strove to expand and intensify it. Where the law commands, "thou shall not kill," Jesus added, "if you are angry with your brother or sister you are liable to [the same] judgment" (Matthew 5:22). Where the law states, "thou shall not commit adultery," Jesus extended it to include "everyone who looks at a woman with lust" (Matthew 5:28). Jesus may have disagreed with the scribes and scholars over the correct interpretation of the law, particularly when it came to such matters as the prohibition against working on the Sabbath. But he never rejected the law. On the contrary, Jesus warned that "whoever breaks one of the least of these commandments and teaches others to do so, will be called least in the kingdom of heaven" (Matthew 5:19).

One would think that Jesus's admonishment not to teach others to break the Law of Moses would have had some impact on Paul. But Paul seems totally unconcerned with anything "Jesus-in-the-flesh" may or may not have said. In fact, Paul shows no interest at all in the historical Jesus. There is almost no trace of Jesus of Nazareth in any of his letters. With the exception of the crucifixion and the Last Supper, which he transforms from a narrative into a liturgical formula, Paul does not narrate a single event from Jesus's life. Nor does Paul ever actually quote Jesus's words (again, with the exception of his rendering of the Eucharistic formula: "This is my body . . ."). Actually, Paul sometimes directly contradicts Jesus. Compare what Paul writes in his epistle to the Romans—"everyone who calls upon the name of the Lord will be saved" (Romans 10:13)—to what Jesus says in the gospel of Matthew: "Not everyone who says to me 'Lord Lord' shall enter the kingdom of heaven" (Matthew 7:21).

Paul's lack of concern with the historical Jesus is not due, as some have argued, to his emphasis on Christological rather than historical concerns. It is due to the simple fact that Paul had no idea who the living Jesus was, nor did he care. He repeatedly boasts that he has not learned about Jesus either from the apostles or from anyone else who may have known him. "But when it pleased God . . . to reveal his son to me, so that I might preach him to the gentiles, I did not confer with anyone, nor did I go up to Jerusalem [to ask permission of] the apostles before me," Paul boasts. "Instead, I went directly to Arabia, and then again to Damascus" (Galatians 1:15–17).

Only after three years of preaching a message that Paul insists he received not from any human being (by which he quite obviously means James and the apostles), but directly from Jesus, did he deign to visit the men and women in Jerusalem who had actually known the man Paul professed as Lord (Galatians 1:12).

Why does Paul go to such lengths not only to break free from the authority of the leaders in Jerusalem, but to denigrate and dismiss them as irrelevant or worse? Because Paul's views about Jesus are so extreme, so beyond the pale of acceptable Jewish thought, that only by claiming that they come directly from Jesus himself could he possibly get away with preaching them. What Paul offers in his letters is not, as some of his contemporary defenders maintain, merely an alternative take on Jewish spirituality. Paul, instead, advances an altogether new doctrine that would have been utterly unrecognizable to the person upon whom he claims it is based. For it was Paul who solved the disciples' dilemma of reconciling Jesus's shameful death on the cross with the messianic expectations of the Jews, by simply discarding those expectations and transforming Jesus into a completely new creature, one that seems almost wholly of his own making: *Christ*.

Although "Christ" is technically the Greek word for "messiah," that is not how Paul employs the term. He does not endow Christ with any of the connotations attached to the term "messiah" in the Hebrew Scriptures. He never speaks of Jesus as "the anointed of Israel." Paul may have recognized Jesus as a descendant of King David, but he does not look to the scriptures to argue that Jesus was the Davidic liberator the Jews had been awaiting. He ignores all the messianic prophecies that the gospels would rely on many years later to prove that Jesus was the Jewish messiah (when Paul does look to the Hebrew prophets—for instance, Isaiah's prophecy about the root of Jesse who will one day serve as "a light to the gentiles" (11:10)—he thinks the prophets are predicting *him*, not Jesus). Most tellingly, unlike the gospel writers (save for John, of course), Paul does not call Jesus *the* Christ (*Yesus ho Xristos*), as though Christ were his title. Rather, Paul calls him "Jesus Christ," or just "Christ," as if it were his surname. This is an extremely un-usual formulation whose closest parallel is in the way Roman em-perors adopted "Caesar" as a cognomen, as in Caesar Augustus.

Paul's Christ is not even human, though he has taken on the likeness of one (Philippians 2:7). He is a cosmic being who existed before time. He is the first of God's creations, through whom the rest of creation was formed (1 Corinthians 8:6). He is God's begot-ten son, God's *physical* progeny (Romans 8:3). He is the new Adam, born not of dust but of heaven. Yet while the first Adam became a living being, "the Last Adam," as Paul calls Christ, has become "a life-giving spirit" (1 Corinthians 15:45–47). Christ is, in short, a comprehensively new being. But he is not unique. He is merely the first of his kind: "the first-born among many brothers" (Ro-mans 8:29). All those who believe in Christ, as Paul does—those who accept Paul's teachings about him—can become one with him in a mystical union (1 Corinthians 6:17). Through their belief, their bodies will be transformed into the glorious body of Christ (Philippians 3:20–21). They will join him in spirit and share in his likeness, which, as Paul reminds his followers, is the likeness of God (Romans 8:29). Hence, as "heirs of God and fellow heirs of Christ," believers can also become divine beings (Romans 8:17). They can become like Christ in his death (Philippians 3:10)—that is, divine and eternal—tasked with the responsibility of judging alongside him the whole of humanity, as well as the angels in heaven (1 Cor-inthians 6:2–3).

Paul's portrayal of Jesus as Christ may sound familiar to con-temporary Christians—it has since become the standard doctrine of the church—but it would have been downright bizarre to Jesus's Jewish followers. The transformation of the Nazarean into a di-vine, preexistent, literal son of God whose death and resurrection launch a new genus of eternal beings responsible for judging the world has no basis in any writings about Jesus that are even remotely contemporary with Paul's (a firm indication that Paul's Christ was likely his own creation). Nothing like what Paul envisions exists in the Q source material, which was compiled around the same time that Paul was writing his letters. Paul's Christ is certainly not the Son of Man who appears in Mark's gospel, written just a few years after Paul's death. Nowhere in the gospels of Matthew and Luke—composed between 90 and 100 C.E.—is Jesus ever considered the literal son of God. Both gospels employ the term "Son of God" exactly as it is used throughout the Hebrew Scriptures: as a royal title, not a description. It is only in the last of the canonized gospels, the gospel of John, written sometime between 100 and 120 C.E., that Paul's vision of Jesus as Christ—the eternal *logos,* the only begotten son of God—can be found. Of course, by then, nearly half a century after the destruction of Jerusalem, Christianity was already a thoroughly Romanized religion, and Paul's Christ had long obliterated any last trace of the Jewish messiah in Jesus. During the decade of the fifties, however, when Paul is writing his letters, his conception of Jesus as Christ would have been shocking and plainly heretical, which is why, around 57 C.E., James and the apostles demand that Paul come to Jerusalem to answer for his deviant teachings.

This would not be Paul's first appearance before the movement's leaders. As he mentions in his letter to the Galatians, he initially met the apostles on a visit to the holy city three years after his conversion, around 40 C.E., when he came face-to-face with Peter and James. The two leaders were apparently thrilled that "the one who had been persecuting us is now proclaiming the message of faith he once tried to destroy" (Galatians 1:23). They glorified God because of Paul and sent him on his way to preach the message of Jesus in the regions of Syria and Cilicia, giving him as his companion and keeper a Jewish convert and close confidant of James named Barnabas.

Paul's second trip to Jerusalem took place about a decade later, sometime around 50 C.E., and was far less cordial than the first. He had been summoned to appear before a meeting of the Apostolic Council to defend his self-designated role as missionary to the gentiles (Paul insists he was not summoned to Jerusalem but went of his own accord because Jesus told him to). With his companion Barnabas and an uncircumcised Greek convert named Titus by his side, Paul stood before James, Peter, John, and the elders of the Jerusalem assembly to strongly defend the message he had been proclaiming to the gentiles.

Luke, writing about this meeting some forty or fifty years later, paints a picture of perfect harmony between Paul and the council's members, with Peter himself standing up for Paul and taking his side. According to Luke, James, in his capacity as leader of the Jerusalem assembly and head of the Apostolic Council, blessed Paul's teachings, decreeing that thenceforth gentiles would be welcomed into the community without having to follow the Law of Moses, so long as they "abstain from things polluted by idols, from prostitution, from [eating] things that have been strangled, and from blood" (Acts 15:1–21). Luke's description of the meeting is an obvious ploy to legitimate Paul's ministry by stamping it with the approval of none other than "the brother of the Lord." However, Paul's own account of the Apostolic Council, written in a letter to the Galatians not long after it had taken place, paints a completely different picture of what happened in Jerusalem.

Paul claims that he was ambushed at the Apostolic Council by a group of "false believers" (those still accepting the primacy of the Temple and Torah) who had been secretly spying on him and his ministry. Although Paul reveals little detail about the meeting, he cannot mask his rage at the treatment he says he received at the hands of "the supposedly acknowledged leaders" of the church: James, Peter, and John. Paul says he "refused to submit to them, not even for a minute," as neither they, nor their opinion of his ministry, made any difference to him whatsoever (Galatians 2:1–10).

Whatever took place during the Apostolic Council, it appears that the meeting concluded with a promise by James, the leader of the Jerusalem assembly, not to compel Paul's gentile followers to be circumcised. Yet what happened soon afterward indicates that he and James were far from reconciled: almost immediately after Paul left Jerusalem, James began sending his own missionaries to Paul's congregations in Galatia, Corinth, Philippi, and most other places where Paul had built a following, in order to correct Paul's unorthodox teachings about Jesus.

Paul was incensed by these delegations, which he viewed, correctly, as a threat to his authority. Almost all of Paul's epistles in the New Testament were written *after* the Apostolic Council and are addressed to congregations that had been visited by these representatives from Jerusalem (Paul's first letter, to the Thessalonians, was written between 48 and 50 C.E.; his last letter, to the Romans, was written around 56 C.E.). That is why these letters devote so much space to defending Paul's status as an apostle, touting his direct connection to Jesus, and railing against the leaders in Jerusalem who, "disguising themselves as apostles of Christ," are, in Paul's view, actually servants of Satan who have bewitched Paul's followers (Corinthians 11:13–15).

Nevertheless, James's delegations seem to have had an impact, for Paul repeatedly lambastes his congregations for abandoning him: "I am amazed at how quickly you have deserted the one who called you" (Galatians 1:6). He implores his followers not to listen to these delegations, or to anyone else for that matter, but only to him: "If anyone else preaches a gospel contrary to the gospel you received [from me], let him be damned" (Galatians 1:9). Even if that gospel comes "from an angel in heaven," Paul writes, his congregations should ignore it (Galatians 1:8). Instead, they should obey Paul and only Paul: "Be imitators of *me,* as I am of Christ" (1 Corinthians 11:1).

Feeling bitter and no longer tethered to the authority of James and the apostles in Jerusalem ("Whatever they are makes no difference to me"), Paul spent the next few years freely expounding his doctrine of Jesus as Christ. Whether James and the apostles in Jerusalem were fully aware of Paul's activities during this period is debatable. After all, Paul was writing his letters in Greek, a language neither James nor the apostles could read. Moreover, Barnabas, James's sole link to Paul, had abandoned him soon after the Apostolic Council for reasons that are unclear (though it bears mentioning that Barnabas was a Levite and as such would probably have been a strict observer of Jewish law). Regardless, by the year 57 C.E., the rumors about Paul's teachings could no longer be ignored. And so, once again, he is summoned to Jerusalem to answer for himself.

This time, James confronts Paul directly, telling him that it has come to his attention that Paul has been teaching believers "to forsake Moses" and "not circumcise their children or observe the customs [of the law]" (Acts 21:21). Paul does not respond to the accusation, though this is exactly what he has been teaching. He has even gone so far as to say that those who let themselves be circumcised will have "cut themselves off from Christ" (Galatians 5:2–4).

To clear up matters once and for all, James forces Paul to take part with four other men in a strict purification ritual in the Temple—the same Temple that Paul believes has been replaced by the blood of Jesus—so that "all will know there is nothing to the rumors said about you, and that you observe and guard the law" (Acts 21:24). Paul obeys; he seems to have no choice in the matter. But as he is completing the ritual, a group of devout Jews recognize him.

"Men of Israel!" they shout. "Help! This is the man who has been teaching everyone everywhere against our people, our law, and this place" (Acts 21:27–28). All at once, a mob descends upon Paul. They seize him and drag him out of the Temple. Just as they are about to beat him to death, a group of Roman soldiers suddenly appears. The soldiers break up the mob and take Paul into custody, not because of the disturbance at the Temple, but because they mistake him for someone else.

"Are you not the Egyptian who some days ago led a revolt in the wilderness of four thousand Sicarii?" a military tribune asks Paul (Acts 21:38).

It seems Paul's arrival in Jerusalem in 57 C.E. could not have come at a more chaotic time. One year earlier, the Sicarii had begun their reign of terror by slaying the high priest Jonathan. They were now wantonly murdering members of the priestly aristocracy, burning down their homes, kidnapping their families, and sowing fear in the hearts of the Jews. The messianic fervor in Jerusalem was at a boil. One by one, claimants to the mantle of the messiah had arisen to liberate the Jews from the yoke of Roman occupation. Theudas the wonder worker had already been cut down by Rome for his messianic aspirations. The rebellious sons of Judas the Galilean, Jacob and Simon, had been crucified. The bandit chief Eleazar son of Dinaeus, who had been ravaging the countryside, slaughtering Samaritans in the name of the God of Israel, had been captured and beheaded by the Roman prefect Felix. And then the Egyptian had suddenly appeared on the Mount of Olives, vowing to bring the walls of Jerusalem tumbling down at his command.

For James and the apostles in Jerusalem, the turmoil could mean only one thing: the end was near; Jesus was about to return. The Kingdom of God they had assumed Jesus would build while he was alive would now finally be established—all the more reason to ensure that those espousing deviant teachings in Jesus's name were brought back into the fold.

In that light, Paul's arrest in Jerusalem may have been unexpected, but considering the apocalyptic expectations in Jerusalem, it was neither ill timed nor unwelcomed. If Jesus were about to return, it would be no bad thing to have Paul waiting for him in a prison cell, where, at the very least, he and his perverse views could be contained until Jesus could judge them himself. But because the arresting soldiers assumed Paul was the Egyptian, they sent him at once to be judged by the Roman governor, Felix, who happened at the time to be in the coastal town of Caesarea dealing with a conflict that had erupted between the city's Jews and its Syrian and Greek inhabitants. Although Felix ultimately cleared Paul of the Egyptian's crimes, he nevertheless threw him in a Caesarean prison, where he languished until Festus replaced Felix as governor and promptly transferred Paul to Rome at his behest.

Festus allowed Paul to go to Rome because Paul claimed to be a Roman citizen. Paul was born in Tarsus, a city whose inhabitants had been granted Roman citizenship by Mark Antony a century earlier. As a citizen, Paul had the right to demand a Roman trial, and Festus, who would serve as governor for an extremely brief and tumultuous period in Jerusalem, seemed happy to grant him one, if for no other reason than to simply be rid of him.

There may have been a more urgent reason for Paul to want to go to Rome. After the embarrassing spectacle at the Temple, in which he was forced to renounce everything he had been preaching for two decades, Paul wanted to get as far as he could from Jerusalem and the ever-tightening noose of control placed around his neck by James and the apostles. Besides, Rome seemed the perfect place for Paul. This was the Imperial City, the seat of the Roman Empire. Surely the Hellenistic Jews who had chosen to make Caesar's home their own would be receptive to Paul's unorthodox teachings about Jesus Christ. Rome already had a small but growing contingent of Christians who lived alongside a fairly sizable Jewish population. A decade before Paul's arrival, conflicts between the two communities had led the emperor Claudius to expel both groups from the city. By the time Paul arrived some time in the early sixties, however, both populations were once again flourishing. The city seemed ripe for Paul's message.

Although Paul was officially under house arrest in Rome, it appears he was able to continue his preaching without much interference from the authorities. Yet by all accounts, Paul had little success in converting Rome's Jews to his side. The Jewish population was not just unreceptive to his unique interpretation of the messiah, they were openly hostile to it. Even the gentile converts did not appear overly welcoming toward Paul. That may be because Paul was not the only "apostle" preaching Jesus in the imperial city. Peter, the first of the Twelve, was also in Rome.

Peter had come to Rome a few years before Paul and likely at James's command to help establish an enduring community of Greek-speaking Jewish believers in the heart of the Roman Empire, a community that would be under the influence of the Jerusalem assembly and taught in accordance with the Jerusalem doctrine: in short, an anti-Pauline community. It is difficult to know just how successful Peter had become in his task before Paul arrived. But according to Acts, the Hellenists in Rome reacted so negatively to Paul's preaching that he decided to cut himself off once and for all from his fellow Jews "who listen but never understand . . . who look but never perceive." Paul vowed from that moment on to preach to none but the gentiles, "for they will listen" (Acts 28:26–29).

No record exists of these final years in the lives of Peter and Paul, the two men who would become the most important figures of Christianity. Strangely, Luke ends his account of Paul's life with his arrival in Rome and he does not mention that Peter was in the city, too. Stranger still, Luke does not bother to record the most significant aspect of the two men's years together in the Imperial City. For in the year 66 C.E., the same year that Jerusalem erupted in revolt, the emperor Nero, reacting to a sudden surge of Christian persecution in Rome, seized Peter and Paul and executed them both for espousing what he assumed was the same faith.

He was wrong.

Chapter Fifteen

The Just One

They called James, the brother of Jesus, "James the Just." In Jerusalem, the city he had made his home after his brother's death, James was recognized by all for his unsurpassed piety and his tireless defense of the poor. He himself owned nothing, not even the clothes he wore—simple garments made of linen, not wool. He drank no wine and ate no meat. He took no baths. No razor ever touched his head, nor did he smear himself with scented oils. It was said he spent so much time bent in worship, beseeching God's forgiveness for the people, that his knees grew hard as a camel's.

To the followers of Jesus, James was the living link to the messiah, the blood of the Lord. To everyone else in Jerusalem, he was simply "the just one." Even the Jewish authorities praised James for his rectitude and his unshakable commitment to the law. Was it not James who excoriated the heretic Paul for abandoning the Torah? Did he not force the former Pharisee to repent of his views and cleanse himself at the Temple? The authorities may not have accepted James's message about Jesus any more than they accepted Paul's, but they respected James and viewed him as a righteous and honorable man. According to the early Christian historian Hegesippus (110–180 C.E.), the Jewish authorities repeatedly asked James

to use his influence among the people to dissuade them from calling Jesus messiah. "We entreat you, restrain the people, for they
have gone astray in regard to Jesus, as if he were the Christ," they
begged. "For we bear you witness, as do all the people, that you are
just and that you do not respect persons. Persuade, therefore, the
multitude not to be led astray concerning Jesus."

Their entreaties went unheeded, of course. For although James
was, as everyone attests, a zealous devotee of the law, he was also a
faithful follower of Jesus; he would never betray the legacy of his
elder brother, not even when he was martyred for it.

The story of James's death can be found in Josephus's *Antiquities*. The year was 62 C.E. All of Palestine was sinking into anarchy.
Famine and drought had devastated the countryside, leaving fields
fallow and farmers starving. Panic reigned in Jerusalem, as the Sicarii murdered and pillaged at will. The revolutionary fervor of the
Jews was growing out of control, even as the priestly class upon
which Rome relied to maintain order was tearing itself apart, with
the wealthy priests in Jerusalem having concocted a scheme to
seize for themselves the tithes that were meant to sustain the lower-
class village priests. Meanwhile, a succession of inept Roman
governors—from the hotheaded Cumanus to the scoundrel Felix
and the hapless Festus—had only made matters worse.

When Festus died suddenly and without an immediate successor, Jerusalem descended into chaos. Recognizing the urgency of
the situation, the emperor Nero hurriedly dispatched Festus's replacement, Albinus, to restore order in the city. But it would take
weeks for Albinus to arrive. The delay gave the newly appointed
high priest, a rash and irascible young man named Ananus, the time
and opportunity to try to fill the vacuum of power in Jerusalem
himself.

Ananus was the son of the extremely influential former high
priest, also named Ananus, whose four other sons (and one son-in-
law, Joseph Caiaphas) had all taken turns serving in the post. It was,
in fact, the elder Ananus, whom Josephus calls "the great hoarder

of money," who instigated the shameless effort to strip the lower priests of their tithes, their sole source of income. With no Roman governor to check his ambitions, the young Ananus began a reckless campaign to rid himself of his perceived enemies. Among his first actions, Josephus writes, was to assemble the Sanhedrin and bring before it "James, the brother of Jesus, the one they call messiah." Ananus charged James with blasphemy and transgression of the law, sentencing him to be stoned to death.

The reaction to James's execution was immediate. A group of the city's Jews, whom Josephus describes as "the most fair-minded and . . . strict in the observance of the law," were outraged by Ananus's actions. They sent word to Albinus, who was en route to Jerusalem from Alexandria, informing him of what had transpired in his absence. In response, Albinus wrote a seething letter to Ananus, threatening to take murderous vengeance upon him the moment he arrived. By the time Albinus entered Jerusalem, however, Ananus had already been removed from his post as high priest and replaced with a man named Jesus son of Damneus, who was himself deposed a year later, just before the start of the Jewish Revolt.

The passage concerning the death of James in Josephus is famous for being the earliest nonbiblical reference to Jesus. As previously noted, Josephus's use of the appellation "James, the brother of Jesus, the one they call messiah," proves that by the year 94 C.E., when the *Antiquities* was written, Jesus of Nazareth was already recognized as the founder of an important and enduring movement. Yet a closer look at the passage reveals that the true focus of Josephus is not Jesus, whom he dismisses as "the one they call messiah," but rather James, whose unjust death at the hands of the high priest forms the core of the story. That Josephus mentions Jesus is no doubt significant. But the fact that a Jewish historian writing to a Roman audience would recount in detail the circumstances of James's death, and the overwhelmingly negative reaction to his execution—not from the Christians in Jerusalem, but from the city's most devout and observant Jews—is a clear indication of just how prominent a figure James was in first-century Palestine. Indeed, James was more than just Jesus's brother. He was, as the historical evidence attests, the undisputed leader of the movement Jesus had left behind.

Hegesippus, who belonged to the second generation of Jesus's followers, affirms James's role as head of the Christian community in his five-volume history of the early Church. "Control of the church," Hegesippus writes, "passed, together with the apostles, to the brother of the Lord, James, whom everyone from the Lord's time till our own has named 'the Just,' for there were many Jameses." In the noncanonical *Epistle of Peter*, the chief apostle and leader of the Twelve refers to James as "Lord and Bishop of the Holy Church." Clement of Rome (30–97 C.E.), who would succeed Peter in the imperial city, addresses a letter to James as "the Bishop of Bishops, who rules Jerusalem, the Holy Assembly of the Hebrews, and all the Assemblies everywhere." In the *Gospel of Thomas,* usually dated somewhere between the end of the first and the beginning of the second century C.E., Jesus himself names James his successor: "The disciples said to Jesus, 'We know that you will depart from us. Who will be our leader?' Jesus said to them, 'Where you are, you are to go to James the Just, for whose sake heaven and earth came into being.'"

The early Church father Clement of Alexandria (150–215 C.E.) claims that Jesus imparted a secret knowledge to "James the Just, to John, and to Peter," who in turn "imparted it to the other apostles," though Clement notes that among the triumvirate it was James who became "the first, as the record tells us, to be elected to the episcopal throne of the Jerusalem church." In his *Lives of Illustrious Men,* Saint Jerome (c. 347–420 C.E.), who translated the Bible into Latin (the Vulgate), writes that after Jesus ascended into heaven, James was "immediately appointed Bishop of Jerusalem by the apostles." In fact, Jerome argues that James's holiness and reputation among the people was so great that "the destruction of Jerusalem was believed to have occurred on account of his death." Jerome is referencing a tradition from Josephus, which is also remarked upon by the third-century Christian theologian Origen (c. 185–254 C.E.) and recorded in the *Ecclesiastical History* of Eusebius of Caesarea (c. 260–c. 339 C.E.), in which Josephus claims that "these things [the Jewish Revolt and the destruction of Jerusalem] happened to the Jews in requital for James the Just, who was a brother of Jesus, known as Christ, for though he was the most Righteous of men, the Jews put him to death." Commenting on this no longer extant passage of Josephus, Eusebius writes: "So remarkable a person must James have been, so universally esteemed for Righteousness, that even the most intelligent of Jews felt this was why his martyrdom was immediately followed by the siege of Jerusalem" (*Ecclesiastical History* 2.23).

Even the New Testament confirms James's role as head of the Christian community: It is James who is usually mentioned first among the "pillars" James, Peter, and John; James who personally sends his emissaries to the different communities scattered in the Diaspora (Galatians 2:1–14); James, to whom Peter reports his activities before leaving Jerusalem (Acts 12:17); James who sits in charge of the "elders" when Paul comes to make supplication (Acts 21:18); James who is the presiding authority over the Apostolic Council, who speaks last during its deliberations, and whose judgment is final (Acts 15:13). In fact, after the Apostolic Council, the apostles disappear from the rest of the book of Acts. But James does not. On the contrary, it is the fateful dispute between James and Paul, in which James publicly shames Paul for his deviant teachings by demanding he make supplication at the Temple, that leads to the climax of the book: Paul's arrest and extradition to Rome.

Three centuries of early Christian and Jewish documentation, not to mention the nearly unanimous opinion of contemporary scholars, recognize James the brother of Jesus as head of the first Christian community—above Peter and the rest of the Twelve; above John, "the disciple whom Jesus loved" (John 20:2); far above Paul, with whom James repeatedly clashed. Why then has James

been almost wholly excised from the New Testament and his role
in the early church displaced by Peter and Paul in the imaginations
of most modern Christians?

Partly it has to do with James's very identity as the brother of
Jesus. Dynasty was the norm for the Jews of Jesus's time. The Jewish Herodian and Hasmonaean families, the high priests and the
priestly aristocracies, the Pharisees, even the bandit gangs all practiced hereditary succession. Kinship was perhaps even more crucial
for a messianic movement like Jesus's, which based its legitimacy on
Davidic descent. After all, if Jesus was a descendant of King David,
then so was James; why should he not lead David's community after
the death of the messiah? Nor was James the sole member of Jesus's family to be given authority in the early church. Jesus's cousin
Simeon, son of Clopas, succeeded James as head of the Jerusalem assembly, while other members of his family, including two grandsons
of Jesus's other brother, Judas, maintained an active leadership role
throughout the first and second centuries of Christianity.

By the third and fourth centuries, however, as Christianity
gradually transformed from a heterogeneous Jewish movement
with an array of sects and schisms into an institutionalized and rig-
idly orthodox imperial religion of Rome, James's identity as Jesus's
brother became an obstacle for those who advocated the perpetual
virginity of his mother Mary. A few overly clever solutions were
developed to reconcile the immutable facts of Jesus's family with
the inflexible dogma of the church. There was, for example, the
well-worn argument that Jesus's brothers and sisters were Joseph's
children from a previous marriage, or that "brother" actually meant
"cousin." But the end result was that James's role in early Christianity was gradually diminished.

At the same time that James's influence was in decline, Peter's
was ascendant. Imperial Christianity, like the empire itself, demanded an easily determinable power structure, one preferably
headquartered in Rome, not Jerusalem, and linked directly to Jesus.

Peter's role as the first bishop of Rome and his status as the chief apostle made him the ideal figure upon which to base the authority of the Roman Church. The bishops who succeeded Peter in Rome (and who eventually became infallible popes) justified the chain of authority they relied upon to maintain power in an ever-expanding church by citing a passage in the gospel of Matthew in which Jesus tells the apostle, "I say to you that you shall be called Peter, and upon this rock I shall build my church" (Matthew 16:18). The problem with this heavily disputed verse, which most scholars reject as unhistorical, is that it is the only passage in the entire New Testament that designates Peter as head of the church. In fact, it is the only passage in any early historical document—biblical or otherwise—that names Peter the successor to Jesus and leader of the community he left behind. By contrast there are at least a dozen passages citing James as such. What historical records do exist about Peter's role in early Christianity are exclusively about his leadership of the assembly in Rome, which, while certainly a significant community, was just one of many assemblies that fell under the overarching authority of the Jerusalem assembly: the "mother assembly." Put another way, Peter may have been bishop of Rome, but James was "Bishop of Bishops."

There is, however, a more compelling reason for James's steady abatement in early Christianity, one that has less to do with his identity as Jesus's brother or his relation to Peter than it does with James's beliefs and his opposition to Paul. Some measure of what James stood for in the early Christian community has already been revealed through his actions in the book of Acts and in his theological disagreements with Paul. But an even more thorough understanding of James's views can be found in his own often overlooked and much maligned epistle, written sometime between 80 and 90 C.E.

Obviously James did not himself write the epistle; he was, like his brother Jesus and most of the apostles, an illiterate peasant with

no formal education. James's epistle was probably written by someone from within his inner circle. Again, that is true of almost every
book in the New Testament, including the gospels of Mark, Matthew, and John, as well as a good number of Paul's letters (Colossians, Ephesians, 2 Thessalonians, 1 and 2 Timothy, and Titus). As
noted, naming a book after someone significant was a common
way of honoring that person and reflecting his views. James may
not have written his own letter, but it no doubt represents what he
believed (the epistle is thought to be an edited and expanded version of a sermon James gave in Jerusalem just before his death in
62 c.e.). The overwhelming consensus is that the traditions contained within the epistle can confidently be traced to James the
Just. That would make James's epistle arguably one of the most
important books in the New Testament. Because one sure way of
uncovering what Jesus may have believed is to determine what his
brother James believed.

The first thing to note about James's epistle is its passionate
concern with the plight of the poor. This, in itself, is not surprising. The traditions all paint James as the champion of the destitute
and dispossessed; it is how he earned his nickname, "the Just." The
Jerusalem assembly was founded by James upon the principle of
service to the poor. There is even evidence to suggest that the first
followers of Jesus who gathered under James's leadership referred
to themselves collectively as "the poor."

What is perhaps more surprising about James's epistle is its bitter condemnation of the rich. "Come now, you wealthy ones, weep
and howl for the miseries that are about to come upon you. Your
riches have rotted and your garments are moth-eaten. Your gold
and silver have corroded, and the venom within them shall be a
witness against you; it shall eat your flesh as though it were fire"
(James 5:1–3). For James there is no path to salvation for the
wealthy who "hoard treasures for the last days," and who "live on
the land in luxury and pleasure" (James 5:3, 5). Their fate is set in
stone. "The rich man will pass away like a flower in the field. For

no sooner does the sun rise with its scorching heat, which withers the field, than the flower dies and its beauty perishes. So it shall be with the rich man" (James 1:11). James goes so far as to suggest that one cannot truly be a follower of Jesus if one does not actively favor the poor. "Do you with your acts of favoritism [toward the rich] really believe in our glorious Lord Jesus Christ?" he asks. "For if you show favoritism, you commit sin and are exposed as a transgressor of the law" (James 2:1, 9).

James's fierce judgment of the rich may explain why he drew the ire of the greedy high priest Ananus, whose father had schemed to impoverish the village priests by stealing their tithes. But in truth, James is merely echoing the words of his brother's Beatitudes: "Woe to you who are rich, for you have received your consolation. Woe to you who are full, for you shall hunger. Woe to you laughing now, for soon you will mourn" (Luke 6:24–25). Actually, much of James's epistle reflects the words of Jesus, whether the topic is the poor ("Has not God chosen the poor in the world to be rich in faith and heirs to the kingdom that he has promised to those who love him?" James 2:5; "Blessed are you who are poor, for the Kingdom of God is yours." Luke 6:20); the swearing of oaths ("Do not swear, either by heaven or earth, or by any other oath; let your yes be yes and your no be no." James 5:12; "Do not swear at all, either by heaven, which is the throne of God, or by the earth, which is God's footstool. . . . Let your yes be yes and your no be no." Matthew 5:34, 37); or the importance of putting one's faith into practice ("Be doers of the word, not just hearers who deceive themselves." James 1:22; "He who hears these words of mine and does them will be like the wise man who built his house on a rock . . . he who hears these words of mine and does not do them is like the foolish man who built his house on sand." Matthew 7:24, 26).

Yet the issue over which James and Jesus are most clearly in agreement is the role and application of the Law of Moses. "Whoever breaks one of the least of these commandments and teaches others to do so, will be called least in the kingdom of heaven," Jesus says in the gospel of Matthew (Matthew 5:19). "Whoever keeps the whole law but trips up on a single point of it is guilty of [violating] it all," James echoes in his epistle (James 2:10).

The primary concern of James's epistle is over how to maintain the proper balance between devotion to the Torah and faith in Jesus as messiah. Throughout the text, James repeatedly exhorts Jesus's followers to remain faithful to the law. "But he who looks to the perfect law—the law of liberty—and perseveres [in following it], being not just hearers who forget, but doers who act [upon it], he shall be blessed in his doing" (James 1:25). James compares Jews who abandon the law after converting to the Jesus movement to those who "look at themselves in the mirror . . . and upon walking away, immediately forget what they looked like" (James 1:23).

There should be little doubt as to whom James is referring in these verses. In fact, James's epistle was very likely conceived as a corrective to Paul's preaching, which is why it is addressed to "the Twelve Tribes of Israel scattered in the Diaspora"—that is, Paul's audience. The epistle's hostility toward Pauline theology is unmistakable. Whereas Paul dismisses the Law of Moses as a "ministry of death, chiseled in letters on a stone tablet" (2 Corinthians 3:7), James celebrates it as "the law of liberty." Paul claims that "one is not justified by the works of the law but only through belief in Jesus Christ" (Galatians 2:16). James emphatically rejects Paul's notion that faith alone engenders salvation. "Can belief save you?" he retorts. "Even the demons believe—and shudder!" (James 2:14,19). Paul writes in his letter to the Romans that "a man is justified by faith apart from works of the law" (Romans 3:28). James calls this the opinion of a "senseless person," countering that "faith apart from works [of the law] is dead" (James 2:26).

What both men mean by "works of the law" is the application of Jewish law in the daily life of the believer. Put simply, Paul views such "works" as irrelevant to salvation, while James views them as a requirement for belief in Jesus as the messiah. To prove his point,

James offers a telling example, one that demonstrates he was specifically refuting Paul in his epistle. "Was not Abraham our father justified by works when he offered up his son Isaac upon the altar?" James says, alluding to the story of Abraham's near sacrifice of Isaac at the behest of the Lord (Genesis 22:9–14). "You see how faith went hand-in-hand with [Abraham's] works, how it was through his works that his faith was made complete? Thus what the scripture says was fulfilled: 'Abraham believed God, and it was reckoned to him as righteousness,' and he was called the friend of God" (James 2:23).

What makes this example so telling is that it is the same one Paul often uses in his letters when making the exact opposite argument. "What then are we to say about Abraham, our father according to the flesh?" Paul writes. "For if Abraham was justified by works, he has something to boast about, though not before God. Rather, what does the scripture say? 'Abraham believed God, and it was reckoned to him as righteousness'" (Romans 4:1–3; see also Galatians 3:6–9).

James may not have been able to read any of Paul's letters but he was obviously familiar with Paul's teachings about Jesus. The last years of his life were spent dispatching his own missionaries to Paul's congregations in order to correct what he viewed as Paul's mistakes. The sermon that became his epistle was just another attempt by James to curb Paul's influence. Judging by Paul's own epistles, James's efforts were successful, as many among Paul's congregations seem to have turned their backs on him in favor of the teachers from Jerusalem.

The anger and bitterness that Paul feels toward these "false apostles [and] deceitful workers," these "servants of Satan" sent to infiltrate his congregations by a man he angrily dismisses as one of the "supposedly acknowledged leaders" of the church—a man he claims "contributed nothing" to him—seeps like poison through the pages of his later epistles (2 Corinthians 11:13; Galatians 2:6). Yet Paul's attempts to convince his congregations not to abandon him would ultimately prove futile. There was never any doubt about where the loyalty of the community would lie in a dispute between a former Pharisee and the flesh and blood of the living Christ. No matter how Hellenistic the Diaspora Jews may have become, their allegiance to the leaders of the mother assembly did not waver. James, Peter, John—these were the pillars of the church. They were the principal characters in all the stories people told about Jesus. They were the men who walked and talked with Jesus. They were among the first to see him rise from the dead; they would be the first to witness him return with the clouds of heaven. The authority James and the apostles maintained over the community during their lifetimes was unbreakable. Not even Paul could escape it, as he discovered in 57 C.E., when he was forced by James to publicly repent of his beliefs by taking part in that strict purification ritual in the Temple of Jerusalem.

As with his account of the Apostolic Council some years earlier, Luke's rendering of this final meeting between James and Paul in the book of Acts tries to brush aside any hint of conflict or animosity by presenting Paul as silently acquiescing to the Temple rite demanded of him. But not even Luke can hide the tension that so obviously exists in this scene. In Luke's account, before James sends Paul to the Temple to prove to the Jerusalem assembly that he "observes and guards the law," he first draws a sharp distinction between "the things that God had done among the gentiles in [Paul's] ministry," and the "many thousands of believers . . . among the Jews [who] are all *zealous for the law*" (Acts 21:20). James then gives Paul "four men who are under a vow" and instructs him to "go through the rite of purification with them, and pay for the shaving of their heads" (Acts 21:24).

What Luke is describing in this passage is called a "Nazirite vow" (Numbers 6:2). Nazirites were strict devotees of the Law of Moses who pledged to abstain from wine and refused to shave their hair or come near a corpse for a set period of time, either as an act of piety or in return for the fulfillment of a wish, such as a healthy child or a safe journey (James himself may have been a Nazirite, as the description of those who take the vow perfectly matches the descriptions of him in the ancient chronicles). Considering Paul's views on the Law of Moses and the Temple of Jerusalem, his forced participation in such a ritual would have been hugely embarrassing for him. The entire purpose of the rite was to demonstrate to the Jerusalem assembly that he no longer believed what he had been preaching for nearly a decade. There is no other way to read Paul's participation in the Nazirite vow except as a solemn renunciation of his ministry and a public declaration of James's authority over him—all the more reason to doubt Luke's depiction of Paul as simply going along with the ritual without comment or complaint.

Interestingly, Luke's may not be the only account of this pivotal moment. An eerily similar story is recounted in the compilation of writings known collectively as the *Pseudo-Clementines*. Although compiled sometime around 300 C.E. (nearly a century before the New Testament was officially canonized), the *Pseudo-Clementines* contain within them two separate sets of traditions that can be dated much earlier. The first is known as the *Homilies,* and comprises two epistles: one by the apostle Peter, the other by Peter's successor in Rome, Clement. The second set of traditions is called the *Recognitions,* which is itself founded upon an older document titled *Ascent of James* that most scholars date to the middle of the second century C.E., perhaps two or three decades after the gospel of John was written.

The *Recognitions* contains an incredible story about a violent altercation that James the brother of Jesus has with someone simply called "the enemy." In the text, James and the enemy are engaged in a shouting match inside the Temple when, all of a sudden, the enemy attacks James in a fit of rage and throws him down the Temple stairs. James is badly hurt by the fall but his supporters quickly come to his rescue and carry him to safety. Remarkably, the enemy who attacked James is later identified as none other than Saul of Tarsus (*Recognitions* 1:70–71).

As with the Lukan version, the story of the altercation between James and Paul in the *Recognitions* has its flaws. The fact that Paul is referred to as Saul in the text suggests that the author believes the event took place before Paul's conversion (though the *Recognitions* never actually refers to that conversion). Yet regardless of the historicity of the story itself, Paul's identity as "the enemy" of the church is repeatedly affirmed, not only in the *Recognitions,* but also in the other texts of the *Pseudo-Clementines*. In the *Epistle of Peter,* for example, the chief apostle complains that "some from among the gentiles have rejected my lawful preaching, attaching themselves to certain lawless and trifling preaching of the man who is my enemy" (Epistle of Peter 2:3). Elsewhere, Peter flatly identifies this "false prophet" who teaches "the dissolution of the law" as Paul, cautioning his followers to "believe no teacher, unless he brings from Jerusalem the testimonial of James the Lord's brother, or whosoever may come after him" (*Recognitions* 4:34–35).

What the *Pseudo-Clementine* documents indicate, and the New Testament clearly confirms, is that James, Peter, John, and the rest of the apostles viewed Paul with wariness and suspicion, if not open derision, which is why they went to such lengths to counteract Paul's teachings, censuring him for his words, warning others not to follow him, even sending their own missionaries to his congregations. No wonder Paul was so keen to flee to Rome after the incident at the Temple in 57 C.E. He was surely not eager to be judged by the emperor for his alleged crimes, as Luke seems to suggest. Paul went to Rome because he hoped he could escape James's authority. But as he discovered when he arrived in the Imperial City and saw Peter already established there, one could not so easily escape the reach of James and Jerusalem.

While Paul spent the last years of his life in Rome, frustrated by the lack of enthusiasm he received for his message (perhaps because the Jews were heeding Peter's call to "believe no teacher, unless he brings from Jerusalem the testimonial of James the Lord's brother"), the Jerusalem assembly under James's leadership thrived. The Hebrews in Jerusalem were certainly not immune to persecution by the religious authorities. They were often arrested and sometimes killed for their preaching. James the son of Zebedee, one of the original Twelve, was even beheaded (Acts 12:3). But these periodic bouts of persecution were rare and seem not to have been the result of a rejection of the law on the part of the Hebrews, as was the case with the Hellenists who were expelled from the city. Obviously, the Hebrews had figured out a way to accommodate themselves to the Jewish priestly authorities, or else they could not have remained in Jerusalem. These were by all accounts law-abiding Jews who kept the customs and traditions of their forefathers but who happened also to believe that the simple Jewish peasant from Galilee named Jesus of Nazareth was the promised messiah.

That is not to say that James and the apostles were uninterested in reaching out to gentiles, or that they believed gentiles could not join their movement. As indicated by his decision at the Apostolic Council, James was willing to forgo the practice of circumcision and other "burdens of the law" for gentile converts. James did not want to force gentiles to first become Jews before they were allowed to become Christians. He merely insisted that they not divorce themselves entirely from Judaism, that they maintain a measure of fidelity to the beliefs and practices of the very man they claimed to be following (Acts 15:12–21). Otherwise, the movement risked becoming a wholly new religion, and that is something neither James nor his brother Jesus could have imagined.

James's steady leadership over the Jerusalem assembly came to an end in 62 C.E., when he was executed by the high priest Ananus, not just because he was a follower of Jesus and certainly not because he transgressed the law (or else "the most fair-minded and . . . strict in the observance of the law" would not have been up in arms about his unjust execution). James was likely killed because he was doing what he did best: defending the poor and weak against the wealthy and powerful. Ananus's schemes to impoverish the lower-class priests by stealing their tithes would not have sat well with James the Just. And so, Ananus took advantage of the brief absence of Roman authority in Jerusalem to get rid of a man who had become a thorn in his side.

One cannot know how Paul felt in Rome when he heard about James's death. But if he assumed the passing of Jesus's brother would relax the grip of Jerusalem over the community, he was mistaken. The leadership of the Jerusalem assembly passed swiftly to another of Jesus's family members, his cousin Simeon, son of Clopas, and the community continued unabated until four years after James's death, when the Jews suddenly rose up in revolt against Rome.

Some among the Hebrews seem to have fled Jerusalem for Pella when the uprising began. But there is no evidence to suggest that the core leadership of the mother assembly abandoned Jerusalem. Rather, they maintained their presence in the city of Jesus's death and resurrection, eagerly awaiting his return, right up to the moment that Titus's army arrived and wiped the holy city and its inhabitants—both Christians and Jews—off the face of the earth. With the destruction of Jerusalem, the connection between the assemblies scattered across the Diaspora and the mother assembly rooted in the city of God was permanently severed, and with it the last physical link between the Christian community and Jesus the Jew. Jesus the zealot.

Jesus of Nazareth.

True God from True God

The balding, gray-bearded old men who began the work of permanently fixing the faith and practice of Christianity met for the first time in the Byzantine city of Nicaea, on the eastern shore of Lake Izmit in present-day Turkey. It was the summer of 325 C.E. The men had been brought together by the emperor Constantine and commanded to come to a consensus on the doctrine of the religion he had recently adopted as his own. Bedecked in robes of purple and gold, an aureate laurel resting on his head, Rome's first Christian emperor called the council to order as though it were a Roman Senate, which is understandable, considering that every one of the nearly two thousand bishops he had gathered in Nicaea to permanently define Christianity was a Roman.

The bishops were not to disband until they had resolved the theological differences among them, particularly when it came to the nature of Jesus and his relationship to God. Over the centuries since Jesus's crucifixion, there had been a great deal of discord and debate among the leaders of the church over whether Jesus was human or divine. Was he, as those like Athanasius of Alexandria claimed, fully God? Or did he, as the followers of Arius seemed to suggest, merely have some measure of divinity within him? Or could he have been, as others in the room argued, just a man— a perfect man, perhaps, but a man nonetheless?

After months of heated negotiations, the council handed to Constantine what became known as the Nicene Creed, outlining for the first time the officially sanctioned, orthodox beliefs of the Christian church. Jesus is the literal son of God, the creed declared. He is Light from Light, true God from true God, begotten not made, of the same substance as the father. As for those who disagreed with the creed, those like the Arians who believed that "there was a time when [Jesus] was not," they were immediately banished from the empire and their teachings violently suppressed.

It may be tempting to view the Nicene Creed as an overtly politicized attempt to stifle the legitimate voices of dissent in the early church. It is certainly the case that the council's decision resulted in a thousand years or more of unspeakable bloodshed in the name of Christian orthodoxy. But the truth is that the council members were merely codifying a creed that was already the majority opinion, not just of the bishops gathered at Nicaea, but of the entire Christian community. Indeed, belief in Jesus as God had been enshrined in the church centuries before the Council of Nicaea, thanks, in no small part, to the overwhelming popularity of the letters of Paul.

After the Temple was destroyed, the holy city burned to the ground, and the remnants of the Jerusalem assembly dispersed, Paul underwent a stunning rehabilitation in the Christian community. With the possible exception of the Q document (which is, after all, a hypothetical text), the only writings about Jesus that existed in 70 C.E. were the letters of Paul. These letters had been in circulation since the fifties. They were written to the Diaspora communities, which, after the destruction of Jerusalem, were the only Christian communities left in the realm. Without the mother assembly to guide the followers of Jesus, the movement's connection to Judaism was broken, and Paul became the primary vehicle

through which a new generation of Christians was introduced to
Jesus the Christ. Even the gospels were deeply influenced by Paul's
letters. One can trace the shadow of Pauline theology in Mark and
Matthew. But it is in the gospel of Luke, written by one of Paul's
devoted disciples, that one can see the dominance of Paul's views,
while the gospel of John is little more than Pauline theology in
narrative form.

Paul's conception of Christianity may have been heretical before 70 C.E. But afterward, his notion of a wholly new religion free
from the authority of a Temple that no longer existed, unburdened
by a law that no longer mattered, and divorced from a Judaism that
had become a pariah was enthusiastically embraced by converts
throughout the Roman Empire. Hence, in 398 C.E., when, according to legend, another group of bishops gathered at a council in the
city of Hippo Regius in modern-day Algeria to canonize what
would become known as the New Testament, they chose to include in the Christian scriptures one letter from James, the brother
and successor of Jesus, two letters from Peter, the chief apostle and
first among the Twelve, three letters from John, the beloved disciple
and pillar of the church, and fourteen letters from Paul, the deviant
and outcast who was rejected and scorned by the leaders in Jerusalem. In fact, more than half of the twenty-seven books that now
make up the New Testament are either by or about Paul.

This should not be surprising. Christianity after the destruction
of Jerusalem had become almost exclusively a gentile religion; it
needed a gentile theology. And that is precisely what Paul provided. The choice between James's vision of a Jewish religion an-
chored in the Law of Moses and derived from a Jewish nationalist
who fought against Rome, and Paul's vision of a Roman religion
that divorced itself from Jewish provincialism and required nothing
for salvation save belief in Christ, was not a difficult one for the
second and third generations of Jesus's followers to make.

Two thousand years later, the Christ of Paul's creation has utterly subsumed the Jesus of history. The memory of the revolu-

tionary zealot who walked across Galilee gathering an army of disciples with the goal of establishing the Kingdom of God on earth, the magnetic preacher who defied the authority of the Temple priesthood in Jerusalem, the radical Jewish nationalist who challenged the Roman occupation and lost, has been almost completely lost to history. That is a shame. Because the one thing any comprehensive study of the historical Jesus should reveal is that Jesus of Nazareth—Jesus the *man*—is every bit as compelling, charismatic, and praiseworthy as Jesus the Christ. He is, in short, someone worth believing in.

Acknowledgments

This book is the result of two decades of research into the New Testament and the origins of the Christian movement conducted at Santa Clara University, Harvard University, and the University of California at Santa Barbara. Although I am obviously indebted to all my professors, I would like to single out my extremely patient Greek professor Helen Moritz, and my brilliant adviser, the late Catherine Bell, at Santa Clara, Harvey Cox and Jon Levinson at Harvard, and Mark Juergensmeyer at UCSB. I am also grateful for the unconditional support I received from my editor Will Murphy and the entire team at Random House. Special thanks to Elyse Cheney, the best literary agent in the world, and to Ian Werrett, who not only translated all the Hebrew and Aramaic passages in the book, but also read multiple drafts and provided vital feedback on the manuscript. But the biggest thanks of all goes, as always, to my beloved wife and best friend Jessica Jackley, whose love and devotion have made me the man I always hoped I could be.

Notes

INTRODUCTION

I am greatly indebted to John P. Meier's epic work, *A Marginal Jew: Rethinking the Historical Jesus*, vols. I–IV (New Haven: Yale University Press, 1991–2009). I first met Father Meier while I was studying the New Testament at Santa Clara University, and it was his definitive look at the historical Jesus, which at the time existed only in its first volume, that planted the seeds of the present book in my mind. Father Meier's book answers the question of why we have so little historical information about a man who so thoroughly changed the course of human history. His thesis—that we know so little about Jesus because in his lifetime he would have been viewed as little more than a marginal Jewish peasant from the backwoods of Galilee—forms the theoretical groundwork for the book you are reading.

Of course, I argue further that part of the reason we know so little about the historical Jesus is that his messianic mission—historic as it may have turned out to be—was not uncommon in first-century Palestine. Hence my reference to Celsus's quote—"I am God, or the servant of God, or a divine spirit . . ."—which can be found in Rudolf Otto's classic study, *The Kingdom of God and the Son of Man* (Boston: Starr King Press, 1957), 13.

A brief word about my use of the term "first-century Palestine" throughout this book. While Palestine was the unofficial Roman designation for the land encompassing modern-day Israel, Palestine, Jordan, Syria, and Lebanon during Jesus's lifetime, it was not until the Romans quashed the Bar Kochba revolt in the middle of the second century C.E that the region was officially named *Syria Palaestina*. Nevertheless, the term "first-century Palestine" has become so commonplace in academic discussions about the era of Jesus that I see no reason not to use it in this book.

For more on Jesus's messianic contemporaries—the so-called false messiahs—
see the works of Richard A. Horsley, specifically "Popular Messianic Movements
Around the Time of Jesus," *Catholic Biblical Quarterly* 46 (1984): 409–32; "Popular Prophetic Movements at the Time of Jesus: Their Principal Features and
Social Origins," *Journal for the Study of the New Testament* 26 (1986): 3–27; and,
with John S. Hanson, *Bandits, Prophets, and Messiahs* (Minneapolis: Winston Press,
1985), 135–189. The reader will note that I rely a great deal on Professor Horsley's work. That is because he is by far the most prominent thinker on the subject of first-century apocalypticism.

Although the so-called Two-Source Theory is almost universally accepted
by scholars, there are a handful of biblical theorists who reject it as a viable explanation for the creation of the four canonized gospels as we know them. For
example, J. Magne, *From Christianity to Gnosis and from Gnosis to Christianity*
(Atlanta: Scholars Press, 1993) views the Two-Source Theory as overly simplistic
and incapable of adequately addressing what he sees as the complex variants
among the Synoptic gospels.

In addition to the story of the fiendish Jewish priest Ananus, there is one
other passage in Josephus's *Antiquities* that mentions Jesus of Nazareth. This is
the so-called Testimonium Flavianum in book 18, chapter 3, in which Josephus
appears to repeat the entire gospel formula. But that passage has been so cor-
rupted by later Christian interpolation that its authenticity is dubious at best,
and scholarly attempts to cull through the passage for some sliver of historicity
have proven futile. Still, the second passage is significant in that it mentions Jesus's crucifixion.

Among Romans, crucifixion originated as a deterrence against the revolt of
slaves, probably as early as 200 B.C.E. By Jesus's time, it was the primary form of
punishment for "inciting rebellion" (i.e., treason or sedition), the exact crime
with which Jesus was charged. See Hubert Cancick et al., eds., *Brill's New Pauly
Encyclopedia of the Ancient World: Antiquity* (Leiden, Netherlands: Brill, 2005), 60
and 966. The punishment applied solely to non-Roman citizens. Roman citizens could be crucified, however, if the crime was so grave that it essentially
forfeited their citizenship.

There are no resurrection appearances in the gospel of Mark, as it is the
unanimous consensus of scholars that the original version of the gospel ended
with Mark 16:8. For more on this, see note to chapter 3 below.

In 313 C.E., the emperor Constantine passed the Edict of Milan, which initiated a period of Christian tolerance in the Roman Empire, wherein property
that was confiscated from Christians by the state was returned and Christians
were free to worship without fear of reprisals from the state. While the Edict of
Milan created space for Christianity to become the official religion of the empire, Constantine never made it so. Julian the Apostate (d. 363 C.E.), the last non-

Christian emperor, actually tried to push the empire back toward paganism by emphasizing that system over and against Christianity and purging the government of Christian leaders, though he never repealed the Edict of Milan. It was not until the year 380 C.E., during the rule of Emperor Flavius Theodosius, that Christianity became the official religion of the Roman Empire.

The very brief outline of Jesus's life and ministry presented at the end of the introduction to this book represents the view of the vast majority of scholars about what can be said with confidence about the historical Jesus. For more, see Charles H. Talbert, ed., *Reimarus: Fragments* (Chico, Calif.: Scholars Press, 1985) and James K. Beilby and Paul Rhodes Eddy, ed., *The Historical Jesus: Five Views* (Downers Grove, Ill.: InterVarsity Press, 2009).

PART I PROLOGUE: A DIFFERENT SORT OF SACRIFICE

Help with the description of the Temple of Jerusalem and the sacrifices therein comes from a variety of sources as well as from my frequent trips to the Temple site. But a few books were particularly helpful in reconstructing the ancient Jewish Temple, including Martin Jaffee, *Early Judaism* (Bethesda: University Press of Maryland, 2006), especially pages 172–88; Joan Comay, *The Temple of Jerusalem* (London: Weidenfeld and Nicolson, 1975); and John Day, ed., *Temple and Worship in Biblical Israel* (New York: T&T Clark, 2005).

Instructions for the Temple's four-horned altar were given to Moses while he and the Israelites rambled across the desert searching for a home: "And you shall make the altar of acacia wood. And you shall affix horns upon its four corners so that it shall be horned; and you shall overlay it with bronze. And you shall make pots for receiving its ashes, and shovels and basins and forks and fire pans; all of its vessels you shall cast in bronze. And you shall make for it a grating, a net made of bronze; and on the net you shall affix four bronze rings to its four corners. And you shall place it under the edge of the altar, so that the net extends halfway down the altar. And you shall make poles for the altar, poles of acacia wood, and overlay them with bronze. And the poles shall be inserted into the rings, so that the poles shall be on the two sides of the altar when it is carried. You shall make it hollow with boards, as it was shown to you on the mountain. Thus it shall be done" (Exodus 27:18).

What does it mean for the Temple to be the sole source of God's divine presence? Consider this: The Samaritans denied the primacy of the Temple of Jerusalem as the sole place of worship. They instead worshipped God on Mount Gerizim. Though this was essentially the only religious difference between the two peoples, it was enough for the Samaritans not to be considered Jews. There were other places of sacrifice for Jews (for instance, in Heliopolis), but these were considered substitutes, not replacements.

For more on Judea as a "Temple-State," see H. D. Mantel in "The High Priesthood and the Sanhedrin in the Time of the Second Temple," *The Herodian Period*, ed. M. Avi-Yonah and Z. Baras, *The World History of the Jewish People* 1.7 (Jerusalem: New Brunswick, 1975), 264–81. Josephus's quote regarding Jerusalem as a theocracy is from *Against Apion,* 2.164–66. For more on the Temple of Jerusalem as a bank, see Neill Q. Hamilton, "Temple Cleansing and Temple Bank," *Journal of Biblical Literature* 83.4 (1964): 365–72. A very concise breakdown of the Temple's revenues can be found in Magen Broshi, "The Role of the Temple in the Herodian Economy," *Jewish Studies* 38 (1987): 31–37.

The Qumran community rejected the Temple of Jerusalem for having fallen into the hands of the corrupt priesthood. Instead, it saw itself as a temporary replacement for the Temple, referring to the community as the "temple of man/men," or *miqdash adam*. Some scholars have argued that this is why the Qumranites were so interested in ritual purity; they believed that their prayers and lustrations were more potent than the rituals and sacrifices in Jerusalem, which had been tainted by the Temple priests. For a detailed discussion of the phrase "temple of man/men" at Qumran, see G. Brooke, *Exegesis at Qumran: 4QFlorilegium in its Jewish Context* (Sheffield, U.K.: Sheffield Academic Press, 1985), 184–93; D. Dimant, "4QFlorilegium and the Idea of the Community as Temple," in *Hellenica et Judaica: Hommage à Valentin Nikiprowetzky*, ed. A. Caquot (Leuben-Paris: Éditions Peeters, 1986), 165–89.

It is Josephus who famously refers to the entire priestly nobility as "lovers of luxury" in *The Jewish War,* though he was not alone in his criticism. There is a similar criticism of the priests in the Dead Sea Scrolls, where they are called the "seekers of smooth things" and those who are "flattery-seekers."

There is a wonderful description of the high priest in the famed *Letter of Aristeas,* written sometime around the second century B.C.E., a translation of which appears in the second volume of James H. Charlesworth, ed., *The Old Testament Pseudepigrapha* (New York: Doubleday, 1985), 7–34. Here is the excerpt: "We were greatly astonished, when we saw Eleazar engaged in the ministration, at the mode of his dress, and the majesty of his appearance, which was revealed in the robe which he wore and the precious stones upon his person. There were golden bells upon the garment which reached down to his feet, giving forth a peculiar kind of melody, and on both sides of them there were pomegranates with variegated flowers of a wonderful hue. He was girded with a girdle of conspicuous beauty, woven in the most beautiful colours. On his breast he wore the oracle of God, as it is called, on which twelve stones, of different kinds, were inset, fastened together with gold, containing the names of the leaders of the tribes, according to their original order, each one flashing forth in an indescribable way its own particular colour. On his head he wore a tiara, as it is called, and upon this in the middle of his forehead an inimitable turban, the royal diadem full of glory with the name of God inscribed in sacred letters on a plate of gold . . . having been judged worthy to wear these emblems in the ministrations. Their appearance created such awe and confusion of mind as to make one feel that one had come into the presence of a man who belonged to a different world. I am convinced that any one who takes part in the spectacle which I have described will be filled with astonishment and indescribable wonder and be profoundly affected in his mind at the thought of the sanctity which is attached to each detail of the service."

CHAPTER ONE: A HOLE IN THE CORNER

For a primer on Rome's policy in dealing with subject populations, and especially its relationship with the high priest and priestly aristocracy in Jerusalem, see Martin Goodman, *The Ruling Class of Judea* (New York: Cambridge University Press, 1987); also Richard A. Horsley, "High Priests and the Politics of Roman Palestine," *Journal for the Study of Judaism* 17.1 (1986): 23–55. Goodman's *Rome and Jerusalem: The Clash of Ancient Civilizations* (London: Penguin, 2007) provides an indispensable discussion of the remarkably tolerant attitude of Rome toward the Jews while also providing a range of Roman views about Jewish exceptionalism. It is from Goodman's book that the quotations from Cicero, Tacitus, and Seneca are pulled (pages 390–91). Further discussion of Roman attitudes toward Jewish practices can be found in Eric S. Gruen, "Roman Perspectives on the Jews in the Age of the Great Revolt," in *The First Jewish Revolt,* ed. Andrea M. Berlin and J. Andrew Overman (New York: Routledge, 2002), 27–42. For more on the religious practices and cults of Rome, see Mary Beard, John North, and Simon Price, *Religions of Rome: A Sourcebook,* 2 vols. (Cambridge: Cambridge University Press, 1998).

The act of "utter annihilation" (*herem* in Hebrew), in which God commands the wholesale slaughter of "all that breathes," is a recurring theme in the Bible, as I explain in my book *How to Win a Cosmic War* (New York: Random House, 2009), 66–69. It is "ethnic cleansing as a means of ensuring cultic purity," to quote the great biblical scholar John Collins, "The Zeal of Phinehas: The Bible and the Legitimation of Violence," *Journal of Biblical Literature* 122.1 (2003): 7.

For precise taxes and measures taken by Rome upon the Jewish peasantry, see Lester L. Grabbe, *Judaism from Cyrus to Hadrian,* 2 vols. (Minneapolis: Fortress Press, 1992), 334–37; also Horsley and Hanson, *Bandits, Prophets, Messiahs,* 48–87. Grabbe notes that some scholars have cast doubt on whether the Jewish population was forced to pay tribute to Rome, though no one questions whether the Jews were forced to finance the Roman civil war between Pompey and Julius Caesar. On the subject of mass urbanization and the transfer of populations from rural to urban centers, see Jonathan Reed, "Instability in Jesus' Galilee: A Demographic Perspective," *Journal of Biblical Literature* (2010) 129.2: 343–65.

CHAPTER TWO: KING OF THE JEWS

The term "messiah" in the Hebrew Bible is used in reference to King Saul (1 Samuel 12:5), King David (2 Samuel 23:1), King Solomon (1 Kings 1:39), and the priest Aaron and his sons (Exodus 29:1–9), as well as the prophets Isaiah (Isaiah 61:1) and Elisha (1 Kings 19:15–16). The exception to this list can be found in Isaiah 45:1, where the Persian king Cyrus, though he does not know the God of the Jews (45:4), is called messiah. In all, there are thirty-nine occurrences of the word "messiah" in the Hebrew Bible that refer specifically to the anointing of someone or something, such as Saul's shield (2 Samuel 1:21) or the Tabernacle (Numbers 7:1). And yet not one of these occurrences refers to the messiah as a future salvific character who would be appointed by God to rebuild the Kingdom of David and restore Israel to a position of glory and power. That view of the messiah, which seems to have been fairly well established by the time of Jesus, was actually shaped during the tumultuous period of the Babylonian Exile in the sixth century B.C.E.

Although there is little doubt that the bandit gangs of Galilee represented an apocalyptic, eschatological, and millenarian movement, Richard Horsley and John Hanson view these as three distinct categories, and as a result they refuse to label the bandits a "messianic" movement. In other words, the authors contend that "messianic" and "eschatological" must not be viewed as equivalents. Yet, as I discuss in this section, there is no reason to believe that such a distinction existed in the minds of the Jewish peasant, who, far from having a sophisticated understanding of messianism, would have most likely lumped all of these "distinct categories" into a vague expectation of the "End Times." In any case, Horsley and Hanson themselves admit that "many of the essential conditions for banditry and messianic movements are the same. In fact, there might well have been no difference between them had there not been among the Jews a tradition of popular kingship and historical prototypes of a popular 'anointed one.'" *Bandits, Prophets, and Messiahs*, 88–93.

For Caesar as Son of God, see Adela Yarbro Collins, "Mark and His Readers: The Son of God Among Greeks and Romans," *Harvard Theological Review* 93.2 (2000): 85–100. Two zealous rabbis, Judas son of Sepphoraeus and Matthias son of Margalus, led an uprising that attacked the Temple and tried to destroy the eagle that Herod placed atop the Temple gates. They and their students were captured and tortured to death by Herod's men.

The complexities of Jewish sectarianism in first-century Judaism are tackled nicely by Jeff S. Anderson in his cogent analysis *The Internal Diversification of Second Temple Judaism* (Lanham, Md: University Press of America, 2002).

Josephus says Simon of Peraea called himself "king," by which Horsley and Hanson infer that he was part of the "popular messianic movements" that erupted after Herod's death. See *Bandits, Prophets, and Messiahs,* 93. Again, for me there seems to be no reason to assume any distinction whatsoever in the minds of the Jewish peasantry between "messiah" and "king," insofar as both titles relied not on the scriptures, which the vast majority of Jews could neither access nor read, but rather on popular traditions and stories of messianic movements from Jewish history, as well as on oracles, popular images, fables, and oral traditions. Of course, some scholars go so far as to refuse to consider "king" to mean messiah. In other words, they make a distinction between, as Craig Evans puts it, "political royal claimants and messianic royal claimants." Among this camp is M. De Jong, *Christology in Context: The Earliest Christian Response to Jesus* (Philadelphia: Westminster Press, 1988). But Evans is right to argue that when dealing with any royal aspirant in first-century Palestine, "the presumption should be that any Jewish claim to Israel's throne is in all probability a messianic claimant in some sense." I couldn't agree more. See Craig Evans, *Jesus and His Contemporaries* (Leiden, Netherlands: Brill, 1995), 55.

CHAPTER THREE: YOU KNOW WHERE I AM FROM

On the population of ancient Nazareth, see the relevant entry in the *Anchor Bible Dictionary* (New York: Doubleday, 1992). See also E. Meyers and J. Strange, *Archaeology, the Rabbis, and Early Christianity* (Nashville: Abingdon, 1981) and John Dominic Crossan, *The Historical Jesus: The Life of a Mediterranean Jewish Peasant* (New York: HarperCollins, 1992), 18. Scholars disagree about just how many people lived in Nazareth at the time of Jesus, with some claiming fewer than a couple hundred, and others saying as many as a couple thousand. My instinct is to hedge toward the middle of the scale; hence my estimate of a population consisting of about one hundred families. For more about provincial life in the Galilee of Jesus see Scott Korb, *Life in Year One: What the World Was Like in First-Century Palestine* (New York: Riverhead, 2011).

Despite the stories in the gospels about Jesus preaching in his hometown's synagogue, no archaeological evidence has been unearthed to indicate the presence of a synagogue in ancient Nazareth, though there very well could have been a small structure that served as such (remember that "synagogue" in Jesus's time could mean something as simple as a room with a Torah scroll). It should also be remembered that by the time the gospels were written, the Temple of Jerusalem had been destroyed and the sole gathering place for Jews was the synagogue. So it makes sense that Jesus is constantly presented as teaching in the synagogue in every town he visits.

No inscriptions have been found in Nazareth to indicate that the population was particularly literate. Scholars estimate that between 95 and 97 percent of the Jewish peasantry at the time of Jesus could neither read nor write. On that point see Crossan, *Historical Jesus*, 24–26.

On Nazareth as the place of Jesus's birth, see John P. Meier, *A Marginal Jew*, vol. 1, 277–78; E. P. Sanders, *The Historical Figure of Jesus* (New York: Penguin, 1993); and John Dominic Crossan, *Jesus: A Revolutionary Biography* (New York: HarperOne, 1995), 18–23.

For more on messianic views at the time of Jesus, see Gershom Scholem, *The Messianic Idea in Judaism* (New York: Schocken Books, 1971), 1–36. Scholem outlines two distinct messianic trends within early Judaism: the restorative and the utopian. Restorative messianism seeks a return to an ideal condition in the glorified past; in other words, it considers the improvement of the present era to be directly linked to the glories of the past. But while the restorative pole finds its hope in the past, it is nevertheless directly concerned with the desire of an even better future that will bring about "a state of things which has never yet existed." Related to the restorative pole is utopian messianism. More apocalyptic in character, utopian messianism seeks catastrophic change with the coming of the messiah: that is, the annihilation of the present world and the initiation of a messianic age. Restorative messianism can be seen in the kingly traditions that look to the Davidic ideal—it seeks to establish a kingdom in the present time—while the utopian messianism is associated with the priestly figure found in the Dead Sea Scrolls at Qumran. Of course, neither of these messianic trends existed independently of the other. On the contrary, both poles existed in some form in nearly every messianic group. Indeed, it was the tension between these two messianic trends that created the varying character of the messiah in Judaism. For more on Jewish messianism, see studies by Richard Horsley, including "Messianic Figures and Movements in First-Century Palestine," *The Messiah*, ed. James H. Charlesworth (Minneapolis: Fortress Press, 1992), 295; "Popular Messianic Movements Around the Time of Jesus," *Catholic Biblical Quarterly* 46 (1984): 447–95; and "'Like One of the Prophets of Old': Two Types of Popular Prophets at the Time of Jesus," *Catholic Biblical Quarterly* 47 (1985): 435–63. All three of Horsley's studies have been vital in my examination of messianic ideas around the time of Jesus. I also recommend the relevant entry in *The Anchor Bible Dictionary*, ed. D. N. Freedman et al. (New York: Doubleday, 1992); and *The Encyclopedia of the Jewish Religion*, ed. J. Werblowsky et al. (New York: Holt, Rinehart and Winston, 1966).

It would seem that the Qumran community did indeed await two different messiahs. The Community Rule suggests this in 9:12 when it speaks of the coming of "the Prophet and the Messiahs of Aaron and Israel." Clearly a differentiation is being made between the kingly and priestly messianic figures. This notion is further developed in the Rule of the Congregation. In this scroll a banquet is described in the "last days" in which the messiah of Israel sits in a subordinate position to the priest of the congregation. While the text does not use the word "messiah" to refer to the priest, his superior position at the table indicates his eschatological power. These texts have led scholars to deduce that the Qumran community believed in the coming of a kingly messiah and a priestly messiah, with the latter dominating over the former. See James Charlesworth, "From Jewish Messianology to Christian Christology; Some Caveats and Perspectives," *Judaisms and Their Messiahs at the Turn of the Christian Era,* ed. Jacob Neusner et al. (Cambridge: Cambridge University Press, 1987), 225–64.

It should be noted that nowhere in the Hebrew Scriptures is the messiah explicitly termed the physical descendant of David, i.e., "Son of David." But the imagery associated with the messiah and the fact that it is thought that his chief task is to reestablish David's kingdom permanently linked messianic aspirations to Davidic lineage. This is in large part due to the so-called Davidic covenant, based on the prophet Nathan's prophecy: "Your [David's] house and your kingdom shall be made sure for ever before me; your throne shall be established forever" (2 Samuel 7:16).

Jesus's lineage from King David is stated over and over again, not just throughout the gospels but also in the letters of Paul, in which Jesus is repeatedly described as "of the seed of David" (Romans 1:3–4; 2 Timothy 2:8). Whether it was true is impossible to say. Many people claimed lineage to the greatest Israelite king (who lived a thousand years before Jesus of Nazareth), and frankly none of them could either prove such lineage or disprove it. But obviously the link between Jesus and David was vital for the early Christian community because it helped prove that this lowly peasant was in fact the messiah.

It is widely accepted that the original text of Mark ended with 16:8 and that Mark 16:9–20 was a later addition to the text. Per Norman Perrin: "It is the virtually unanimous opinion of modern scholarship that what appears in most translations of the gospel of Mark 16:9–20 is a pastiche of material taken from other gospels and added to the original text of the gospel as it was copied and transmitted by the scribes of the ancient Christian communities." Perrin, *The Resurrection According to Matthew, Mark, and Luke* (Philadelphia: Fortress Press: 1977), 16. However, there are still some who question this assumption, arguing that a book cannot end with the Greek word γαρ, as Mark 16:8 does. That view has been debunked by P. W. van der Horst, "Can a Book End with ΓΑΡ? A Note on Mark XVI.8," *Journal of Theological Studies* 23 (1972): 121–24. Horst notes numerous texts in antiquity that do in fact end in this manner (e.g., Plotinus's 32nd treatise). In any case, anyone who reads Mark in the original Greek can tell that a different hand wrote the final eight verses.

For prophecies claiming that "when the messiah comes, no one will know where he is from," see 1 Enoch 48:6 and 4 Ezra 13:51–52. For a complete breakdown of the so-called messianic "proof texts," see J.J.M. Roberts, "The Old Testament's Contribution to Messianic Expectations," *The Messiah,* 39–51. According to Roberts, these texts fall into five categories. First, there are those passages that appear to be prophecies *ex eventu.* Roberts cites Balaam's oracle in Numbers 24:17 ("a star will come forth out of Jacob") as an instance in which a prophecy that seems to find its fulfillment in the early monarchical period (in this case, the celebration of David's victories as king of Israel over Moab and Edom, as is indicated in verses 17b and 18) has been forced to function as a prophecy regarding future divine kingship. Such a futuristic interpretation, argues Roberts, ignores the original setting of the prophecy. The second category deals with prophetic passages that seem to have settings in the enthronement ceremonies of the anointed kings. For instance, Psalm 2 ("You are my son . . . / this day I become your father") and Isaiah 9:6 ("For a child has been born to us . . . and his title will be Wonderful Counselor, Mighty Hero, Eternal Father, Prince of Peace") were most likely composed for specific occasions to serve both religious and political functions. The political usage of these texts is apparent in their claims of the authoritative power of the king and his direct link to God. They also establish a link between the responsibilities of the king toward his people and the commands of God. The king who serves in God's stead must display God's justice. Even so, such statements as are found in these verses would no doubt create a powerful tool for kingly propaganda. The third category of the messianic proof texts do indeed speak of a future ruler and are perhaps the verses most frequently quoted by those who want to give a salvific interpretation to the messiah of the Hebrew scriptures (Micah 5:1–5; Zechariah 9:1–10). These texts speak of the embodiment of the Davidic ideal, *metaphorically* (not physically) referred to as a king of the Davidic line, who will restore the monarchy of Israel to its former glory. But for Roberts, the promises of a future king (e.g., Micah's promise of a king rising from the humility of Bethlehem) "imply a serious criticism of the current occupant of the Davidic throne as less than an adequate heir to David." Such criticism is apparent throughout the prophetic texts (see Isaiah 1:21–26, 11:1–9, 32:1–8). Roberts uses the same approach in the fourth group of messianic proof texts envisioning a future king. These texts, primarily Jeremiah and Ezekiel, Roberts places at the end of the Judean kingdom, when a restoration of the Davidic dynasty was a response to growing existential concerns over the future of Israel as a theocracy. The final category deals with the postexilic texts. According to Roberts, upon return from exile, the Jews were faced with a destroyed Temple, a disgraced priesthood, and no Davidic king. The prophetic texts of Zechariah and Haggai dealt with these problems in oracles that placed Zerubbabel in the position of restoring Israel's monarchy and Temple (Haggai 2:20–23; Zechariah 4:6–10). Roberts believes that the prophecies regarding the restoration of the crown and the Temple (e.g., Zechariah 6:9–15) refer solely to the actions of Zerubbabel and are an optimistic response to the terrible circumstances that existed in the postexilic period. He also traces the later priestly expectations of the messiah to the texts of this period that include a restoration of the priesthood under Joshua (Zechariah 3:1–10). Roberts is convinced by his study of the messianic proof texts that the idea of a salvific messiah is not explicitly stated in the Hebrew scriptures but is rather a later development of Jewish eschatology that was adopted by the Pharisees, perhaps in the second or first century B.C.E., and later incorporated into "normative Judaism."

CHAPTER FOUR: THE FOURTH PHILOSOPHY

Some scholars believe that *tekton* means not "woodworker" but any artisan who deals in the building trades. While Mark 6:3 is the only verse that calls Jesus a *tekton,* Matthew 13:55 states that Jesus's father was a *tekton.* Considering the strictures of the day, the verse is likely meant to indicate that Jesus was a *tekton,* too (though this passage in Matthew does not actually name Jesus's father). Some scholars believe that artisans and day laborers in the time of Jesus should be considered akin to a lower middle class in the social hierarchy of Galilee, but that view has been disproven by Ramsay MacMullen in *Roman Social Relations: 50 B.C. to A.D. 384* (New Haven:Yale University Press, 1974).

Many studies have been done about the language of Jesus and of first-century Palestine in general, but none are better than those of Joseph Fitzmyer. See "Did Jesus Speak Greek?" *Biblical Archaeology Review* 18.5 (September/October 1992): 58–63; and "The Languages of Palestine in the First Century A.D.," in *The Language of the New Testament,* ed. Stanley E. Porter (Sheffield, UK: Sheffield Academic Press, 1991), 126–62. Other fine studies on the language of Jesus include James Barr, "Which Language Did Jesus Speak? Some Remarks of a Semitist," *Bulletin of the John Rylands Library* 53.1 (Autumn 1970): 14–15; and Michael O. Wise, "Languages of Palestine," in *Dictionary of Jesus and the Gospels,* ed. Joel B. Green and Scot McKnight (Downers Grove, Ill.: InterVarsity Press, 1992), 434–44.

John Meier makes an interesting comment about the passage in Luke in which Jesus stands at the synagogue reading the Isaiah scroll: "Anyone who would wish to defend Luke's depiction of the Isaiah reading as historically reliable even in its details would have to explain (1) how Jesus managed to read from an Isaiah scroll a passage made up of Isaiah 61:1a, b, d; 58:6d; 61:2a, with the omission of 61:1c, 2d; (2) why it is that Jesus read a text of Isaiah that is basically that of the Greek Septuagint, even when at times the Septuagint diverges from the Masoretic text." See Meier, *Marginal Jew,* vol. 1, 303. Nevertheless, Meier actually believes that Jesus was not illiterate and that he even may have had some kind of formal education, though he provides an enlightening account of the debate on both sides of the argument (271–78).

Regarding Jesus's brothers, arguments have been made by some Catholic (and a few Protestant) theologians that the Greek word *adelphos* (brother) could possibly mean "cousin" or "step-brother." While that may be true, nowhere in the entire New Testament is the word *adelphos* ever used to mean either (and it is used some 340 times). Mark 6:17 uses the word *adelphos* to mean "half brother" when he refers to Philip's relationship to Herod Antipas, but even this usage implies "physical brother."

One interesting sidenote about Jesus's family is that they were all named after great heroes and patriarchs of the Bible. Jesus's name was Yeshu, short for Yeshua or Joshua, the great Israelite warrior whose wholesale slaughter of the tribes inhabiting Canaan cleansed the land for the Israelites. His mother was Miriam, named after the sister of Moses. His father, Joseph, was named after the son of Jacob, who would become known as Israel. His brothers, James, Joseph, Simon, and Judas, were all named after biblical heroes. Apparently the naming of children after the great patriarchs became customary after the Maccabean revolt and may indicate a sense of awakened national identity that seemed to have been particularly marked in Galilee.

The argument in Matthew that Jesus's virgin birth was prophesied in Isaiah holds no water at all, since scholars are nearly unanimous in translating the passage in Isaiah 7:14 not as "behold a virgin shall conceive" but "behold, a young maiden (*alma*) will conceive." There is no debate here: *alma* is Hebrew for a young woman. Period.

For one particularly controversial argument about Jesus's illegitimate birth, see Jane Schaberg, *The Illegitimacy of Jesus* (San Francisco: Harper and Row, 1978). Schaberg claims Mary was very likely raped, though it is not clear how she comes to that conclusion.

Celsus's story about the soldier Panthera is from his second-century tract *True Discourse,* which has been lost to history. Our only access to it comes from Origen's polemical response to the work titled *Against Celsus,* written sometime in the middle of the third century C.E.

It should be noted that both Matthew and Luke recount the "son of Mary" passage in Mark 6:3, but both fix Mark's statement by pointedly referring to Jesus as "the carpenter's son" (Matthew 13:55) and "the son of Joseph" (Luke 4:22) respectively. There are variant readings of Mark that insert "the son of the carpenter" in this verse, but it is generally agreed that these are later additions. The original of Mark 6:3 undoubtedly calls Jesus "son of Mary." It is possible, though highly unlikely, that Jesus was called "son of Mary" because Joseph had died so long ago that he was forgotten. But John Meier notes that there is only a single case in the entire Hebrew Scriptures in which a man is referred to as his mother's son. That would be the sons of Zeruiah—Joab, Abishai, and Asahel—who were soldiers in King David's army (1 Samuel 26:6; 2 Samuel 2:13). All three are repeatedly referred to as "sons of Zeruiah." See Meier, *Marginal Jew,* vol. 1, 226.

For more on the question of whether Jesus was married, see William E. Phipps, *Was Jesus Married?* (New York: Harper and Row, 1970) and *The Sexuality of Jesus* (New York: Harper and Row, 1973). Karen King, a professor at Harvard University, has recently unearthed a tiny scrap of papyrus, which she dates to the fourth century, that contains a Coptic phrase that translates to "Jesus said to them, my wife . . ." At the time of this writing, the fragment had yet to be authenticated, though even if it is not a forgery, it would only tell us what those in the fourth century believed about Jesus's marital status.

There are some great stories about the boy Jesus in the gnostic gospels, especially *The Infancy Gospel of Thomas,* in which a petulant Jesus flaunts his magical powers by bringing clay birds to life or striking dead neighborhood kids who fail to show him deference. The best and most complete collection of the gnostic gospels in English is *The Nag Hammadi Library,* ed. Marvin W. Meyer (New York: Harper and Row, 1977).

For more on Sepphoris, see the relevant entry by Z. Weiss in *The New Encyclopedia of Archaeological Excavations in the Holy Land,* ed. Ephraim Stern (New York: Simon and Schuster; Jerusalem: Israel Exploration Society, 1993), 1324–28. For Sepphoris as a major commercial center in Galilee, see Arlene Fradkin, "Long-Distance Trade in the Lower Galilee: New Evidence from Sepphoris," in *Archaeology and the Galilee,* Douglas R. Edwards and C. Thomas McCollough, eds. (Atlanta: Scholars Press, 1997), 107–16. There is some debate as to whether the *miqva'ot* (ritual baths) discovered in Sepphoris were actually ritual baths; Hanan Eshel at Bar Ilan is among those who do not think they were. See "A Note on 'Miqvaot' at Sepphoris," *Archaeology and the Galilee,* 131–33. See also Eric Meyers, "Sepphoris: City of Peace," in *The First Jewish Revolt: Archaeology, History, and Ideology,* ed. Andrea M. Berlin and Andrew J. Overman (London: Routledge, 2002), 110–20. I actually find Eshel's argument quite convincing, though the majority of scholars and archaeologists do not.

There is no way to be certain of the exact date of Antipas's declaration and rebuilding of Sepphoris as his royal seat. Eric Meyer says that Antipas moved to Sepphoris almost immediately after the Romans razed the city in 6 B.C.E.; see Eric M. Meyers, Ehud Netzer, and Carol L. Meyers, "Ornament of All Galilee," *The Biblical Archeologist,* 49.1 (1986): 4–19. However, Shirley Jackson Case places the date much later, at around 10 C.E., in "Jesus and Sepphoris," *Journal of Biblical Literature* 45 (1926): 14–22. For better or worse, the closest we can place Antipas's entry into Sepphoris is around the turn of the first century. It should be noted that Antipas renamed the city *Autocratoris,* or "Imperial City," after he made it the seat of his tetrarchy.

For more on Jesus's life in Sepphoris, see Richard A. Batey, *Jesus and the Forgotten City: New Light on Sepphoris and the Urban World of Jesus* (Grand Rapids, Mich.: Baker Book House, 1991). Archaeological work by Eric Meyers has cast some doubt on the widely held notion that the city was razed by Varus, as Josephus claims in *War* 2:68. See "Roman Sepphoris in the Light of New Archeological Evidence and Research," *The Galilee in Late Antiquity,* ed. Lee I. Levine (New York: Jewish Theological Seminary of America, 1992), 323.

Although it seems that Judas was actually from the town of Gamala in the Golan, he was nevertheless known to all as "Judas the Galilean." There is a great deal of debate about the relationship between Hezekiah and Judas the Galilean, and while it cannot be definitively proven that Judas the Galilean was the same person as Judas the bandit who was Hezekiah's son, that is certainly the assumption that Josephus makes (twice!), and I do not see a reason to doubt him. See *War* 2.56 and *Antiquities* 17.271–72. For more on Judas's genealogical connection to Hezekiah, see the relevant entry in Geza Vermes, *Who's Who in the Age of Jesus* (New York: Penguin, 2006), 165–67; also J. Kennard, "Judas the Galilean and His Clan," *Jewish Quarterly Review* 36 (1946): 281–86. For the opposing view, see Richard A. Horsley, "Menahem in Jerusalem: A Brief Messianic Episode Among the Sicarii—Not 'Zealot Messianism,'" *Novum Testamentum* 27.4 (1985): 334–48. On Judas the Galilean's innovation and his effect on the revolutionary groups that would follow, see Morton Smith, "The Zealots and the Sicarii," *Harvard Theological Review* 64 (1971): 1–19.

The biblical concept of zeal is best defined as "jealous anger," and it is derived from the divine character of God, whom the Bible calls "a devouring fire, a jealous God" (Deuteronomy 4:24). The most celebrated model of biblical zeal is Phinehas, the grandson of Aaron (Moses's brother), whose example of spontaneous individual action as an expression of God's jealous anger and as atonement for the sins of the Jewish nation became the model of personal righteousness in the Bible (Numbers 25). See my *How to Win a Cosmic War,* 70–72. Also see relevant entry in *The Anchor Bible Dictionary,* 1043–54.

Once again, Richard Horsley rejects the proposition that Judas the Galilean had messianic aspirations. But his rejection is based on two assumptions: first, that Judas the Galilean is not descended from Hezekiah the bandit chief, which we have already questioned above; and second, that Josephus does not directly call Judas "king" or "messiah" but instead calls him "sophist," a term with no messianic connotations. See *Menahem in Jerusalem,* 342–43. However, Josephus clearly derides Judas for what he calls his "royal aspirations." What else could this mean but that Judas had messianic (i.e., kingly) ambitions? What's more, Josephus uses the same term, "sophist," to describe both Mattathias (*Antiquities* 17.6), who was overtly connected to messianic aspirations during the Maccabean revolt, and Menahem (*Jewish War* 2.433–48), whose messianic pretensions are not in dispute. On this point I agree with Martin Hengel when he writes that "a dynasty of leaders proceeded from Judas [of Galilee], among whom messianic pretension became evident at least in one, Menahem, allows one to surmise that the 'Fourth Sect' had a messianic foundation already in its founder." See *The Zealots* (London: T&T Clark, 2000), 299. However, I disagree with Hengel that the members of the Fourth Philosophy can be adequately labeled Zealots. Rather, I contend that they preached zealotry as a biblical doctrine demanding the removal of foreign elements from the Holy Land, which is why I use the term "zealot," with a lowercase z, to describe them. For more on Josephus's use of the term "sophist," see note 71 in Whiston's translation of *The Jewish War,* book 2, chapter 1, section 3.

CHAPTER FIVE: WHERE IS YOUR FLEET TO SWEEP THE ROMAN SEAS?

There is very little historical evidence about the life of Pontius Pilate before his tenure as prefect in Jerusalem, but Ann Wroe has written an interesting account titled *Pontius Pilate* (New York: Random House, 1999), which, while not a scholarly book, is definitely a fun read. With regard to the difference between a Roman prefect and a procurator, the short answer is that there was none, at least not in a small and fairly insignificant province like Judea. Josephus calls Pilate a procurator in the *Antiquities* 18.5.6, whereas Philo refers to him as prefect. The terms were probably interchangeable at the time. I have chosen to simply use the term "governor" to mean both prefect and procurator.

For more on Pilate's introduction of the shields into the Temple of Jerusalem, I recommend G. Fuks, "Again on the Episode of the Gilded Roman Shields at Jerusalem," *Harvard Theological Review* 75 (1982): 503–7, and P. S. Davies, "The Meaning of Philo's Text About the Gilded Shields," *Journal of Theological Studies* 37 (1986): 109–14.

A great deal has been written about the reasons why the Jews rebelled against Rome. No doubt there was a combination of social, economic, political, and religious grievances that ultimately led to the Jewish War, but David Rhoads outlines six principal causes in his book *Israel in Revolution: 6–74* C.E. (Philadelphia: Fortress Press, 1976): (1) the Jews were defending the Law of God; (2) the Jews believed God would lead them to victory; (3) the Jews wanted to rid the holy land of foreigners and gentiles; (4) the Jews were trying to defend God's city, Jerusalem, from desecration; (5) the Jews wanted to cleanse the Temple; and (6) the Jews hoped it would usher in the end time and the coming of the messiah. However, some scholars (and I include myself in this category) emphasize the eschatological motivations of the Jews over these other reasons. See for example A. J. Tomasino, "Oracles of Insurrection: The Prophetic Catalyst of the Great Revolt," *Journal of Jewish Studies* 59 (2008): 86–111. Others caution about putting too much weight on the role that apocalyptic fervor played in stirring the Jews to revolt. See for instance Tessa Rajak, "Jewish Millenarian Expectations," *The First Jewish Revolt,* ed. Andrea M. Berlin and J. Andrew Overman (New York: Routledge, 2002), 164–88. Rajak writes: "Expectation of an imminent End . . . was not the normal mindset of first-century Judaism." However, I think the evidence to the contrary far outweighs this view, as the link between messianism and the Jewish Revolt could not be clearer in Josephus's account of the Jewish War.

Concerning the list of messianic aspirants that arose in the buildup to the Jewish War, P. W. Barnett suggests that the fact that Josephus fails to call these messianic figures *baselius,* or "king" (with the exception of "the Egyptian"), proves that they thought of themselves not as messiahs but rather as "sign prophets." But Barnett notes that even these sign prophets "anticipated some great act of eschatological redemption," which, after all, is the inherent right of the messiah. See P. W. Barnett, "The Jewish Sign Prophets," *New Testament Studies* 27 (1980): 679–97. James S. McLaren tries (and, in my opinion, fails) to avoid relying too much on the idea that the Jews expected "divine assistance" to defeat the Romans or that they were fueled by messianic fervor, by claiming that the Jews "were simply optimistic that they would succeed," in the same way that, say, the Germans were optimistic that they would defeat Britain. Yet what else did "optimism" mean in first-century Palestine but confidence in God? See "Going to War Against Rome: The Motivation of the Jewish Rebels," in *The Jewish Revolt Against Rome: Interdisciplinary Perspectives,* ed. M. Popovic, *Supplements to the Journal for the Study of Judaism* 154 (Leiden, Netherlands: Brill, 2011), 129–53.

It should be noted that while "the Samaritan" called himself "messiah," he did not mean it exactly in the Jewish sense of the word. The Samaritan equivalent of "messiah" is *Taheb.* However, the Taheb was directly related to the messiah. In fact, the words were synonymous, as evidenced by the Samaritan woman in the gospel of John who tells Jesus, "I know that the messiah is coming. When he will come, he will show us all things" (John 4:25).

Josephus is the first to use the Latin word "Sicarii" (Josephus, *Jewish War* 2.254–55), though it is obvious he borrows the term from the Romans. The word "Sicarii" appears in Acts 21:38 in reference to the "false prophet" known as "the Egyptian," for whom Paul is mistaken. Acts claims the Egyptian had four thousand followers, which is a more likely figure than the thirty thousand that Josephus claims in *Jewish War* 2.247–70 (though in *Antiquities* 20.171, Josephus provides a much smaller number).

Although Josephus describes the Sicarii as "a different type of bandit," he uses the words "Sicarii" and "bandits" interchangeably throughout *The Jewish War*. In fact, at times he uses the term "Sicarii" to describe groups of bandits who do not use daggers as weapons. It is likely that his reason for differentiating the Sicarii from "the other bandits" was to keep all the various bandit gangs distinct for narrative's sake, though a case can be made that after the rise of Menahem in the first year of the war, the Sicarii became a recognizably separate group—the same group that seized control of Masada. See Shimon Applebaum, "The Zealots: The Case for Revaluation," *Journal of Roman Studies* 61 (1971): 155–70. In my opinion, the best and most up-to-date study of the Sicarii is Mark Andrew Brighton, *The Sicarii in Josephus's Judean War: Rhetorical Analysis and Historical Observations* (Atlanta: Society of Biblical Scholarship, 2009).

Other views on the Sicarii include Emil Schurer, *A History of the Jewish People in the Time of Jesus Christ*, 3 vols. (Edinburgh: T&T Clark, 1890), for whom the Sicarii are a fanatical offshoot of the Zealot Party; Martin Hengel, *The Zealots* (Edinburgh: T&T Clark, 1989), who disagrees with Schurer, arguing that the Sicarii were just an ultra-violent subgroup of the bandits; Solomon Zeitlin, "Zealots and Sicarii," *Journal of Biblical Literature* 81 (1962): 395–98, who believes the Sicarii and the Zealots were two distinct and "mutually hostile" groups; Richard A. Horsley, "Josephus and the Bandits," *Journal for the Study of Judaism* 10 (1979): 37–63, for whom the Sicarii are just a localized phenomenon, part of the larger movement of "social banditry" that was rife in the Judean countryside; and Morton Smith, "Zealots and Sicarii: Their Origins and Relation," *Harvard Theological Review* 64 (1971): 7–31, whose view that labels such as Sicarii and Zealot were not static designations but rather indicated a generalized and widespread yearning for the biblical doctrine of zeal is wholeheartedly adopted in this book.

In the *Antiquities*, written some time after *The Jewish War*, Josephus suggests that it was the Roman proconsul Felix who spurred the Sicarii to murder the high priest Jonathan for his own political purposes. Some scholars, most notably Martin Goodman, *The Ruling Class of Judea* (Cambridge: Cambridge University Press, 1987), continue to argue this point, viewing the Sicarii as little more than hired assassins or mercenaries. This is unlikely. First of all, the explanation given in the *Antiquities* contradicts Josephus's earlier, and likely more reliable, account in *The Jewish War*, which makes no mention of Felix's hand in the assassination of Jonathan. In fact, the description of Jonathan's murder in the *Antiquities* fails to mention the role of the Sicarii at all. Instead, the text refers to assassins generally as "bandits" (*lestai*). In any case, the account of Jonathan's murder in *The Jewish War* is written deliberately to emphasize the ideological/religious motivations of the Sicarii (hence their slogan "No lord but God!"), and as a prelude to the much more significant murders of the high priest Ananus ben Ananus (62 C.E.) and Jesus ben Gamaliel (63–64 C.E.), which ultimately launch the war with Rome.

Tacitus's quote about Felix comes from Geza Vermes, *Who's Who in the Age of Jesus* (London: Penguin, 2005), 89. Josephus's quote about every man hourly expecting death is from *The Jewish War* 7.253.

Rome actually assigned one more procurator to succeed Gessius Florus: Marcus Antonius Julianus. But that was during the years of the Jewish Revolt, and he never seems to have set foot in Jerusalem.

Agrippa's speech is from *The Jewish War* 2.355–78. As moving as the speech may be, it is obviously Josephus's own creation.

CHAPTER SIX: YEAR ONE

For more on the history of Masada and its changes under Herod, see Solomon Zeitlin, "Masada and the Sicarii," *Jewish Quarterly Review* 55.4 (1965): 299–317.

Josephus seems to deliberately avoid using the word "messiah" to refer to Menahem, but in describing Menahem's posturing as a popularly recognized "anointed king," he is no doubt describing phenomena that, according to Richard Horsley, "can be understood as concrete examples of popular 'messiahs' and their movements." Horsley, "Menahem in Jerusalem," 340.

For some great examples of the coins struck by the victorious Jewish rebels, see Ya'akov Meshorer, *Treasury of Jewish Coins from the Persian Period to Bar Kokhba* (Jerusalem and Nyack, N.Y.: Amphora Books, 2001).

The speech of the Sicarii leader was made by Eleazar ben Yair and can be found in Josephus, *The Jewish War* 7.335. Tacitus's description of the era in Rome being "rich in disasters" comes from Goodman, *Rome and Jerusalem,* 430.

The Zealot Party was led by a revolutionary priest named Eleazar son of Simon. Some scholars argue that this Eleazar was the same Eleazar the Temple Captain who seized control of the Temple at the start of the revolt and ceased all sacrifices on behalf of the emperor. For this view, see Rhoads, *Israel in Revolution;* also Geza Vermes, *Who's Who in the Age of Jesus,* 83. Vermes claims this was the same Eleazar who attacked and killed Menahem. That is unlikely. The Temple Captain was named Eleazar son of Ananias, and, as both Richard Horsley and Morton Smith have shown, he had no connection to the Eleazar son of Simon who took over the leadership of the Zealot Party in 68 C.E. See Smith, "Zealots and Sicarii," *Harvard Theological Review* 64 (1971): 1–19, and Horsley, "The Zealots: Their Origin, Relationship and Importance in the Jewish Revolt," *Novum Testamentum* 28 (1986): 159–92.

Most of the information we have about John of Gischala comes from Josephus, with whom John was on extremely unfriendly terms. Thus the portrait of John that comes out of Josephus's writings is of a mad tyrant who put all of Jerusalem in danger with his thirst for power and blood. No contemporary scholar takes this description of John seriously. For a better portrait of the man, see Uriel

Rappaport, "John of Gischala: From Galilee to Jerusalem," *Journal of Jewish Studies* 33 (1982): 479–93. With regard to John's zealousness and his eschatological ideals, Rappaport is correct to note that while it is difficult to know his exact religiopolitical outlook, his alliance with the Zealot Party suggests, at the very least, that he was sympathetic to zealot ideology. In any case, John eventually managed to overpower the Zealots and take control over the inner Temple, though, by all accounts, he allowed Eleazar son of Simon to remain at least nominally in charge of the Zealot Party, right up to the moment in which Titus invaded Jerusalem.

For a description of the famine that ensued in Jerusalem during Titus's siege, see Josephus, *The Jewish War* 5.427–571, 6.271–76. Josephus, who was writing his history of the war for the very man who won it, presents Titus as trying desperately to restrain his men from killing wantonly and in particular from destroying the Temple. This is obviously nonsense. It is merely Josephus pandering to his Roman audience. Josephus also sets the number of Jews who died in Jerusalem at one million. This is clearly an exaggeration.

For complete coverage of the exchange rate among ancient currencies in first-century Palestine, see Fredric William Madden's colossal work, *History of Jewish Coinage and of Money in the Old and New Testament* (London: Bernard Quaritch, 1864). Madden notes that Josephus refers to the shekel as equal to four Attic drachms (drachmas), meaning two drachmas equals one-half shekel (238). See also J. Liver, "The Half-Shekel Offering in Biblical and Post-Biblical Literature," *Harvard Theological Review* 56.3 (1963): 173–98.

Some scholars argue, unconvincingly, that no perceptible shift occurred in the Roman attitude toward Jews; see, for example, Eric S. Gruen, "Roman Perspectives on the Jews in the Age of the Great Revolt," *First Jewish Revolt,* 27–42. With regard to the symbol of parading the Torah during the Triumph, I think Martin Goodman said it best in *Rome and Jerusalem*: "There could not be a clearer demonstration that the conquest was being celebrated not just over Judea but over Judaism" (453). For more on Judaism after the destruction of the Temple, see Michael S. Berger, "Rabbinic Pacification of Second-Century Jewish Nationalism," *Belief and Bloodshed*, ed. James K. Wellman, Jr. (Lanham, Md.: Rowman and Littlefield, 2007), 48.

It is vital to note that the earliest manuscripts we have of the gospel of Mark end the first verse at "Jesus the Christ." It was only later that a redactor added the phrase "the Son of God." The significance of the gospels' being written in Greek should not be overlooked. Consider that the Dead Sea Scrolls, the most contemporary set of Jewish writings to survive the destruction of Jerusalem, whose themes and topics are very close to those of the New Testament, were written almost exclusively in Hebrew and Aramaic.

PART II PROLOGUE: ZEAL FOR YOUR HOUSE

The story of Jesus's triumphal entry into Jerusalem and the cleansing of the Temple can be found in Matthew 21:1–22, Mark 11:1–19, Luke 19:29–48, and John 2:13–25. Note that John's gospel places the event at the start of Jesus's ministry, whereas the Synoptics place it at the end. That Jesus's entry into Jerusalem reveals his kingly aspirations is abundantly clear. Recall that Solomon also mounts a donkey in order to be proclaimed king (1 Kings 1:32–40), as does Absalom when he tries to wrest the throne from his father, David (2 Samuel 19:26). According to David Catchpole, Jesus's entry into Jerusalem fits perfectly into a family of stories detailing "the celebratory entry to a city by a hero figure who has previously achieved his triumph." Catchpole notes that this "fixed pattern of triumphal entry" has precedence not only among the Israelite kings (see for example Kings 1:32–40) but also in Alexander's entry into Jerusalem, Apollonius's entry into Jerusalem, Simon Maccabaeus's entry into Jerusalem, Marcus Agrippa's entry into Jerusalem, and so on. See David R. Catchpole, "The 'Triumphal' Entry," *Jesus and the Politics of His Day*, ed. Ernst Bammel and C.F.D. Moule (New York: Cambridge University Press, 1984), 319–34.

Jesus explicitly uses the term *lestai* to signify "den of thieves," instead of the more common word for thieves, *kleptai* (see Mark 11:17). While it may seem obvious that in this case Jesus is not using the term in its politicized sense as "bandit"—meaning someone with zealot tendencies—some scholars believe that Jesus is in fact referring specifically to bandits in this passage. Indeed, some link Jesus's cleansing of the Temple to an insurrection led by bar Abbas that took place there around the same time (see Mark 15:7). The argument goes like this: Since bar Abbas is *always* characterized with the epithet *lestai,* Jesus's use of the term must be referring to the slaughter that took place around the Temple during the bandit insurrection he led. Therefore, the best translation of Jesus's admonition here is not "den of thieves," but rather "cave of bandits," meaning "zealot stronghold," and thus referring specifically to bar Abbas's insurrection. See George Wesley Buchanan, "Mark 11:15–19: Brigands in the Temple," *Hebrew Union College Annual* 30 (1959): 169–77. This is an intriguing argument, but there is a simpler explanation for Jesus's use of the word *lestai* instead of *kleptai* in this passage. The evangelist is likely quoting the prophet Jeremiah (7:11) in its Septuagint (Greek) translation: "Has this house, which is called by my name, become a den of robbers in your eyes? Behold, I myself have seen it, utters the LORD!" That translation uses the phrase *spaylayon laystoun* to mean "den of thieves," which makes sense in that the Septuagint was written long before *lestai* became a byword for "bandits"—indeed, long before there was any such thing as a bandit in Judea or Galilee. Here, *lestai* is the preferred Greek translation of the Hebrew word *paritsim,* which is poorly attested in the Hebrew Bible and is used, at most, twice in the entire text. The word *paritsim* can mean something like "violent ones," though in Ezekiel 7:22, which also uses the Hebrew word *paritsim,* the Septuagint translates the word into the Greek by using *afulaktos,* which means something like "unguarded." The point is that the Hebrew word *paritsim* was obviously problematic for the Septuagint translators, and any attempt to limit the meaning of the Hebrew or Greek words to a specific meaning or an overly circumscribed semantic range is difficult, to say the least. Thus, it is likely that when Jesus uses the word *lestai* in this passage, he means nothing more complicated than "thieves," which, after all, is how he viewed the merchants and money changers at the Temple.

The tangled web that bound the Temple authorities to Rome, and the notion that an attack on one would have been considered an attack on the other, is an argument made brilliantly by S.G.F. Brandon, *Jesus and the Zealots* (Manchester: Manchester University Press, 1967), 9. Brandon also notes correctly that the Romans would not have been ignorant of the cleansing incident, since the Roman garrison in the Antonia Fortress overlooked the Temple courts. For the opposing view to Brandon's analysis, see Cecil Roth, "The Cleansing of the Temple and Zechariah XIV.21," *Novum Testamentum* 4 (1960): 174–81. Roth seems to deny any nationalist or zealot significance whatsoever either in Jesus's entry into Jerusalem or in his cleansing of the Temple, which he reinterprets in a "spiritual and basically non-political sense," claiming that Jesus's main concern was stripping the Temple of any "mercantile operations." Other scholars take this argument one step further and claim that the "cleansing" incident never even happened, at least not as it has been recorded by all four gospel writers, because it so contrasts with Jesus's message of peace. See Burton Mack, *A Myth of Innocence: Mark and Christian Origins* (Philadelphia: Fortress Press, 1988). Once again this seems like a classic case of scholars refusing to accept an obvious reality that does not fit into their preconceived Christological conceptions of who Jesus was and what Jesus meant. Mack's thesis is expertly refuted by Craig Evans, who demonstrates not only that the Temple cleansing incident can be traced to the historical Jesus, but also that it could not have been understood in any other way than as an act of profound political significance. See Evans, *Jesus and His Contemporaries* (Leiden, Netherlands: Brill, 1995), 301–18. However, elsewhere Evans disagrees with me regarding Jesus's prediction of the Temple's destruction. He not only believes that the prediction can be traced to Jesus, whereas I view it as being put in Jesus's mouth by the gospel writers, he also thinks it may have been the principal factor that motivated the high priest to take action against him. See Craig Evans, "Jesus and Predictions of the Destruction of the Herodian Temple in the Pseudepigrapha, Qumran Scrolls, and Related Texts," *Journal for the Study of the Pseudepigrapha* 10 (1992): 89–147.

Both Josephus and the Babylonian Talmud indicate that the sacrificial animals used to be housed on the Mount of Olives, but that sometime around 30 C.E., Caiaphas transferred them into the Court of Gentiles. Bruce Chilton believes that Caiaphas's innovation was the impetus for Jesus's actions at the Temple as well as the principal reason for the high priest's desire to have Jesus arrested and executed; see Bruce Chilton, "The Trial of Jesus Reconsidered," in *Jesus in Context*, ed. Bruce Chilton and Craig Evans (Leiden, Netherlands: Brill, 1997), 281–500.

The question posed to Jesus about the legality of paying tribute to Caesar can be found in Mark 12:13–17, Matthew 22:15–22, and Luke 20:20–26. The episode does not appear in John's gospel because there the cleansing event is placed among Jesus's first acts and not at the end of his life. See Herbert Loewe, *Render unto Caesar* (Cambridge: Cambridge University Press, 1940). The Jewish authorities who try to trap Jesus by asking him about the payment of tribute are variously described in the Synoptic gospels as Pharisees and Herodians (Mark 12:13; Matthew 22:15), or as "scribes and chief priests" (Luke 20:20). This lumping together of disparate authorities indicates a startling ignorance on the part of the gospel writers (who were writing their accounts some forty to sixty years after the events they describe) about Jewish religious hierarchy in first-century Palestine. The scribes were lower- or middle-class scholars, while the chief priests were aristocratic nobility; the Pharisees and Herodians were about as far apart economically, socially, and (if by Herodians Mark suggests a Sadducean connection) theologically as can be imagined. It almost seems as though the gospel writers are throwing out these formulae simply as bywords for "the Jews."

That the coin Jesus asks for, the denarius, is the same coin used to pay the tribute to Rome is definitively proven by H. St. J. Hart, "The Coin of 'Render unto Caesar,'" *Jesus and the Politics of His Day*, 241–48.

Among the many scholars who have tried to strip Jesus's answer regarding the tribute of its political significance are J.D.M. Derrett, *Law in the New Testament* (Eugene, Ore.: Wipf and Stock, 2005) and F. F. Bruce, "Render to Caesar," *Jesus and the Politics of His Day*, 249–63. At least Bruce recognizes the significance of the word *apodidomi*, and indeed it is his analysis of the verb that I reference above. Helmut Merkel is one of many scholars who see Jesus's answer to the religious authorities as a nonanswer; "The Opposition Between Jesus and Judaism," *Jesus and the Politics of His Day*, 129–44. Merkel quotes the German scholar Eduard Lohse in refuting Brandon and those, like myself, who believe that Jesus's answer betrays his zealot sentiments: "Jesus neither allowed himself to be lured into conferring divine status on the existing power structure, nor concurred with the revolutionaries who wanted to change the existing order and compel the coming of the Kingdom of God by the use of force." First of all, it should be noted that the use of force is not the issue here. Whether Jesus agreed with the followers of Judas the Galilean that only the use of arms could free the Jews from Roman rule is not what is at stake in this passage. All that is at stake here is the question of where Jesus's views fell on the most decisive issue of the day, which also happened to be the fundamental test of zealotry: Should the Jews pay tribute to Rome? Those scholars who paint Jesus's answer to the religious authorities as apolitical are, to my mind, totally blind to the political and religious context of Jesus's time, and, more important, to the fact that the issue of the tribute is quite clearly meant to be connected to Jesus's provocative entry into Jerusalem, of which there can be no apolitical interpretation.

For some reason, the *titulus* above Jesus's head has been viewed by scholars and Christians alike as some sort of joke, a sarcastic bit of humor on the part of Rome. The Romans may be known for many things, but humor isn't one of them. As usual, this interpretation relies on a prima facie reading of Jesus as a man with no political ambitions whatsoever. That is nonsense. All criminals sentenced to execution received a *titulus* so that everyone would know the crime for which they were being punished and thus be deterred from taking part in similar activity. That the wording on Jesus's *titulus* was likely genuine is demonstrated by Joseph A. Fitzmeyer, who notes that "If [the *titulus*] were invented by Christians, they would have used *Christos,* for early Christians would scarcely have called their Lord 'King of the Jews.'" See *The Gospel According to Luke I–IX* (Garden City, N.Y.: Doubleday, 1981), 773. I will speak more about Jesus's "trial" in subsequent chapters, but suffice it to say that the notion that a no-name Jewish peasant would have received a personal audience with the Roman governor, Pontius Pilate, who had probably signed a dozen execution orders that day alone, is so outlandish that it cannot be taken seriously.

Oddly, Luke refers to the two crucified on either side of Jesus not as *lestai* but as *kakourgoi,* or "evildoers" (Luke 23:32).

CHAPTER SEVEN: THE VOICE CRYING OUT IN THE WILDERNESS

All four gospels give varying accounts of John the Baptist (Matthew 3:1–17; Mark 1:2–15; Luke 3:1–22; John 1:19–42). It is generally agreed that much of this gospel material, including John's infancy narrative in Luke, was derived from independent "Baptist traditions" preserved by John's followers. On this, see Charles Scobie, *John the Baptist* (Minneapolis: Fortress Press, 1964), 50–51, and Walter Wink, *John the Baptist in the Gospel Tradition* (Eugene, Ore.: Wipf and Stock, 2001), 59–60. However, Wink thinks only some of this material came from John's unique sources. He argues that the infancy narratives of John and Jesus were likely developed concurrently. See also Catherine Murphy, *John the Baptist: Prophet of Purity for a New Age* (Collegeville, Minn.: Liturgical Press, 2003).

Although, according to Matthew, John warns the Jews of the coming of the "kingdom of heaven," that is merely Matthew's circumlocution for Kingdom of God. In fact, Matthew uses the phrase "Kingdom of Heaven" throughout his gospel, even in those passages in which he has borrowed from Mark. In other words, we can be fairly certain that "Kingdom of God" and "Kingdom of Heaven" mean the same thing and that both derived in some part from the teachings of John the Baptist.

There are many inaccuracies in the gospel account of John's execution (Mark 6:17–29; Matthew 14:1–12; Luke 9:7–9). For one, the evangelists refer to Herodias as the wife of Philip, when she was actually the wife of Herod. It was Salome who was Philip's wife. Any attempt by conservative Christian commentators to make up for this blatant error—for instance, by referring to Antipas's half brother as "Herod Philip" (a name that does not appear in any records)—falls flat. The gospels also seem to confuse the place of John's execution (the fortress of Machaerus) with Antipas's court, which at the time would have been in Tiberias. Finally, it should be mentioned that it is inconceivable that a royal princess would have performed for Antipas's guests, considering the strictures of the day for Jewish women of any status. There are, of course, many apologetic attempts to rescue the gospel story of John's beheading and to argue for its historicity (for example, Geza Vermes, *Who's Who in the Age of Jesus*, 49), but I agree with Rudolf Bultmann, *History of the Synoptic Tradition* (San Francisco: Harper and Row, 1968), 301–2, and Lester L. Grabbe, *Judaism from Cyrus to Hadrian*, vol. 2, 427–28, both of whom argue that the gospel story is far too fanciful and riddled with too many errors to be taken as historical.

For parallels between Mark's account of John's execution and the book of Esther, see Roger Aus, *Water into Wine and the Beheading of John the Baptist* (Providence: Brown Judaic Studies, 1988). The story also echoes Elijah's conflict with Jezebel, the wife of King Ahab (1 Kings 19–22).

Josephus's account of John the Baptist's life and death can be found in *Antiquities* 18.116–19. King Aretas IV was the father of Antipas's first wife, Phasaelis, whom Antipas divorced in order to marry Herodias. It is unclear whether Antipas was exiled to Spain, as Josephus states in *The Jewish War* 2.183, or to Gaul, as he alleges in *Antiquities* 18.252.

A catalogue of ablutions and water rituals in Jewish scripture and practice can be found in R. L. Webb, *John the Baptizer and Prophet: A Socio-Historical Study* (Sheffield, U.K.: Sheffield Academic Press, 1991), 95–132. For more on the use of water in Jewish conversion rituals, see Shaye J. D. Cohen, "The Rabbinic Conversion Ceremony," *Journal of Jewish Studies* 41 (1990): 177–203. There were a few notable individuals in first-century Palestine who practiced ritual acts of immersion, most famously the ascetic known as Bannus, who lived as a hermit in the desert and who bathed himself morning and night in cold water as a means of ritual purification; see Josephus, *Life* 2.11–12.

Josephus writes at length about the Essenes in both the *Antiquities* and *The Jewish War,* but the earliest evidence about the Essenes comes via Philo of Alexandria's *Hypothetica,* written between 35 and 45 C.E. Pliny the Elder also speaks of the Essenes in his *Natural History,* written circa 77 C.E. It is Pliny who states that the Essenes lived near Engeddi, on the western shore of the Dead Sea, although most scholars believe the Essenes were located at Qumran. Pliny's error may be due to the fact that he was writing after the war with Rome and the destruction of Jerusalem, after which the Qumran site was abandoned. Nevertheless, a huge debate has erupted among scholars over whether the community at Qumran was in fact Essene. Norman Golb is perhaps the best-known scholar who rejects the Qumran hypothesis. Golb views the Qumran site not as an Essene community but rather as a Hasmonaean fortress. He believes that the documents found in the caves near Qumran—the so-called Dead Sea Scrolls—were not written by the Essenes but brought there for safekeeping from Jerusalem. See Norman Golb, *Who Wrote the Dead Sea Scrolls? The Search for the Secret Qumran* (New York: Scribner, 1995), and "The Problem of Origin and Identification of the Dead Sea Scrolls," *Proceedings of the American Philosophical Society* 124 (1980): 1–24. Golb and his contemporaries make some valid points, and it must be admitted that some of the documents found in the caves at Qumran were not written by the Essenes and do not reflect Essene theology. The fact is that we cannot be certain whether the Essenes lived at Qumran. That said, I agree with the great Frank Moore Cross, who argued that the burden of proof rests not with those who connect the Essenes with Qumran, but with those who do not. "The scholar who would 'exercise caution' in identifying the sect of Qumran with the Essenes places himself in an astonishing position," Moore writes; "he must suggest seriously that two major parties formed communistic religious communities in the same district of the desert of the Dead Sea and lived together in effect for two centuries, holding similar bizarre views, performing similar or rather identical lustrations, ritual meals, and ceremonies. He must suppose that one, carefully described by classical authors, disappeared without leaving building remains or even potsherds behind: the other, systematically ignored by classical authors, left extensive ruins, and indeed a great library. I prefer to be reckless and flatly identify the men of Qumran with their perennial houseguest, the Essenes." Frank Moore Cross, *Canaanite Myth and Hebrew Epic: Essays in the History of the Religion of Israel* (Cambridge, Mass.: Harvard University Press, 1973), 331–32. Everything you could ever want to know and more about Essene purity rituals can be found in Ian C. Werrett, *Ritual Purity and the Dead Sea Scrolls* (Leiden, Netherlands: Brill, 2007).

Among those who believe that John the Baptist was a member of the Essene community are Otto Betz, "Was John the Baptist an Essene?" *Understanding the Dead Sea Scrolls,* ed. Hershel Shanks (New York: Random House, 1992), 205–14;

W. H. Brownlee, "John the Baptist in the New Light of Ancient Scrolls," *The Scrolls and the New Testament,* ed. Krister Stendahl (New York: Harper, 1957), 71–90; and J.A.T. Robinson, "The Baptism of John and the Qumran Community: Testing a Hypothesis," *Twelve New Testament Studies* (London: SCM Press, 1962), 11–27. Among those who disagree are H. H. Rowley, "The Baptism of John and the Qumran Sect," *New Testament Essays: Studies in Memory of Thomas Walter Manson, 1893–1958,* ed. A.J.B. Higgins (Manchester: Manchester University Press, 1959), 218–29; Bruce D. Chilton, *Judaic Approaches to the Gospels* (Atlanta: Scholars Press, 1994), 17–22; and Joan E. Taylor, *The Immerser: John the Baptist Within Second Temple Judaism* (Grand Rapids, Mich.: Eerdmans, 1997).

It should be noted that while Isaiah 40:3 was applied to both John and the Essenes, there were important distinctions in the way the passage seems to have been interpreted by both. For more on John's possible childhood "in the wilderness," see Jean Steinmann, *Saint John the Baptist and the Desert Tradition* (New York: Harper, 1958). Regardless of whether John was a member of the Essenes, it is clear that there are a number of parallels between the two, including setting, asceticism, priestly lineage, water immersion, and the sharing of property. Individually, none of these parallels definitively proves a connection, but together they make a strong case for certain affinities between the two that should not be easily dismissed. In any case, John would not need to have been an actual member of the Essene community to be influenced by their teachings and ideas, which were pretty well integrated into the Jewish spirituality of the time.

Although it is never explicitly stated that John's baptism was not meant to be repeated, one can infer that to be the case for two reasons: first, because the baptism seems to require an administrator, like John, as opposed to most other water rituals, which were self-administered; and second, because John's baptism assumes the imminent end of the world, which would make its repetition somewhat difficult, to say the least. See John Meier, *Marginal Jew,* vol. 2, 51.

John Meier makes a compelling case for accepting the historicity of the phrase "baptism for the forgiveness of sins." See *Marginal Jew,* vol. 2, 53–54. Josephus's claim to the contrary can be found in *Antiquities* 18.116. Robert L. Webb argues that John's baptism was a "repentance-baptism which functioned to initiate [the Jews] into the group of prepared people, the true Israel," meaning John did in fact form his own distinct sect; see *John the Baptizer and Prophet,* 197 and 364. Bruce Chilton completely dismantles Webb's argument in "John the Purifier," 203–20.

The heavenly affirmation "This is my son, the Beloved" is from Psalms 2:7, in which God addresses David on the occasion of his enthronement as king in Jerusalem (Beloved was David's nickname). As John Meier rightly notes, this moment "does not mirror some inner experience that Jesus had at the time; it mirrors the desire of the first-generation Christian church to define Jesus as soon as the primitive Gospel story begins—all the more so because this definition was needed to counter the impression of Jesus's subordination to John, implicit in the tradition of the former being baptized by the latter." *Marginal Jew,* vol. 2, 107.

Among those scholars who make a convincing case that Jesus began his ministry as a disciple of John are P. W. Hollenbach, "Social Aspects of John the Baptizer's Preaching Mission in the Context of Palestinian Judaism," *Aufstieg und Niedergang der römischen Welt (ANRW)* 2.19.1 (1979): 852–53, and "The Conversion of Jesus: From Jesus the Baptizer to Jesus the Healer," *ANRW* 2.25.1 (1982): 198–200, as well as Robert L. Webb, "Jesus' Baptism: Its Historicity and Implications," *Bulletin for Biblical Research* 10.2 (2000): 261–309. Webb summarizes the relationship between John and Jesus thus: "Jesus was baptized by John and probably remained with him for some time in the role of disciple. Later, in alignment and participation with John and his movement, Jesus also engaged in a baptizing ministry near John. Although he was still a disciple of John, Jesus perhaps should be viewed at this point as John's right-hand man or protégé. While tensions may have arisen between John's disciples and those around Jesus, the two men viewed themselves as working together. Only later, after the arrest of John, did a shift take place in which Jesus moved beyond the conceptual framework of John's movement in certain respects. Yet Jesus always appears appreciative of the foundation that John's framework initially provided for him."

Regarding Jesus's sojourn in the wilderness, one must remember that "the wilderness" is more than a geographic location. It is where the covenant with Abraham was made, where Moses received the Law of God, where the Israelites wandered for a generation; it is where God dwelt and where he could be found and communed with. The gospel's use of the term "forty days"—the number of days Jesus is said to have spent in the desert—is not meant to be read as a literal number. In the Bible, "forty" is a byword for "many," as in "it rained for forty days and nights." The implication is that Jesus stayed in the wilderness for a long time.

I disagree with Rudolf Otto, who claims that "John did not preach the coming of the kingdom of heaven, but of the coming judgment of wrath"; *The Kingdom of God and the Son of Man,* 69. It is Otto's point that John was concerned chiefly with the coming judgment of God, what he calls "the Day of Yahweh," whereas Jesus's focus was on the redemptive nature of God's kingdom on earth. Yet even Jesus marks John's activities as part of the inauguration of the Kingdom of God on earth: "The Law and Prophets were [in effect] until John; afterward, the Kingdom of God is proclaimed" (Luke 16:16).

CHAPTER EIGHT: FOLLOW ME

Josephus's description of the Galileans can be found in *The Jewish War* 3.41–42. Richard Horsley expertly details the history of Galilean resistance, even when it came to the "political-economic-religious subordination to the Hasmonean high priesthood in Jerusalem," in *Galilee: History, Politics, People* (Valley Forge, Pa.: Trinity Press International, 1995). Horsley writes that "the Temple itself, temple dues, and rule by the high priesthood would all have been foreign to the Galileans, whose ancestors had rebelled centuries earlier against the Solomonic monarchy and the Temple. Thus the Galileans, like the Idumeans, would have experienced the laws of the Judeans superimposed on their own customs as the means to define and legitimate their subordination to Jerusalem rule" (51). Hence Luke's assertion that Jesus's parents went to the Temple for Passover every year quite clearly reflects a Lukan agenda rather than Galilean practices (Luke 2:41–51). See also Sean Freyne, *Galilee, Jesus, and the Gospels* (Dublin: Gill and MacMillan, 1988), 187–89.

On the distinctive accent of the Galileans, see Obery M. Hendricks, *The Politics of Jesus* (New York: Doubleday, 2006), 70–73. For the implications of the term "people of the land," see the comprehensive study done by Aharon Oppenheimer, *The 'Am Ha-Aretz: A Study in the Social History of the Jewish People in the Hellenistic-Roman Period* (Leiden, Netherlands: Brill, 1977).

For more on Jesus's family as followers, see John Painter, *Just James: The Brother of Jesus in History and Tradition* (Columbia: University of South Carolina Press), 14–31.

The Greek word for "disciples," *hoi mathetai,* can mean both male and female disciples. Obviously the sight of unaccompanied women following an itinerant preacher and his mostly male companions from town to town would have caused a scandal in Galilee, and in fact there are numerous passages in the gospels in which Jesus is accused of consorting with "loose women." Some variants of the gospel of Luke say Jesus had seventy, not seventy-two, disciples. The discrepancy is irrelevant, as numbers in the Bible—especially evocative numbers such as three, twelve, forty, and seventy-two—are meant to be read symbolically, not literally, with the exception of the twelve disciples, which should be read both ways.

There can be no doubt that Jesus specifically designated twelve individuals to represent the twelve tribes of Israel. However, there is much confusion about the actual names and biographies of the Twelve. Thank God for John Meier, who presents everything there is to know about the Twelve in *Marginal Jew,* vol. 3, 198–285. That the Twelve were unique and set apart from the rest of the disciples is clear: "And when it was day, he called his disciples to him and from them he chose twelve whom he named apostles" (Luke 6:13). Some scholars insist that the Twelve was a creation of the early church, but that is unlikely. Otherwise, why make Judas one of the Twelve? See Craig Evans, "The Twelve Thrones of Israel: Scripture and Politics in Luke 22:24–30," in *Luke and Scripture: The Function of Sacred Tradition in Luke-Acts,* ed. Craig Evans and J. A. Sanders (Minneapolis: Fortress Press, 1993), 154–70; Jacob Jervell, "The Twelve on Israel's Thrones: Luke's Understanding of the Apostolate," in *Luke and the People of God: A New Look at Luke-Acts,* ed. Jacob Jervell (Minneapolis: Augsburg Publishing House, 1972), 75–112; and R. P. Meyer, *Jesus and the Twelve* (Grand Rapids, Mich.: Eerdmans, 1968).

For more on Jesus's anticlerical message, see John Meier, *Marginal Jew,* vol. 1, 346–47. Meier notes that by the time the gospels were written there were no more priests in Judaism. After the destruction of the Temple, the spiritual heirs of the Pharisees—the rabbinate—became the primary Jewish opponents of the new Christian movement, and so it is natural that the gospels would have made them appear as Jesus's chief enemies. This is all the more reason why the few hostile encounters that Jesus is presented as having with the Temple priests should be seen as genuine. Helmut Merkel expands on the division between Jesus and the Temple priesthood in "The Opposition Between Jesus and Judaism," *Jesus and the Politics of His Day,* 129–44. Interestingly, Jesus is seen in conversation with the Sadducees only once, during a debate around the resurrection on the last day; Mark 12:18–27.

CHAPTER NINE: BY THE FINGER OF GOD

A comprehensive treatment of Jesus's individual miracles can be found in H. van der Loos, *The Miracles of Jesus* (Leiden, Netherlands: Brill, 1965).

For more on Honi and Hanina ben Dosa, see Geza Vermes, "Hanina ben Dosa: A Controversial Galilean Saint from the First Century of the Christian Era," *Journal of Jewish Studies* 23 (1972): 28–50, and *Jesus the Jew* (Minneapolis: Fortress Press, 1981), 72–78. For a more general study of miracle workers in the time of Jesus, see William Scott Green, "Palestinian Holy Men: Charismatic Leadership and Rabbinic Tradition," *ANRW* 19.2 (1979): 619–47. A very good critique of scholarly work on Hanina can be found in Baruch M. Bokser, "Wonder-Working and the Rabbinic Tradition: The Case of Hanina ben Dosa," *Journal of Jewish Studies* 16 (1985): 42–92.

The earliest work on Apollonius is the third-century text by Philostratus of Athens titled *The Life of Apollonius of Tyana.* For an English translation, see F. C. Conybeare, ed., *Philostratus: The Life of Apollonius of Tyana* (London: Heinemann, 1912). Conybeare's book also includes a translation of a later work on Apollonius by Hierocles titled *Lover of Truth,* which expressly compares Apollonius to Jesus of Nazareth. See also Robert J. Penella, *The Letters of Apollonius of*

Tyana (Leiden, Netherlands: Brill, 1979). For an analysis of the parallels between Apollonius and Jesus, see Craig A. Evans, "Jesus and Apollonius of Tyana," in *Jesus and His Contemporaries,* 245–50.

Research done by Harold Remus indicates no difference in the way pagans and early Christians described either miracles or the miracle workers; "Does Terminology Distinguish Early Christian from Pagan Miracles?" *Journal of Biblical Literature* 101.4 (1982): 531–51; see also Meier, *Marginal Jew,* vol. 2, 536. More on Eleazar the exorcist can be found in Josephus, *Antiquities* 8.46–48.

A survey of magic and the laws against it in the Second Temple period is provided by Gideon Bohak, *Ancient Jewish Magic: A History* (London: Cambridge University Press, 2008). As in the fable of Rumpelstiltskin, there was a general belief that knowledge of another's name establishes a certain power over him. Magical prayers quite often derived their power from the name of whoever was being cursed or blessed. Per Bultmann: "The idea . . . that to know the name of the demon gives power over it is a well-known and widespread motif." See *History of the Synoptic Tradition,* 232. Ulrich Luz cites as a Hellenistic example the story of Chonsu, "the God who drives out demons," as an instance of demon recognition; "The Secrecy Motif and the Marcan Christology," *The Messianic Secret,* ed. Christopher Tuckett (Philadelphia: Fortress Press, 1983), 75–96.

Joseph Baumgarten discusses the relationship between illness and demon possession and provides a host of references to other articles on the topic in "The 4Q Zadokite Fragments on Skin Disease," *Journal of Jewish Studies* 41 (1990): 153–65.

Additional useful studies on magic in the ancient world are Matthew W. Dickie, *Magic and Magicians in the Greco-Roman World* (London: Routledge, 2001); Naomi Janowitz, *Magic in the Roman World* (London: Routledge, 2001); and Ann Jeffers, *Magic and Divination in Ancient Palestine and Syria* (Leiden, Netherlands: Brill, 1996). The word "magic" comes from the Greek term *mageia,* which has its roots in the Persian term for priest, *magos.* As in "the Magi."

Contrary to popular perception, Jesus's miracles were not meant to confirm his messianic identity. In all the biblical prophecies ever written about the messiah, there is no characterization of him as either a miracle worker or an exorcist; the messiah is king, his task is to restore Israel to glory and destroy its enemies, not heal the sick and cast out demons (indeed, there are no such things as demons in the Hebrew Bible).

Justin Martyr, Origen, and Irenaeus are quoted in Anton Fridrichsen, *The Problem of Miracle in Primitive Christianity* (Minneapolis: Augsburg Publishing House, 1972), 87–95. Perhaps the most famous argument made about Jesus as a magician is Morton Smith's controversial thesis, *Jesus the Magician* (New York: Harper and Row, 1978). Smith's argument is actually quite simple: Jesus's miraculous actions in the gospels bear a striking resemblance to what we see in the "magical texts" of the time, which indicates that Jesus may have been seen by his fellow Jews and by the Romans as just another magician. Other scholars, most notably John Dominic Crossan, agree with Morton's analysis. See Crossan, *Historical Jesus,* 137–67. Smith's argument is sound and it does not deserve the opprobrium it has received in some scholarly circles, though my objections to it are clear in the text. For parallels between the miracle stories in the gospels and those in rabbinic writings, see Craig A. Evans, "Jesus and Jewish Miracle Stories," in *Jesus and His Contemporaries,* 213–43.

Regarding the law for cleansing lepers, it should be noted that the Torah allows for those who are poor to substitute two turtledoves or two pigeons for two of the lambs (Leviticus 14:21–22).

CHAPTER TEN: MAY YOUR KINGDOM COME

For a clear and concise treatment of the notion of the Kingdom of God in the New Testament, see Joachim Jeremias, *New Testament Theology: The Proclamation of Jesus* (New York: Charles Scribner's Sons, 1971). Jeremias calls the Kingdom of God the "central theme of the public proclamation of Jesus." See also Norman Perrin, *The Kingdom of God in the Teaching of Jesus* (Philadelphia: Westminster Press, 1963) and *Rediscovering the Teachings of Jesus* (New York: Harper and Row, 1967). Perrin refers to the Kingdom of God as being the very heart of the message of Jesus: "all else in his teaching takes its point of departure from this central, awe-inspiring—or ridicule-inspiring, according to one's perspective— conviction."

According to John Meier, "outside of the Synoptic Gospels and the mouth of Jesus, [the term Kingdom of God] does not seem to have been widely used by either Jews or Christians in the early 1st century A.D."; *Marginal Jew,* vol. 2, 239. The Hebrew Bible never uses the phrase the "Kingdom of God," but it does use "Kingdom of Yahweh" in 1 Chronicles 28:5, wherein David speaks of Solomon sitting on the throne of the Kingdom of Yahweh. I think it is safe to say that this phrase means the same thing as Kingdom of God. That said, the exact phrase "Kingdom of God" is found only in the apocryphal text *The Wisdom of Solomon* (10:10). Examples of God's kingship and his right to rule are, of course, everywhere in the Hebrew Bible. For example, "God will reign as king forever and ever" (Exodus 15:18). Perrin thinks the impetus for the use of the word "kingdom" in the Lord's Prayer can be seen in an Aramaic Kaddish prayer found in an ancient synagogue in Israel, which he claims was in use during Jesus's lifetime. The prayer states: "Magnified and sanctified be his great name in the world which he has created according to his will. May he establish his kingdom in your lifetime and in your days and in the lifetime of all the house of Israel even speedily and at a near time." See *Kingdom of God in the Teaching of Jesus,* 19.

Like many other scholars, Perrin is convinced that Jesus uses the term "Kingdom of God" in an eschatological sense. But Richard Horsley notes that while God's actions with regard to the Kingdom may be thought of as "final," that does not necessarily imply an eschatological event. "The symbols surrounding the Kingdom of God do not refer to 'the last,' 'final,' 'eschatological,' and 'all-transforming' 'act' of God," Horsley writes. "If the original kernel of any of the sayings about 'the son of man coming with the clouds of heaven' . . . stem from Jesus, then, like the image in Daniel 7:13 to which they refer, they are symbolizations of the vindication of the persecuted and suffering righteous." Horsley's point is that the Kingdom of God may be properly understood in eschatological terms but only insofar as that implies God's final and definitive activity on earth. He correctly observes that once we abandon the notion that Jesus's preaching about the Kingdom of God refers to an End Times, we can also abandon the historic debate about whether Jesus thought of the Kingdom as a present or as a future thing. See *Jesus and the Spiral of Violence: Popular Jewish Resistance in Roman Palestine* (Minneapolis: Fortress Press, 1993), 168–69. Nevertheless, for those interested in the "present or future" debate, John Meier, who himself believes the Kingdom of God was meant as an eschatological event, lays out the argument on both sides in *Marginal Jew,* vol. 2, 289–351. Among those who disagree with Meier are John Dominic Crossan, *Jesus: A Revolutionary Biography*, 54–74; Marcus J. Borg, *Jesus: A New Vision* (New York: HarperCollins, 1991), 1–21; and, of course, me. In the words of Werner Kelber, "the Kingdom spells the ending of an older order of things." See *The Kingdom in Mark* (Philadelphia: Fortress Press, 1974), 23.

For more on the "Jewishness" of Jesus of Nazareth, see Amy-Jill Levine, *The Misunderstood Jew* (New York: HarperOne, 2006). Jesus's statements against gentiles can be pretty firmly accepted as historical, considering that the early Christians were actively courting gentiles for conversion and would not have been well served in their efforts by such verses in the gospels. It is true that Jesus believed that gentiles would ultimately be allowed into the Kingdom of God once it was established. But as John Meier notes, Jesus seemed to have considered this to be the case only at the end of Israel's history, when the gentiles would be allowed entry into the kingdom as subservient to the Jews. *Marginal Jew*, vol. 3, 251.

I agree with Richard Horsley that the commandments to "love your enemies" and "turn the other cheek" in the gospel of Luke are likely closer to the original Q material than the parallel statements in Matthew, which juxtapose Jesus's commandments with the Hebrew Bible's command for "an eye for an eye" (*lex talionis*). See *Jesus and the Spiral of Violence,* 255–65.

Regarding Matthew 11:12, I have included here the variant version of the verse—"the Kingdom of Heaven has been coming violently"—both because I am convinced it is the original form of the verse and because it fits better with the context of the passage. The standard version of the passage reads:"From the days of John the Baptist until now the Kingdom of Heaven operates by force, and forceful men snatch it away."That is the translation by Rudolf Otto in *The Kingdom of God and the Son of Man,* 78. Note that this version of the verse is more often imprecisely translated as "From the days of John the Baptist until now the Kingdom of Heaven *suffers violence,* and *violent men* snatch it away," though even those translations will include a variant reading to indicate the active voice that I use in my translation. The problem lies in the verb *biazomai,* which means "to use violence or force." In the present perfect tense, *biazomai* can mean "to have violence done to one," but it is not the perfect tense that is operative in this passage. Similarly, in the passive voice *biazomai* can mean "to suffer violence," but again, it is not the passive voice that is used in Matthew 11:12. According to the UBS Lexicon, the word *biazomai* in this passage is actually in the Greek middle voice and thus means "to exercise violence." A clue to how to translate the passage in Matthew 11:12 can be found in the parallel passage in Luke 16:16. Luke, perhaps wanting to avoid the controversy, omits altogether the first half of the verse—"the Kingdom of God operates through force/ violence." However, in the latter half of the verse he uses the exact same word, *biazetai,* actively in the phrase "everyone uses violence in entering it." Ultimately the usual translation, "the kingdom of heaven suffers violence," agrees neither with the time when Jesus spoke the words nor with the context in which he lived. And context is everything. See *Analytic Greek New Testament* (Grand Rapids, Mich.: Baker Book House, 1981). Also see note on Matthew 11:12 in *Thayer's Greek-English Lexicon of the New Testament* (Ann Arbor: University of Michigan Press, 1996) and *Greek-English Lexicon of the New Testament,* ed. Johannes P. Louw and Eugene A. Nida (Grand Rapids, Mich.: United Bible Societies, 1988). Louw and Nida correctly note that "in many languages it may be difficult, if not impossible, to speak of the kingdom of heaven 'suffering violent attacks,'" though they do concede that "some active form may be employed, for example, 'and violently attack the kingdom of heaven' or '. . . the rule of God.'"

CHAPTER ELEVEN: WHO DO YOU SAY I AM?

On the expectation among the Jews in first-century Palestine for Elijah's return and the inauguration of the messianic age, see John J. Collins, *Apocalypticism in the Dead Sea Scrolls* (London: Routledge, 1997). On Jesus's deliberate imitation of Elijah, see John Meier, *Marginal Jew,* vol. 3, 622–26.

Unlike Matthew and Luke, who report a change in the physical appearance of Jesus in the transfiguration (Matthew 17:2; Luke 9:29), Mark claims that Jesus was transfigured in a way that only affected his clothes (9:3). The parallels to

Exodus in the transfiguration account are clear: Moses takes Aaron, Nadab, and Abihu to Mount Sinai, where he is engulfed by a cloud and given the Law and the design for building God's tabernacle. Like Jesus, Moses is transformed on the mountain in the presence of God. But there is a great difference between the two stories. Moses received the Law from God himself, whereas Jesus only sees Moses and Elijah while physically receiving nothing. The difference between the two stories serves to highlight Jesus's superiority over Moses. Moses is transformed because of his confrontation with God's glory, but Jesus is transformed by his own glory. The point is driven home for Morton Smith by the fact that Moses and Elijah, the Law and the Prophets, appear as Jesus's subordinates. See "The Origin and History of the Transfiguration Story," *Union Seminary Quarterly Review* 36 (1980): 42. Elijah, too, went up a mountain and experienced the spirit of God passing over him. "The Lord said, 'Go out and stand on the mountain in the presence of the Lord, for the Lord is about to pass by.' Then a great and powerful wind tore the mountains apart and shattered the rocks before the Lord, but the Lord was not in the wind. After the wind there was an earthquake, but the Lord was not in the earthquake. After the earthquake came a fire, but the Lord was not in the fire. And after the fire came a gentle whisper" (1 Kings 19:11–12). It should be noted that Smith thinks the transfiguration story to be "from the world of magic." His thesis deals with his concept of Jesus as a magician "like other magicians." Smith, therefore, believes the transfiguration to be some hypnotically induced mystical event that required silence; consequently, the spell was broken when Peter spoke. Mark's attempt to use this story as a confirmation of Jesus's messiahship is, for Smith, an error on the part of the evangelist. All of this demonstrates Mark's notion that Jesus surpasses both characters in glory. This is of course not a new notion in New Testament Christology. Paul explicitly states Jesus's superiority over Moses (Romans 5:14; 1 Corinthians 10:2), as does the writer of Hebrews (3:1–6). In other words, Mark is simply stating a familiar belief of the early Church that Jesus is the new Moses promised in Deuteronomy 18:15. See also Morna D. Hooker, "'What Doest Thou Here, Elijah?' A Look at St. Mark's Account of the Transfiguration," *The Glory of Christ in the New Testament,* ed. L. D. Hurst et al. (Oxford: Clarendon Press, 1987), 59–70. Hooker sees great significance in the fact that Mark's gospel presents Elijah first, stating that Moses was with him.

The term "messianic secret" is a translation of the German word *Messiasgeheimnis* and is derived from William Wrede's classic study, *The Messianic Secret,* trans. J.C.G. Greig (London: Cambridge University Press, 1971). Theories about the messianic secret can be divided into two schools of thought: those who believe the secret can be derived from the historical Jesus and those who consider it a creation of either the evangelist or the early Markan community. Wrede argued that the messianic secret is a product of the Markan community and a redaction element of the gospel itself. He claimed that the messianic secret stems from an attempt by Mark to reconcile a primitive Christian belief in first-century Jerusalem that regarded Jesus as becoming messiah only after the resurrection, with the view that Jesus was messiah throughout his life and ministry. The problem with Wrede's theory is that there is nothing in Mark 16:1–8 (the original ending of the gospel of Mark) to suggest a transformation in the identity of Jesus other than his inexplicable disappearance from the tomb. In any case, it is difficult to explain how the resurrection, an idea that was alien to messianic expectations in first-century Palestine, could have raised the belief that Jesus was messiah. The point of Wrede's study was to use the "messianic secret" to show that, in his words, "Jesus actually did not give himself out as messiah" in his lifetime, an intriguing and probably correct hypothesis. Those who disagree with Wrede and argue that the messianic secret can actually be traced to the historical Jesus include Oscar Cullman, *Christology of the New Testament* (Philadelphia: Westminster Press, 1963), 111–36, and James D. G. Dunn, "The Messianic Secret in Mark," *The Messianic Secret,* ed. Christopher Tuckett (Philadelphia: Fortress Press, 1983), 116–36. For more general information about the messianic secret, see James L. Blevins, *The Messianic Secret in Markan Research, 1901–1976* (Washington, D.C.: University Press of America, 1981), and Heikki Raisanen, *The "Messianic Secret" in Mark* (Edinburgh: T&T Clark, 1990). Raisanen correctly argues that many of the theories offered for the "messianic secret" generally presume the notion that "the theological viewpoint of Mark's gospel is based on a *single* secrecy theology." He believes, and most contemporary scholars agree, that the "messianic secret" can be understood only when the secrecy concept is "broken down . . . into parts which are only relatively loosely connected with each other"; Raisanen, *Messianic Secret,* 242–43.

For a brief précis on the many messianic paradigms that existed in first-century Palestine, see Craig Evans, "From Anointed Prophet to Anointed King: Probing Aspects of Jesus' Self-Understanding," *Jesus and His Contemporaries,* 437–56.

Although many contemporary scholars would agree with me that the use of the title Son of Man can be traced to the historical Jesus, there remains a great deal of debate over how many, and which, of the Son of Man sayings are authentic. Mark indicates three primary functions of Jesus's interpretation of this obscure title. First, it is used in the descriptions of a future figure that comes in judgment (Mark 8:38, 13:26, 14:62). Second, it is used when speaking of Jesus's expected suffering and death (Mark 8:31, 9:12, 10:33). And finally, there are a number of passages in which the Son of Man is presented as an earthly ruler with the authority to forgive sins (Mark 2:10, 2:28). Of these three, perhaps the second is most influential in Mark. Some scholars, including Hermann Samuel Reimarus, *The Goal of Jesus and His Disciples* (Leiden, Netherlands: Brill, 1970), accept the historicity only of the noneschatological, so-called lowly sayings. Others, including Barnabas Lindars, *Jesus Son of Man* (London: SPCK Publishing, 1983), accept as authentic only those among the "sayings traditions" (Q and Mark) that reproduce the underlying *bar enasha* idiom (there are nine of them) as a mode of self-reference. Still others believe only the apocalyptic sayings to be authentic: "The authentic passages are those in which the expression is used in that apocalyptic sense which goes back to Daniel," writes Albert Schweitzer, *The Quest of the Historical Jesus* (New York: Macmillan, 1906), 283. And of course there are those scholars who reject nearly all of the Son of Man sayings as inauthentic. Indeed, that was more or less the conclusion of the famed "Jesus Seminar" conducted by Robert W. Funk and Roy W. Hoover, *The Five Gospels: The Search for the Authentic Words of Jesus* (New York: Polebridge Press, 1993). A comprehensive analysis of the centuries-long debate about the Son of Man is provided by Delbert Burkett in his indispensable monograph *The Son of Man Debate* (New York: Cambridge University Press, 1999). An interesting comment by Burkett is that the Gnostics apparently understood "son" literally, believing that Jesus was stating his filial relation to the gnostic "aeon" or god Anthropos, or "Man."

Geza Vermes demonstrates that *bar enasha* is never a title in any Aramaic sources; "The Son of Man Debate," *Journal for the Study of the New Testament* 1 (1978): 19–32. It should be mentioned that Vermes is among a handful of scholars who believe that "Son of Man" in its Aramaic expression is just a circumlocution for "I"—an indirect and deferential way to refer to oneself, as in when Jesus says, "Foxes have holes and birds of the air have nests but the Son of Man has [that is, *I have*] no place to lay his [*my*] head" (Matthew 8:20 | Luke 9:58). See also P. Maurice Casey, *Son of Man: The Interpretation and Influence of Daniel 7* (London: SPCK Publishing, 1979). But as Burkett notes, the basic problem with the circumlocution theory is that "the idiom requires a demonstrative pronoun ('*this* man') which the gospel expression lacks." *The Son of Man Debate,* 96. Others take the opposite tack, claiming that "Son of Man" does not refer to Jesus at all but to some other figure, someone Jesus expected would follow him. "When the Son of Man comes in his glory, and the holy angels with him, he shall sit upon the throne of his glory" (Matthew 25:31). Prominent proponents of the theory that Jesus was referring to someone else as the Son of Man include Julius Wellhausen and Rudolf Bultmann. However, that, too, is unlikely; the context of most of Jesus's Son of Man sayings makes it clear that he is speaking about himself, as when he compares himself to John the Baptist: "John came neither eating nor drinking and they say, 'He has a demon.' The Son of Man [i.e., *I*] came eating and drinking and they say 'Look! A glutton and drunk'" (Matthew 11:18–19 | Luke 7:33–34). Among those who believe that "the Son of Man" is an Aramaic idiomatic expression meaning either "a man" in general, or more specifically "a man like me," are Barnabas Lindars, *Jesus Son of Man,* and Reginald Fuller, "The Son of Man: A Reconsideration," *The Living Texts: Essays in Honor of Ernest W. Saunders,* ed. Dennis E. Groh and Robert Jewett (Lanham, Md.: University Press of America, 1985), 207–17. These scholars note that God addresses the prophet Ezekiel as *ben adam,* meaning a human being but perhaps implying an ideal human. For the lack of unified conception among the Jews of the Son of Man, see Norman Perrin, "Son of Man," *Interpreter's Dictionary of the Bible* (Nashville: Abingdon, 1976), 833–36, and Adela Yarbro Collins, "The Influence of Daniel on the New Testament," *Daniel,* ed. John J. Collins (Minneapolis: Fortress Press, 1993), 90–123.

Although the "one like a son of man" is never identified as the messiah, it seems that the Jewish scholars and rabbis of the first century understood him as such. Whether Jesus also understood Daniel's "one like a son of man" to be a messianic figure is unclear. Not all scholars believe that Daniel is referring to a distinct personality or a specific individual when he uses the phrase "son of man." He may be using the term as a symbol for Israel as victorious over its enemies. The same is true of Ezekiel, where "son of man" may be not a distinct individual named Ezekiel but a symbolic representative of the ideal man. In fact, Maurice Casey thinks even the "son of man" in *Enoch* is not a distinct individual but simply a generic "man"; see "The Use of the Term 'Son of Man' in the Similitudes of Enoch," *Journal for the Study of Judaism* 7.1 (1976): 11–29. I do not disagree with this position, but I do think there is a significant difference between the way the generic term is used in, say, Jeremiah 51:43—"Her cities have become an object of horror, and a land of drought and a desert, a land in which no man lives, nor any son of man [*ben adam*] passes"—and the way it is used in Daniel 7:13 to refer to a singular figure.

Both Enoch and 4 Ezra explicitly identify the son of man figure with the messiah, but in 4 Ezra he is also called "my son" by God: "For my son the messiah shall be revealed with those who are with him, and those who remain shall rejoice four hundred years. And after these years my son the Messiah shall die, and all who draw human breath" (4 Ezra 7:28–29). There's no question that 4 Ezra was written at the end of the first century, or perhaps the beginning of the second century C.E. However there has long been a debate over the dating of the *Similitudes.* Because no copies of the *Similitudes* were found among the many copies of Enoch found at Qumran, most scholars are convinced that it was not written until well after the destruction of the Temple in 70 C.E. See Matthew Black, *The Book of Enoch or 1 Enoch: A New English Edition with Commentary and Textual Notes* (Leiden, Netherlands: Brill, 1985). See also David Suter, "Weighed in the Balance: The Similitudes of Enoch in Recent Discussion," *Religious Studies Review* 7 (1981): 217–21, and J. C. Hindly, "Towards a Date for the Similitudes of Enoch: A Historical Approach," *New Testament Studies* 14 (1967–68): 551–65.

Hindly offers a date between 115 and 135 C.E. for the *Similitudes*, which is a bit late, in my opinion. For better or worse, the best date we can give for the *Similitudes* is sometime after the destruction of Jerusalem in 70 C.E., but before the composition of the gospel of Matthew in around 90 C.E.

On the parallels between the Enoch Son of Man and the gospel Son of Man in the material that is unique to Matthew, see Burkett, *The Son of Man Debate*, 78; see also John J. Collins, "The Heavenly Representative: The 'Son of Man' in the Similitudes of Enoch," in *Ideal Figures in Ancient Judaism: Profiles and Paradigms*, ed. John J. Collins and George Nickelsburg (Chico, Calif.: Scholars Press, 1980), 111–33. On the Son of Man as a preexistent heavenly being in the fourth gospel, see Delbert Burkett, *The Son of the Man in the Gospel of John* (Sheffield, U.K.: Sheffield Academic Press, 1991) and R. G. Hamerton-Kelly, *Pre-Existence, Wisdom, and the Son of Man* (Cambridge: Cambridge University Press, 1973). It should be noted that neither in the *Similitudes* nor in 4 Ezra is "Son of Man" used as a title, certainly not the way Jesus uses it.

Jesus standing before Caiaphas quotes not only Daniel 7:13 but also Psalms 110:1 ("The Lord says to my lord, 'Sit at my right hand until I make your enemies your footstool'"). The integration of Daniel 7:13 and Psalms 110:1 in Jesus's reply to the high priest may at first seem somewhat disjointed. But according to T. F. Glasson, Jesus is making a natural connection. Glasson notes that in Daniel, the coming of the Son of Man "with the clouds of heaven" symbolizes the establishment of the Kingdom of God on earth. Thus, once Jesus is exalted to the right hand of God, the kingdom he preached in 1:15 will emerge as the "new community of the saints." According to Glasson, the reference to the Psalms demonstrates Jesus's personal exaltation, while the reference to Daniel indicates the inauguration of the kingdom on earth—an event that must begin with his death and resurrection. This idea is quite in league with Jesus's threefold interpretation of the Son of Man. In other words, Glasson believes that this is the moment when the two titles, messiah and Son of Man, come together for Jesus. See Thomas Francis Glasson, "Reply to Caiaphas (Mark 14:62)," *New Testament Studies* 7 (1960): 88–93. Mary Ann L. Beavis notes the parallels between the story of Jesus before Caiaphas and the previous confession made by Peter. Both scenes begin with a question of Jesus's identity (8:27, 14:60), and both end with a Son of Man discourse. Furthermore, in both instances Jesus's reinterpretation of the messianic title is met with a resounding condemnation (8:32–33, 14:63–65); see Mary Ann L. Beavis, "The Trial Before the Sanhedrin (Mark 14:53–65): Reader Response and Greco-Roman Readers," *Catholic Biblical Quarterly* 49 (1987): 581–96.

CHAPTER TWELVE: NO KING BUT CAESAR

As tempting as it may be to dismiss the betrayal of Judas Iscariot as nothing more than a narrative embellishment, the fact is that it is a detail attested to by all four gospel writers, though each presents a different reasoning for his betrayal.

Mark and Matthew make it clear that "the crowd" had been expressly sent by the Sanhedrin, and Luke adds the presence of the Temple captains to the arresting party to make the point clearer. Only the gospel of John indicates the presence of Roman troops in the arresting party. That is highly unlikely, as no Roman soldier would seize a criminal and deliver him to the Sanhedrin unless he was ordered to do so by his prefect, and there is no reason to think that Pilate became involved in Jesus's situation until Jesus was brought before him. Although Mark seems to suggest that the one wielding the sword was not a disciple but "a certain one of those standing by" (Mark 14:47), the rest of the gospels make it clear that this was indeed a disciple who cut off the servant's ear. In fact, John identifies the sword-wielding disciple as Simon Peter (John 18:8–11). Luke's discomfort with a Jesus who seems to resist arrest is ameliorated by his insistence that Jesus stopped the melee and healed the poor servant's ear before allowing himself to be taken away (Luke 22:49–53). That said, it is Luke who specifically claims that the disciples were commanded by Jesus to bring *two* swords to Gethsemane (Luke 22:35–38).

On Eusebius, see Pamphili Eusebius, *Ecclesiastical History* III.3, quoted in George R. Edwards, *Jesus and the Politics of Violence* (New York: Harper and Row, 1972), 31. Eusebius's account has been challenged by some contemporary scholars including L. Michael White, *From Jesus to Christianity* (New York: HarperOne, 2004), 230.

Raymond Brown outlines the argument for a set of pregospel passion narratives in his encyclopedic two-volume work *The Death of the Messiah* (New York: Doubleday, 1994), 53–93. Contra Brown is the so-called Perrin School, which rejects the notion of a pre-Markan passion narrative and claims that the narrative of the trial and crucifixion was shaped by Mark and adapted by all the canonized gospels, including John. See *The Passion in Mark: Studies on Mark 14-16,* ed. W. H. Kelber (Philadelphia: Fortress Press, 1976).

For the use of crucifixion among the Jews, see Ernst Bammel, "Crucifixion as a Punishment in Palestine," *The Trial of Jesus,* ed. Ernst Bammel (Naperville, Ill.: Alec R. Allenson, 1970), 162–65. Josef Blinzler notes that by Roman times there was some sense of uniformity in the process of crucifixion, especially when it came to the nailing of the hands and feet to a crossbeam. There was usually a flogging beforehand, and at least among the Romans it was expected that the criminal would carry his own cross to the site of the crucifixion. See Blinzler, *The Trial of Jesus* (Westminster, Md.: Newman Press, 1959).

Josephus notes that the Jews who tried to escape Jerusalem as it was besieged by Titus were first executed, then crucified; *The Jewish War* 5.449–51. Martin Hengel writes that although crucifixion was a punishment reserved for non-Roman citizens, there were instances of Roman citizens being crucified. But these were deliberately done in response to crimes that were deemed treasonous. In other words, by giving the citizen a "slave's punishment," the message was that the crime was so severe that it forfeited the criminal's Roman citizenship. See Hengel, *Crucifixion in the Ancient World and the Folly of the Message of the Cross* (Philadelphia: Fortress Press, 1977), 39–45. Cicero's quote is from Hengel, 37. See also J. W. Hewitt, "The Use of Nails in the Crucifixion," *Harvard Theological Review* 25 (1932): 29–45.

Regarding Jesus's trial before Caiaphas in the gospels, Matthew and Mark claim that Jesus was brought to the courtyard (*aule*) of the high priest and not to the Sanhedrin. Unlike Mark, Matthew specifically names the high priest Caiaphas. John claims that Jesus was first taken to the previous high priest, Ananus, before being transferred to Ananus's son-in-law and the present high priest, Caiaphas. It is interesting to note that Mark treats as false the claim that Jesus will bring down the Temple and build another without human hands. As Matthew, Luke-Acts, and John make clear, that is precisely what Jesus threatened to do (Matthew 26:59–61; Acts 6:13–14; John 2:19). In fact, a version of that very statement can be found in the Gospel of Thomas: "I shall destroy this house, and no one will be able to rebuild it." Even Mark puts Jesus's threat into the mouths of the passersby who mock him on the cross. If the statement were false, as Mark contends, where would the passersby have heard it? From the closed night session of the Sanhedrin? Unlikely. Indeed, such a statement seems to have been part of the post–70 C.E. Christological foundation of the Church, which considered the Christian community to be the "temple made not with human hands." There can be no doubt that whatever Jesus's actual words may have been, he had in fact threatened the Temple in some way. Mark himself attests to this: "Do you see these buildings? Not one stone will be left upon another; all will be thrown down" (Mark 13:2). For more on Jesus's threats to the Temple, see Richard Horsley, *Jesus and the Spiral of Violence,* 292–96. With all this in mind, Mark's apologetic overlay in the trial before the Sanhedrin comes across as a ridiculously contrived attempt to show the injustice of those who made accusations against Jesus, regardless of whether those accusations were true, which in this case they most certainly were.

Raymond Brown lists twenty-seven discrepancies between the trial of Jesus before the Sanhedrin and later rabbinic procedure; *Death of the Messiah,* 358–59. D. R. Catchpole examines the argument against the historicity of the trial in "The Historicity of the Sanhedrin Trial," *Trial of Jesus,* 47–65. That nocturnal trials were, at the very least, unusual is demonstrated by Acts 4:3–5, in which Peter and John are arrested at night but must wait until daylight to be judged before the Sanhedrin. Luke, who wrote that passage in Acts, tries to fix his fellow evangelists' blunder by arguing for two Sanhedrin meetings: one on the night Jesus was arrested and another "when day came." In Acts 12:1–4, Peter is arrested during Passover but not brought before the people for judgment until after the feast is over, though Solomon Zeitlin takes exception to the idea that the Sanhedrin could not meet on the eve of the Sabbath; Zeitlin, *Who Crucified Jesus?* (New York: Bloch, 1964). One could argue here for John's sequence of events, wherein the Sanhedrin met days before arresting Jesus, but considering that in John, Jesus's triumphal entry into Jerusalem and his cleansing of the Temple, which all scholars agree was the impetus for his arrest, were among the first acts of his ministry, John's logic falls apart.

On the argument about whether the Jews had the right under Roman occupation to put criminals to death, see Raymond Brown, *Death of the Messiah,* vol. 1, 331–48. Catchpole's conclusion on this issue is, in my opinion, the correct one: "The Jews could try [a death penalty case], but they could not execute." See "The Historicity of the Sanhedrin trial," *The Trial of Jesus,* 63. G.W.H. Lampe suggests that an official record of Jesus's "trial" before Pilate could have been preserved, considering the preservation of similar *acta* of Christian martyrs. Apparently several Christian writers mention an *Acta Pilati* existing in the second and third centuries. But even if that were true (and it very likely is not), there is no reason to believe that such a document would represent anything other than a Christological polemic. See G.W.H. Lampe, "The Trial of Jesus in the *Acta Pilati,*" *Jesus and the Politics of His Day,* 173–82.

Plutarch writes that "every wrongdoer who goes to execution carries his own cross."

PART III PROLOGUE: GOD MADE FLESH

The evidence that Stephen was a Diaspora Jew comes from the fact that he is designated as the leader of the Seven, the "Hellenists" who fell into conflict with the "Hebrews," as recounted in Acts 6 (see below for more on the Hellenists). Stephen's stoners were freedmen, themselves Hellenists, but recent émigrés to Jerusalem theologically aligned with the Jewish leadership in Jerusalem. See Marie-Éloise Rosenblatt, *Paul the Accused* (Collegeville, Minn.: Liturgical Press, 1995), 24.

The earliest sources we have for belief in the resurrection of the dead can be found in the Ugaritic and Iranian traditions. Zoroastrian scriptures, primarily the Gathas, present the earliest and perhaps most well-developed concept of the resurrection of the individual when it speaks of the dead "rising in their bodies" at the end of time (Yasna 54). Egyptians believed that the Pharaoh would be resurrected, but they did not accept the resurrection of the masses.

Stanley Porter finds examples of bodily resurrection in Greek and Roman religions but claims there is little evidence of the notion of physical resurrection of the dead in Jewish thought. See Stanley E. Porter, Michael A. Hayes, and David Tombs, *Resurrection* (Sheffield, U.K.: Sheffield Academic Press, 1999). Jon Douglas Levenson disagrees with Porter, arguing that belief in the resurrection of the body is rooted in the Hebrew Bible and is not, as some have argued, merely part of the Second Temple period or the apocalyptic literature written after 70 C.E.; *Resurrection and the Restoration of Israel* (New Haven: Yale University Press, 2006). Levenson argues that after the destruction of Jerusalem there was a growing belief among the rabbinate that the redemption of Israel required the flesh-and-blood resurrection of the dead. But even he admits that the vast majority of the resurrection traditions found in Judaism are not about individual exaltation but about national restoration. In other words, this is about a metaphorical resurrection of the Jewish people as a whole, not the literal resurrection of mortals who had died and come back again as flesh and blood. Indeed, Charlesworth notes that if by "resurrection" we mean "the concept of God's raising the body and soul after death (meant literally) to a new and eternal life (not a return to mortal existence)," then there is only one passage in the entire Hebrew Bible that fits such a criterion—Daniel 12:2–3: "Many of those who sleep in the dust of the earth shall awake, some to everlasting life, and some to shame and everlasting contempt." The many other passages that have been interpreted as referencing the resurrection of the dead simply do not pass scrutiny. For instance, Ezekiel 37—"Thus said the Lord God to these bones: I will cause breath to enter you and you shall live again . . ."—explicitly refers to these bones as "the House of Israel." Psalm 30, in which David writes, "I cried out to you and you healed me. O Lord, you brought me up from Sheol, preserved me from going down into the pit" (30:2–4), is very obviously about healing from illness, not literally being raised from death. The same holds true for the story of Elijah resurrecting the dead (1 Kings 17:17–24), or, for that matter, Jesus raising Lazarus (John 11:1–46), both of which fall into the category of healing stories, not resurrection stories, as the person "resurrected" will presumably die again. Charlesworth, however, does find evidence of belief in the resurrection of the dead into immortality in the Dead Sea Scrolls, especially in a scroll called *On Resurrection* (4Q521), which claims that God, through the messiah, will bring the dead to life. Interestingly, this seems to fit with Paul's belief that believers in the risen Christ will also be resurrected: "and the dead in Christ shall rise" (1 Thessalonians 4:15–17). See James H. Charlesworth et al., *Resurrection: The Origin and Future of a Biblical Doctrine* (London: T&T Clark, 2006). Those scrolls that seem to imply that the Righteous Teacher of Qumran will rise from the dead are speaking not about a literal resurrection of the body but about a metaphorical rising from disenfranchisement for a people who had been divorced from the Temple. There is something like a resurrection idea in the *pseudepigrapha*—for instance, in 1 Enoch 22–27, or in 2 Maccabees 14, in which Razis tears out his entrails and God puts them back again. Also, *The Testament of Judah* implies that Abraham, Isaac, and Jacob will rise to live again (25:1). With regard to ideas of the resurrection in the Mishnah, Charlesworth correctly notes that such passages are too late (post–second century C.E.) to be quoted as examples of Jewish beliefs prior to 70 C.E., though he admits it is conceivable that "the tradition in Mishnah Sanhedrin defined the beliefs of some pre-70 Pharisees."

Rudolf Bultmann finds evidence for the concept of the dying and rising son-deity in the so-called mystery religions of Rome. He states that "gnosticism above all is aware of the notion of the Son of God become man—and the heavenly redeemer man." See *Essays: Philosophical and Theological* (New York: Macmillan, 1995), 279. But I think Martin Hengel is right to note that the great wave of interest in "mystery religions" that arose in the Roman Empire, and the synthesis with Judaism and proto-Christianity that resulted, did not take place until the second century. In other words, it may have been Christianity that influenced the dying and rising deity concept in gnosticism and the mystery religions, not the other way around. See Martin Hengel, *The Son of God* (Eugene, Ore.: Wipf and Stock, 1976), 25–41.

Other important texts for the historical and cultural study of resurrection in the ancient world include Geza Vermes, *The Resurrection: History and Myth* (New York: Doubleday, 2008) and N. T. Wright, *The Resurrection of the Son of God* (Minneapolis: Fortress Press, 2003).

There can be no question whatsoever that Psalm 16 is self-referential, as the first person singular form is used from the beginning: "Preserve me, O God, for in thee I take refuge." The Hebrew word translated here as "godly one" is *chasid*. It seems obvious to me that David's reference to himself as "godly one" has more to do with his piety and devotion to God than it does with the deification of either David himself (which would have been unimaginable) or any future Davidic figure. Of course, Luke would have been using the Septuagint of Psalm 16:8–11, which translates the Hebrew *chasid* into the Greek *hosion*, meaning "holy one," which, given the context and meaning of the psalm, should be seen as synonymous with "godly one." It may be a huge stretch of the imagination to consider this psalm to be about the messiah, but it is ridiculous to interpret it as predicting Jesus's death and resurrection.

Stephen's lengthy defense in the book of Acts is obviously Luke's composition; it was written six decades after Stephen's death. But it bears scrutiny, nonetheless, as Luke was himself a Diaspora Jew—a Greek-speaking Syrian convert from the city of Antioch—and his perception of who Jesus was would have aligned with Stephen's.

Among the more egregious errors in Stephen's slipshod account of the biblical story: Stephen speaks of Abraham buying the tomb at Schechem for his grandson Jacob to be buried in, whereas the Bible says it was Jacob who bought the tomb at Schechem (Genesis 33:19), though he himself was buried with Abraham in Hebron (Genesis 50:13). Stephen contends that Moses saw the burning bush on Mount Sinai, when in fact it appeared to him on Mount Horeb, which, despite some arguments to the contrary, was not the same place as Sinai (Exodus 3:1). He then goes on to state that an angel gave the law to Moses, when it was God himself who gave Moses the law. It is possible, of course, that Luke has been influenced by the Jubilean tradition, which claims that Moses was given the law by the "Angel of the Presence." Jubilees 45.15–16 states, "and Israel blessed his sons before he died and told them everything that would befall them in the land of Egypt; and he made known to them what would come upon them in the last days, and blessed them and gave to Joseph two portions in the land. And he slept with his fathers, and he was buried in the double cave in the land of Canaan, near Abraham his father in the grave which he dug for himself in the double cave in the land of Hebron. And he gave all his books and the books of his fathers to Levi his son that he might preserve them and renew them for his children until this day." Interestingly, Jubilees also suggests that the Torah was written down by Moses, which is the oldest witness to the tradition of Mosaic authorship for the Torah.

For more on the significance of the phrase "the right hand of God," see entry in David Noel Freedman et al., *Eerdmans Dictionary of the Bible* (Cambridge: Eerdmans, 2000). Per Freedman, the signet ring was worn on the royal right hand (Jeremiah 22:24); the elder son received the greater blessing via the right hand (Genesis 48:14, 17); the position of honor was at one's right hand (Psalm 110:1); and the right hand of God performs acts of deliverance (Exodus 15:6), victory (Psalms 20:6), and might (Isaiah 62:8). Thomas Aquinas's remarks are from *Summa Theologica*, question 58.

CHAPTER THIRTEEN: IF CHRIST HAS NOT BEEN RISEN

There were, in actuality, two (though some say three) veils that divided the Holy of Holies from the rest of the Temple: an outer veil that hung at the entrance to the inner sanctuary, and an inner veil within the sanctuary itself that separated the *hekal,* or portal, from the smaller chamber within which the spirit of God dwelt. Which veil is meant by the gospels is irrelevant, since the story is legend, though it should be noted that only the outer veil would have been visible to anyone but the high priest. See Daniel Gurtner, *Torn Veil: Matthew's Exposition of the Death of Jesus* (Cambridge: Cambridge University Press, 2007).

Although the historical evidence and the New Testament both clearly demonstrate that the followers of Jesus remained in Jerusalem after his crucifixion, it is interesting to note that the gospel of Matthew has the risen Jesus telling the disciples to meet him back in Galilee (Matthew 28:7).

Oscar Cullman, *The State in the New Testament* (New York: Charles Scribner's Sons, 1956); *The Christology of the New Testament* (Philadelphia: Westminster Press, 1959); John Gager, *Kingdom and Community: The Social World of the Early Christians* (Englewood Cliffs, N.J.: Prentice Hall, 1975); and Martin Dibelius, *Studies in the Acts of the Apostles* (New York: Charles Scribner's Sons, 1956), have all demonstrated that the early followers of Jesus were unsuccessful in persuading other Jerusalemites to their movement. Gager notes correctly that, in general, "early converts did not represent the established sectors of Jewish society" (26). Dibelius suggests that the Jerusalem community wasn't even interested in missionizing outside Jerusalem but led a quiet life of piety and contemplation as they awaited Jesus's second coming.

Gager explains the success of the early Jesus movement, despite its many doctrinal contradictions, by relying on a fascinating sociological study by L. Festinger, H. W. Riecken, and S. Schachter titled *When Prophecy Fails: A Social and Psychological Study of a Modern Group That Predicted the Destruction of the World* (New York: Harper and Row, 1956), which, in Gager's words, demonstrates that "under certain conditions a religious community whose fundamental beliefs are disconfirmed by events in the world will not necessarily collapse and disband. Instead it may undertake zealous missionary activity as a response to its sense of cognitive dissonance, i.e., a condition of distress and doubt stemming from the disconfirmation of an important belief" (39). As Festinger himself puts it in his follow-up study, *A Theory of Cognitive Dissonance* (Stanford: Stanford University Press, 1957): "the presence of dissonance gives rise to pressures to reduce or eliminate the dissonance. The strength of the pressure to reduce the dissonance is a function of the magnitude of the dissonance" (18).

There is a great deal of debate about what exactly "Hellenist" meant. It could have meant that these were gentile converts to Christianity, as Walter Bauer argues in *Orthodoxy and Heresy in Earliest Christianity* (Mifflintown, Pa.: Sigler Press, 1971). H. J. Cadbury agrees with Bauer. He thinks the Hellenists were gentile Christians who may have come from Galilee or other gentile regions and who were not favorably disposed toward the Law. See "The Hellenists," *The Beginnings of Christianity*, vol. 1, ed. K. Lake and H. J. Cadbury (London: Macmillan, 1933), 59–74. However, the term "Hellenist" most likely refers to Greek-speaking Jews from the Diaspora, as Martin Hengel convincingly demonstrates in *Between Jesus and Paul* (Eugene, Ore.: Wipf and Stock, 1983). Marcel Simon agrees with Hengel, though he also believes (contra Hengel) that the term had derogatory connotations among the Jews of Judea for its Greek (that is, pagan) accommodations. Simon notes that Hellenism is numbered among Justin Martyr's list of heresies in *Trypho* (80.4). See *St. Stephen and the Hellenists in the Primitive Church* (New York: Longmans, 1958).

That the Seven were leaders of an independent community in the early church is proven by the fact that they are presented as actively preaching, healing, and performing signs and wonders. They are not waiters whose main responsibility is food distribution, as Luke suggests in Acts 6:1–6.

Hengel writes that "the Aramaic-speaking part of the community was hardly affected" by the persecution of the Hellenists, and he notes that, considering the fact that the Hebrews stayed in Jerusalem until at least the outbreak of war in 66 C.E., they must have come to some sort of accommodation with the priestly authorities. "In Jewish Palestine, only a community which remained strictly faithful to the law could survive in the long run"; *Between Jesus and Paul*, 55–56.

Another reason to consider the Jesus movement in the first few years after the crucifixion to be an exclusively Jewish mission is that among the first acts of the apostles after Jesus's death was to replace Judas Iscariot with Matthias (Acts 1:21–26). This may indicate that the notion of the reconstitution of Israel's tribes was still alive immediately after the crucifixion. Indeed, among the first questions the disciples ask the risen Jesus is whether, now that he was back, he intended to "restore the kingdom to Israel." That is, will you perform now the messianic function you failed to perform during your lifetime? Jesus brushes off the question: "it is not for you to know the times or the season that the Father has put down in his power [to accomplish such things]" (Acts 1:7).

CHAPTER FOURTEEN: AM I NOT AN APOSTLE?

Of the letters in the New Testament that are attributed to Paul, only seven can be confidently traced to him: 1 Thessalonians, Galatians, 1 and 2 Corinthians, Romans, Philippians, and Philemon. Letters attributed to Paul but probably not written by him include Colossians, Ephesians, 2 Thessalonians, 1 and 2 Timothy, and Titus.

There is some debate over the date of Paul's conversion. The confusion rests with Paul's statement in Galatians 2:1 that he went to the Apostolic Council in Jerusalem "after fourteen years." Assuming that the council was held around the year 50 C.E., that would place Paul's conversion around 36 or 37 C.E. This is the date favored by James Tabor, *Paul and Jesus* (New York: Simon and Schuster, 2012). However, some scholars believe that by "after fourteen years," Paul means fourteen years after his *initial* appearance before the Apostles, which he claims took place three years after his conversion. That would place his conversion closer to 33 C.E., a date favored by Martin Hengel, *Between Jesus and Paul,* 31. Adolf Harnack, in *The Mission and Expansion of Christianity in the First Three Centuries* (New York: Harper and Row, 1972), calculates that Paul was converted eighteen months after Jesus's death, but I think that is far too early a date for Paul's conversion. I agree with Tabor and others that Paul's conversion was more likely sometime around 36 or 37 C.E., fourteen years before the Apostolic Council.

That these lines of Paul in the letter to the Galatians regarding the "so-called pillars of the church" were directed specifically toward the Jerusalem-based Apostles and not some unnamed Jewish Christians with whom he disagreed is definitely proven by Gerd Ludemann in his indispensable works *Paul: The Founder of Christianity* (New York: Prometheus Books, 2002), especially pages 69 and 120; and, with M. Eugene Boring, *Opposition to Paul in Jewish Christianity* (Minneapolis: Fortress Press, 1989). See also Tabor, *Paul and Jesus,* 19; and J.D.G. Dunn, "Echoes of the Intra-Jewish Polemic in Paul's Letter to the Galatians," *Journal of Biblical Literature* 112/3 (1993): 459–77.

There has been a fierce debate recently about the role of Paul in creating what we now consider Christianity, with a number of contemporary scholars coming to Paul's defense and painting him as a devout Jew who remained loyal to his Jewish heritage and faithful to the laws and customs of Moses but who just happened to view his mission as adapting messianic Judaism to a gentile audience. The traditional view of Paul among scholars of Christianity could perhaps best be summed up by Rudolf Bultmann, *Faith and Understanding* (London: SCM Press, 1969), who famously described Paul's doctrine of Christ as "basically a wholly new religion, in contrast to the original Palestinian Christianity." Scholars who more or less agree with Bultmann include Adolf Harnak, *What Is Christianity?* (New York: G. P. Putnam's Sons, 1902); H. J. Schoeps, *Paul: The Theology of the Apostle in the Light of Jewish History* (Philadelphia: Westminster Press, 1961); and Gerd Ludemann, *Paul: The Founder of Christianity.* Among the recent scholars who see Paul as a loyal Jew who merely tried to translate Judaism for a gentile audience are L. Michael White, *From Jesus to Christianity,* and my former professor Marie-Éloise Rosenblatt, *Paul the Accused* (Collegeville, Minn.: Liturgical Press, 1995).

Ultimately, there is some truth in both views. Those who believe that Paul was the creator of Christianity as we know it, or that it was he who utterly divorced the new faith from Judaism, often do not adequately take into consideration the eclecticism of Diaspora Judaism or the influence of the Greek-speaking Hellenists, from whom Paul, himself a Greek-speaking Hellenist, likely first heard about Jesus of Nazareth. But to be clear, the Hellenists may have deemphasized the Law of Moses in their preaching, but they did not demonize it; they may have abandoned circumcision as a requirement for conversion, but they did not relegate it to dogs and evildoers and suggest those who disagree should be castrated, as Paul does (Galatians 5:12). Regardless of whether Paul adopted his unusual doctrine from the Hellenists or invented it himself, however, what even his staunchest defenders cannot deny is just how deviant his views are from even the most experimental Jewish movements of his time.

That Paul is speaking about himself when he cites Isaiah 49:1–6 regarding "the root of Jesse" serving as "a light to the Gentiles" is obvious, since even Paul admits that Jesus did not missionize to the gentiles (Romans 15:12).

Research done by N. A. Dahl demonstrates just how unusual Paul's use of the term *Xristos* (Christ) was. Dahl notes that for Paul, *Xristos* is never a predicate, never governed by a genitive, never a title but always a designation, and never used in the appositional form, as in *Yesus ha Xristos*, or Jesus *the* Christ. See N. A. Dahl, *Jesus the Christ: The Historical Origins of Christological Doctrine* (Minneapolis: Fortress Press, 1991).

It was not unusual to be called Son of God in ancient Judaism. God calls David his son: "today I have begotten you" (Psalms 2:7). He even calls Israel his "first-born son" (Exodus 4:22). But in every case, Son of God is meant as a title, not a description. Paul's view of Jesus as the literal son of God is without precedence in second Temple Judaism.

Luke claims that Paul and Barnabas separated because of a "sharp contention," which Luke claims was over whether to take Mark with them on their next missionary trip but which is obviously tied to what happened in Antioch shortly after the Apostolic Council. While Peter and Paul were in Antioch, they engaged in a fierce public feud because, according to Paul, Peter stopped sharing a table with gentiles as soon as a delegation sent by James arrived in the city, "for fear of the circumcision faction" in Jerusalem (Galatians 2:12). Of course, Paul is our only source for this event, and there are plenty of reasons for doubting his version of the story, not the least of which is the fact that sharing a table with gentiles is in no way forbidden under Jewish law. It is more likely that the argument was about the keeping of Jewish dietary laws—that is, not eating gentile food—an argument in which Barnabas sided with Peter.

Luke says Paul was sent to Rome to escape a Jewish plot to have him killed. He also claims that the Roman tribune ordered nearly five hundred of his soldiers to personally accompany Paul to Caesarea. This is absurd and can be flatly ignored.

Claudius expelled the Jews from Rome, according to the historian Suetonius, "because the Jews of Rome were indulging in constant riots at the instigation of Chrestus." It is widely believed that by Chrestus, Suetonius meant Christ, and that this spat among the Jews was between the city's Christian and non-Christian Jews. As F. F. Bruce notes, "we should remind ourselves that, while we with our hindsight can distinguish between Jews and Christians as early as the reign of Claudius, no such distinction could have been made at that time by the Roman authorities." F. F. Bruce, "Christianity Under Claudius," *Bulletin of the John Rylands Library* 44 (March 1962): 309–26.

CHAPTER FIFTEEN: THE JUST ONE

The description of James and the entreaties of the Jews are both taken from the account of the Palestinian Jewish Christian Hegesippus (100–180 C.E.). We have access to Hegesippus's five books of early Church history only through passages cited in the third-century text of *Ecclesiastical History* by Eusebius of Caesarea (c. 260–c. 339 C.E.), an archbishop of the Church under the Emperor Constantine.

How reliable a source Hegesippus may be is a matter of great debate. On the one hand, there are a number of statements by Hegesippus whose historicity the majority of scholars accept without dispute, including his assertion that "control of the Church passed together with the Apostles, to the brother of the Lord James, whom everyone from the Lord's time till our own has named the Just, for there were many Jameses, but this one was holy from his birth" (Eusebius, *Ecclesiastical History* 2.23). This claim is backed up with multiple attestations (see below) and can even be traced in the letters of Paul and in the book of Acts. However, there are some traditions in Hegesippus that are confused and downright incorrect, including his claim that James was allowed to "enter the Sanctuary alone." If by "Sanctuary" Hegesippus means the Holy of Holies (and there is some question as to whether that is indeed what he means), then the statement is patently false; only the high priest could enter the Holy of Holies. There is also a variant tradition of James's death in Hegesippus that contradicts what scholars accept as the more reliable account in Josephus's *Antiquities*. As recorded in the *Ecclesiastical History*, it was James's response to the request of the Jews to help dissuade the people from following Jesus as messiah that ultimately leads to his death: "And [James] answered with a loud voice: Why do you ask me concerning Jesus, the Son of Man? He himself sits in heaven at the right hand of the great power, and is about to come upon the clouds of heaven! So they went up and threw down the just man, and said to each other: Let us stone James the Just. And they began to stone him, for he was not killed by the fall; but he turned and knelt down and said: I entreat you, Lord God our father, forgive them, for they know not what they do."

What is fascinating about this story is that it seems to be a variant of the story of Stephen's martyrdom in the book of Acts, which was itself swiped from Jesus's response to the high priest Caiaphas in the gospel of Mark. Note also the parallel between James's death speech and that of Jesus's on the cross in Luke 23:24.

Hegesippus ends the story of James's martyrdom thus: "And one of them, one of the fullers, took the club with which he beat out clothes and struck the just man on the head. And thus he suffered martyrdom. And they buried him on the spot, by the temple, and his monument still remains by the temple. He became a true witness, both to Jews and Greeks, that Jesus is the Christ. And immediately Vespasian besieged them" (Eusebius, *Ecclesiastical History* 2.23.1–18). Again, while scholars are almost unanimous in preferring Josephus's account of James's death to Hegesippus, it bears mentioning that the latter tradition is echoed in the work of Clement of Alexandria, who writes: "there were two Jameses, one the Just, who was thrown down from the parapet [of the Temple] and beaten to death with the fuller's club, the other the James [son of Zebedee] who was beheaded" (Clement, *Hypotyposes,* Book 7).

Josephus writes of the wealthy priestly aristocracy seizing the tithes of the lower priests in *Antiquities* 20.180–81: "But as for the high priest, Ananias, he increased in glory every day, and this to a great degree, and had obtained the favor and esteem of the citizens in a signal manner; for he was a great hoarder up of money: he therefore cultivated the friendship of Albinus, and of the high priest [Jesus, son of Danneus], by making them presents; he also had servants who were very wicked, who joined themselves to the boldest sort of the people, and went to the thrashing-floors, and took away the tithes that belonged to the priests by violence, and did not refrain from beating such as would not give these tithes to them. So the other high priests acted in the like manner, as did those his servants, without any one being able to prohibit them; so that [some of the] priests, that of old were wont to be supported with those tithes, died for want of food." This Ananias was probably Ananus the Elder, father to the Ananus who killed James.

Josephus's account of James's martyrdom can be found in *Antiquities* 20.9.1. Not everyone is convinced that James was executed for being a Christian. Maurice Goguel, for instance, argues that if the men executed along with James were also Christians then their names would have been preserved in Christian tradition; Goguel, *Birth of Christianity* (New York: Macmillan, 1954). Some scholars, myself included, believe that he was executed for condemning Ananus's seizure of the tithes meant for the lower-class priests; see S.G.F. Brandon, "The Death of James the Just: A New Interpretation," *Studies in Mysticism and Religion* (Jerusalem: Magnus Press, 1967): 57–69.

Whether the Jews were outraged by the unlawful procedure of the trial or by the unjust verdict is difficult to decipher from Josephus's account. The fact that they complain to Albinus about the illegality of Ananus's calling the Sanhedrin without a procurator in Jerusalem seems to suggest that it was the procedure of the trial they objected to, not the verdict. However, I agree with John Painter who notes that "the suggestion that what the group objected to was

Ananus taking the law into his own hands when Roman authority was required for the imposition of the death penalty (see John 18:31) does not fit an objection raised by 'the most fair-minded . . . and strict in the observance of the law'. . . . Rather it suggests that those who were fair-minded and strict in their observance of the law regarded as unjust the verdict that James and the others had transgressed the law." See John Painter, "Who Was James?" in *The Brother of Jesus: James the Just and His Mission*, Bruce Chilton and Jacob Neusner, eds. (Louisville, Ky.: Westminster John Knox Press, 2001), 10–65; 49.

Pierre-Antoine Bernheim agrees: "Josephus, by indicating the disagreement of the 'most precise observers of the law,' probably wanted to emphasize not the irregularity of the convening of the Sanhedrin in terms of the rules imposed by the Romans but the injustice of the verdict in relation to the law of Moses as this was interpreted by the most widely recognized experts . . ." *James, the Brother of Jesus* (London: SCM Press, 1997), 249.

While some scholars—for instance, Craig C. Hill, *Hellenists and Hebrews* (Minneapolis: Fortress Press, 1992)—disagree with Painter and Bernheim, arguing that the complaint of the Jews had nothing to do with James himself, most (myself included) are convinced that the Jews' complaint was about the injustice of the verdict, not the process of the trial; see also F. F. Bruce, *New Testament History* (New York: Doubleday, 1980), especially pages 372–73.

Hegesippus's quote regarding the authority of James can be found in Eusebius, *Ecclesiastical History* 2.23.4–18. It is unclear whether Hegesippus means that control of the church passed to the apostles and to James, or that control over the apostles also passed to James. Either way, James's leadership is affirmed. Gerd Ludemann actually thinks the phrase "with the apostles" is not original but was added by Eusebius to conform with the mainstream view of apostolic authority. See *Opposition to Paul in Jewish Christianity* (Philadelphia: Fortress Press, 1989).

The material from Clement of Rome is taken from the so-called *Pseudo-Clementines*, which, while compiled sometime around 300 C.E., reflects far earlier Jewish-Christian traditions that can be traced through the text's two primary documents: the *Homilies* and the *Recognitions*. The *Homilies* contain two epistles: *The Epistle of Peter*, from which the reference to James as "Lord and Bishop of the Holy Church" is cited, and the *Epistle of Clement*, which is addressed to James "the Bishop of Bishops, who rules Jerusalem, the Holy Assembly of the Hebrews, and all the Assemblies everywhere." The *Recognitions* is itself probably founded upon an older document titled *Ascent of James*, which most scholars trace to the mid-100s. Georg Strecker thinks the *Ascent* was written in Pella, where the Jerusalem-based Christians allegedly congregated after the destruction of Jerusalem. See his entry "The Pseudo-Clementines," in *New Testament Apocrypha*, vol. 2, Wilhelm Schneemelker, ed. (London: Cambridge University Press, 1991), 483–541.

The passage from the *Gospel of Thomas* can be found in Chapter 12. Incidentally the surname "James the Just" also appears in the *Gospel of the Hebrews;* see *The Nag Hammadi Library* for the complete text of both. Clement of Alexandria is quoted in Eusebius, *Ecclesiastical History* 2.1.2–5. Obviously the title of bishop in describing James is anachronistic, but the implication of the term is clear. Jerome's *Lives of Illustrious Men* can be found in an English translation by Ernest Cushing Richardson in *A Select Library of the Nicene and Post-Nicene Fathers of the Christian Church*, vol. 3 (Edinburgh: T&T Clark, 1892). The no longer extant passage in Josephus blaming the destruction of Jerusalem on James's unjust death is cited by Origen in *Contra Celsus* 1.47, by Jerome in *Lives* and in his *Commentary on Galatians*, and by Eusebius in *Ecclesiastical History* 2.23.

That James is in the position of presiding authority in the Apostolic Council is proven by the fact that he is the last to speak and begins his judgment with the word *krino*, or "I decree." See Bernheim, *James, Brother of Jesus*, 193. As Bernheim correctly notes, the fact that Paul, when referencing the three pillars of the church, always mentions James first is due to his preeminence. This is affirmed by later redactions of the text in which copyists have reversed the order to put Peter before James in order to place him as head of the church. Any question of James's preeminence over Peter is put to rest in the passage of Galatians 2:11–14 in which emissaries sent by James to Antioch compel Peter to stop eating with Gentiles, while the ensuing fight between Peter and Paul leads Barnabas to leave Paul and return to James.

Bernheim outlines the role of dynastic succession and its use among the early Christian church in *James, Brother of Jesus*, 216–17. It is Eusebius who mentions that Simeon, son of Clopas, succeeded James: "After the martyrdom of James and the taking of Jerusalem which immediately ensued, it is recorded that those apostles and disciples of the Lord who were still surviving met together from all quarters and, *together with our Lord's relatives after the flesh* (for the most part of them were still alive), took counsel, all in common, as to whom they should judge worthy to be the successor of James; and, what is more, that they all with one consent approved Simeon the son of Clopas, of whom also the book of the Gospels makes mention, as worthy of the throne of the community in that place. He was a cousin—at any rate so it is said—of the Savior; for indeed Hegesippus relates that Clopas was Joseph's brother" (*Ecclesiastical History* 3.11; italics mine). Regarding the grandsons of Jesus's other brother, Judas, Hegesippus writes that they "ruled the churches, inasmuch as they were both martyrs and of the Lord's family" (*Ecclesiastical History* 3.20).

It should be noted that the famous statement of Jesus calling Peter the rock upon which he will found his church is rejected as unhistorical by most scholars. See for example Pheme Perkins, *Peter, Apostle for the Whole Church* (Philadelphia: Fortress Press, 2000); B. P. Robinson, "Peter and His Successors: Tradition and

Redaction in Matthew 16:17–19," *Journal for the Study of the New Testament* 21 (1984), 85–104; and Arlo J. Nau, *Peter in Matthew* (Collegeville, Minn.: Liturgical Press, 1992). John Painter demonstrates that no tradition exists concerning Peter's leadership of the Jerusalem church. Such traditions that exist are only concerning Rome. See Painter, "Who Was James?" 31.

Some scholars think that Peter was the head of the church until he was forced to flee Jerusalem. See, for instance, Oscar Cullman, *Peter: Disciple. Apostle. Martyr* (London: SCM Press, 1953). But that view is based mostly on an erroneous reading of Acts 12:17, in which Peter, before being forced to flee from Jerusalem, tells John Mark to inform James of his departure to Rome. Cullman and others argue that this is the moment in which leadership of the Jerusalem church transfers from Peter to James. However, as John Painter demonstrates, the proper reading of Acts 12:17 is that Peter is merely informing James (his "boss," if you will) of his activities before fleeing Jerusalem. There is nothing in this passage, or for that matter, in any passage in Acts, which suggests Peter ever led the Jerusalem church. See Painter, "Who was James?" 31–36.

Cullman also claims that the church under Peter was far more lax in its observance of the law before James took over and made the observance more rigid. The only evidence for this view comes from Peter's conversion of the Roman Cornelius. While this is a story whose historicity is doubtful, it still does not prove a laxity of the law on the part of Peter, and it most definitely does not indicate Peter's leadership of the Jerusalem assembly. The book of Acts makes it abundantly clear that there was a wide divergence of views among Jesus's first followers over the rigidity of the law. Peter may have been less rigid than James when it came to observance of the law, but so what? As Bernheim notes: "There is no reason to suppose that the Jerusalem church was less liberal in 48/49 [than it was] at the beginning of the 30s," *James, Brother of Jesus*, 209.

Wiard Popkes details the evidence for a first-century dating of James's epistle in "The Mission of James in His Time," *The Brother of Jesus*, 88–99. Martin Dibelius disagrees with the first-century dating. He believes that the epistle is actually a hodgepodge of Jewish-Christian teachings that should be dated to the second century. See Martin Dibelius, *James* (Philadelphia: Fortress Press, 1976). It is interesting to note that James's epistle is addressed to "the Twelve Tribes of Israel scattered in the Diaspora." James seems to continue to presuppose the fulfillment that the tribes of Israel will be restored to their full number and Israel liberated. Scholars believe that the reason so much of James's epistle has echoes in the gospel of Matthew is that embedded within the gospel is a tradition, often referred to as M, that can traced to James.

Bruce Chilton writes about the Nazirite vow that Paul is forced to undergo in "James in Relation to Peter, Paul, and Jesus," *The Brother of Jesus*, 138–59. Chilton believes that not only was James a Nazirite, but Jesus was one, too. Indeed, he believes the reference to Jesus as the Nazarean is a corruption of the term Nazirite. Note that Acts 18:18 portrays Paul as taking part in something similar to a Nazirite vow. After setting off by ship for Syria, Paul lands at Cenchreae, in the eastern port of Corinth. There, Luke writes that, "he had his hair cut, for he was under a vow." Although Luke is clearly referring to a Nazirite vow here, he seems to be confused about the nature and practice of it. The entire point of the ritual was to cut the hair at the end of the vow. Luke gives no hint as to what Paul's vow may have been, but if it was for a safe journey to Syria he had not reached his destination and thus had not fulfilled his vow. Moreover, Paul's Nazirite vow is not taken at the Temple and does not involve a priest.

John Painter outlines all of the anti-Pauline material in the *Pseudo-Clementines,* including the altercation at the Temple between Paul and James, in "Who Was James?" 38–39. Painter also addresses Jesus's expansion of the Law of Moses in 55–57.

The community that continued to follow the teachings of James in the centuries after the destruction of Jerusalem referred to itself as the Ebionites, or "the Poor," in honor of James's focus on the poor. The community may have been called the Ebionites even during James's lifetime, as the term is found in the second chapter of James's epistle. The Ebionites insisted on circumcision and strict adherence to the law. Well into the fourth century they viewed Jesus as just a man. They were one of the many heterodox communities who were marginalized and persecuted after the Council of Nicaea in 325 C.E. essentially made Pauline Christianity the orthodox religion of the Roman Empire.

Bibliography

BOOKS

Anderson, Jeff S. *The Internal Diversification of Second Temple Judaism.* Lanham, Md.: University Press of America, 2002.

Aslan, Reza. *How to Win a Cosmic War: God, Globalization, and the End of the War on Terror.* New York: Random House, 2009.

Aus, Roger. *Water into Wine and the Beheading of John the Baptist.* Providence: Brown Judaic Studies, 1988.

Avi-Yonah, M., and Z. Baras, eds. *The World History of the Jewish People: The Herodian Period.* Jerusalem: New Brunswick, 1975.

Bammel, Ernst, ed. *The Trial of Jesus.* Naperville, Ill.: Alec R. Allenson, 1970.

Bammel, Ernst, and C.F.D. Moule, eds. *Jesus and the Politics of His Day.* New York: Cambridge University Press, 1984.

Batey, Richard A. *Jesus and the Forgotten City: New Light on Sepphoris and the Urban World of Jesus.* Grand Rapids, Mich.: Baker Book House, 1991.

Bauer, Walter. *Orthodoxy and Heresy in Earliest Christianity.* Mifflintown, Pa.: Sigler Press, 1971.

Beard, Mary, John North, and Simon Price. *Religions of Rome: A Sourcebook.* 2 vols. Cambridge: Cambridge University Press, 1998.

Beilby, James K., and Paul Rhodes Eddy, eds. *The Historical Jesus: Five Views.* Downers Grove, Ill.: InterVarsity Press, 2009.

Berlin, Andrea M., and J. Andrew Overman. *The First Jewish Revolt: Archaeology, History, and Ideology.* New York: Routledge, 2002.

Bernheim, Pierre-Antoine. *James, the Brother of Jesus.* London: SCM Press, 1997.

Black, Matthew. *The Book of Enoch or 1 Enoch: A New English Edition with Commentary and Textual Notes.* Leiden, Netherlands: Brill, 1985.

Blevins, James L. *The Messianic Secret in Markan Research, 1901–1976*. Lanham, Md.: University Press of America, 1981.

Blinzler, Josef. *The Trial of Jesus*. Westminster, Md.: Newman Press, 1959.

Bohak, Gideon. *Ancient Jewish Magic: A History*. London: Cambridge University Press, 2008.

Borg, Marcus J. *Jesus: A New Vision*. New York: HarperCollins, 1991.

Brandon, S.G.F. *Jesus and the Zealots*. Manchester: Manchester University Press, 1967.

Brighton, Mark Andrew. *The Sicarii in Josephus's Judean War: Rhetorical Analysis and Historical Observations*. Atlanta: Society of Biblical Scholarship, 2009.

Brooke, G. *Exegesis at Qumran: 4QFlorilegium in Its Jewish Context*. Sheffield, U.K.: Sheffield Academic Press, 1985.

Brown, Raymond. *The Death of the Messiah*. 2 vols. New York: Doubleday, 1994.

Bruce, F. F. *New Testament History*. New York: Doubleday, 1980.

Bultmann, Rudolf. *Essays: Philosophical and Theological*. New York: Macmillan, 1995.

————. *Faith and Understanding*. London: SCM Press, 1969.

————. *History of the Synoptic Tradition*. San Francisco: Harper and Row, 1968.

Burkett, Delbert. *The Son of Man Debate*. New York: Cambridge University Press, 1999.

————. *The Son of the Man in the Gospel of John*. Sheffield, U.K.: Sheffield Academic Press, 1991.

Cadbury, H. J., and K. Lake, eds. *The Beginnings of Christianity*. Vol. 1. London: Macmillan, 1933.

Casey, P. Maurice. *Son of Man: The Interpretation and Influence of Daniel 7*. London: SPCK Publishing, 1979.

Charlesworth, James H., ed. *The Messiah*. Minneapolis: Fortress Press, 1992.

————, ed. *The Old Testament Pseudepigrapha*. Garden City, N.Y.: Doubleday, 1985.

————, et al. *Resurrection: The Origin and Future of a Biblical Doctrine*. London: T&T Clark, 2006.

Chilton, Bruce D. *Judaic Approaches to the Gospels*. Atlanta: Scholars Press, 1994.

————, and Jacob Neusner, eds. *The Brother of Jesus*. Louisville: Westminster John Knox Press, 2001.

Collins, John J. *Apocalypticism in the Dead Sea Scrolls*. London: Routledge, 1997.

————, ed. *Daniel*. Minneapolis: Fortress Press, 1993.

Collins, John J., and George Nickelsburg. *Ideal Figures in Ancient Judaism: Profiles and Paradigms*. Chico, Calif.: Scholars Press, 1980.

Comay, Joan. *The Temple of Jerusalem*. London: Weidenfeld and Nicolson, 1975.

Conybeare, F. C., ed. *Philostratus: The Life of Apollonius of Tyana*. London: Heinemann, 1912.

Cross, Frank Moore. *Canaanite Myth and Hebrew Epic: Essays in the History of the Religion of Israel*. Cambridge, Mass.: Harvard University Press, 1973.

Crossan, John Dominic. *The Historical Jesus: The Life of a Mediterranean Jewish Peasant*. New York: HarperCollins, 1992.

———. *Jesus: A Revolutionary Biography*. New York: HarperOne, 1995.

Cullman, Oscar. *Christology of the New Testament*. Philadelphia: Westminster Press, 1963.

———. *Peter: Disciple. Apostle. Martyr*. London: SCM Press, 1953.

———. *The State in the New Testament*. New York: Charles Scribner's Sons, 1956.

Dahl, N. A. *Jesus the Christ: The Historical Origins of Christological Doctrine*. Minneapolis: Fortress Press, 1991.

Day, John, ed. *Temple and Worship in Biblical Israel*. New York: T&T Clark, 2005.

De Jong, M. *Christology in Context: The Earliest Christian Response to Jesus*. Philadelphia: Westminster Press, 1988.

Derrett, J.D.M. *Law in the New Testament*. Eugene, Ore.: Wipf and Stock, 2005.

Dibelius, Martin. *James*. Philadelphia: Fortress Press, 1976.

———. *Studies in the Acts of the Apostles*. New York: Charles Scribner's Sons, 1956.

Dickie, Matthew W. *Magic and Magicians in the Greco-Roman World*. London: Routledge, 2001.

Edwards, Douglas R., and C. Thomas McCollough, eds. *Archaeology and the Galilee*. Atlanta: Scholars Press, 1997.

Edwards, George R. *Jesus and the Politics of Violence*. New York: Harper and Row, 1972.

Evans, Craig. *Jesus and His Contemporaries*. Leiden, Netherlands: Brill, 1995.

———, and J. A. Sanders. *Luke and Scripture: The Function of Sacred Tradition in Luke-Acts*. Minneapolis: Fortress Press, 1993.

Festinger, Leon. *A Theory of Cognitive Dissonance*. Stanford: Stanford University Press, 1957.

———, H. W. Riecken, and S. Schachter. *When Prophecy Fails: A Social and Psychological Study of a Modern Group That Predicted the Destruction of the World*. New York: Harper and Row, 1956.

Fitzmeyer, Joseph A. *The Gospel According to Luke I–IX*. Garden City: Doubleday, 1981.

Freyne, Sean. *Galilee, Jesus, and the Gospels*. Dublin: Gill and Macmillan, 1988.

Fridrichsen, Anton. *The Problem of Miracle in Primitive Christianity*. Minneapolis: Augsburg Publishing House, 1972.

Funk, Robert W., and Roy W. Hoover. *The Five Gospels: The Search for the Authentic Words of Jesus*. New York: Polebridge Press, 1993.

Gager, John. *Kingdom and Community: The Social World of the Early Christians*. Englewood Cliffs, N.J.: Prentice Hall, 1975.

Goguel, Maurice. *Birth of Christianity*. New York: Macmillan, 1954.

Golb, Norman. *Who Wrote the Dead Sea Scrolls? The Search for the Secret Qumran*. New York: Scribner, 1995.

Goodman, Martin. *Rome and Jerusalem: The Clash of Ancient Civilizations*. London: Penguin, 2007.

———. *The Ruling Class of Judea*. New York: Cambridge University Press, 1987.

Grabbe, Lester L. *Judaism from Cyrus to Hadrian*. 2 vols. Minneapolis: Fortress Press, 1992.

Groh, Dennis E., and Robert Jewett, eds. *The Living Texts: Essays in Honor of Ernest W. Saunders*. Lanham, Md.: University Press of America, 1985.

Gurtner, Daniel. *Torn Veil: Matthew's Exposition of the Death of Jesus*. Cambridge: Cambridge University Press, 2007.

Hamerton-Kelly, R. G. *Pre-Existence, Wisdom, and the Son of Man*. Cambridge: Cambridge University Press, 1973.

Harnack, Adolf. *The Mission and Expansion of Christianity in the First Three Centuries*. New York: Harper and Row, 1972.

———. *What Is Christianity?* New York: G. P. Putnam's Sons, 1902.

Hendricks, Obery M. *The Politics of Jesus*. New York: Doubleday, 2006.

Hengel, Martin. *Between Jesus and Paul*. Eugene, Ore.: Wipf and Stock, 1983.

———. *Crucifixion in the Ancient World and the Folly of the Message of the Cross*. Philadelphia: Fortress Press, 1977.

———. *The Son of God*. Eugene, Ore.: Wipf and Stock, 1976.

———. *The Zealots*. London: T&T Clark, 2000.

Higgins, A.J.B., ed. *Studies in Memory of Thomas Walter Manson, 1893–1958*. Manchester: Manchester University Press, 1959.

Hill, Craig C. *Hellenists and Hebrews*. Minneapolis: Fortress Press, 1992.

Horsley, Richard, and John S. Hanson. *Bandits, Prophets, and Messiahs*. Minneapolis: Winston Press, 1985.

———. *Galilee: History, Politics, People*. Pennsylvania: Trinity Press International, 1995.

———. *Jesus and the Spiral of Violence: Popular Jewish Resistance in Roman Palestine*. Minneapolis: Fortress Press, 1993.

Hurst, L. D., et al., eds. *The Glory of Christ in the New Testament*. Oxford: Clarendon Press, 1987.

Jaffee, Martin. *Early Judaism*. Bethesda: University Press of Maryland, 2006.

Janowitz, Naomi. *Magic in the Roman World*. London: Routledge, 2001.

Jeffers, Ann. *Magic and Divination in Ancient Palestine and Syria*. Leiden, Netherlands: Brill, 1996.

Jeremias, Joachim. *New Testament Theology: The Proclamation of Jesus*. New York: Charles Scribner's Sons, 1971.

Jervell, Jacob, ed. *Luke and the People of God: A New Look at Luke-Acts*. Minneapolis: Augsburg Publishing House, 1972.

Kelber, Werner. *The Kingdom in Mark*. Philadelphia: Fortress Press, 1974.

———, ed. *The Passion in Mark: Studies on Mark 14–16*. Philadelphia: Fortress Press, 1976.

Korb, Scott. *Life in Year One: What the World Was Like in First-Century Palestine*. New York: Riverhead, 2011.

Levenson, Jon Douglas. *Resurrection and the Restoration of Israel*. New Haven: Yale University Press, 2006.

Levine, Amy-Jill. *The Misunderstood Jew*. New York: HarperOne, 2006.

Levine, Lee I., ed. *The Galilee in Late Antiquity*. New York: Jewish Theological Seminary of America, 1992.

Lindars, Barnabas. *Jesus Son of Man*. London: SPCK Publishing, 1983.

Loewe, Herbert. *Render unto Caesar*. Cambridge: Cambridge University Press, 1940.

Ludemann, Gerd. *Paul: The Founder of Christianity*. New York: Prometheus Books, 2002.

———, and M. Eugene Boring. *Opposition to Paul in Jewish Christianity*. Minneapolis: Fortress Press, 1989.

Mack, Burton. *A Myth of Innocence: Mark and Christian Origins*. Philadelphia: Fortress Press, 1988.

MacMullen, Ramsay. *Roman Social Relations: 50 B.C. to A.D. 384*. New Haven: Yale University Press, 1974.

Madden, Fredric William. *History of Jewish Coinage and of Money in the Old and New Testament*. London: Bernard Quaritch, 1864.

Meier, John P. *A Marginal Jew: Rethinking the Historical Jesus*. 4 vols. New Haven: Yale University Press, 1991–2009.

Meshorer, Ya'akov. *Treasury of Jewish Coins from the Persian Period to Bar Kokhba*. Jerusalem and Nyack, N.Y.: Amphora Books, 2001.

Meyer, Marvin W., ed. *The Nag Hammadi Library*. New York: Harper and Row, 1977.

Meyer, R. P. *Jesus and the Twelve*. Grand Rapids, Mich.: Eerdmans, 1968.

Meyers, Eric, and J. Strange. *Archaeology, the Rabbis, and Early Christianity*. Nashville: Abingdon, 1981.

Murphy, Catherine. *John the Baptist: Prophet of Purity for a New Age*. Collegeville, Minn.: Liturgical Press, 2003.

Nau, Arlo J. *Peter in Matthew*. Collegeville, Minn.: Liturgical Press, 1992.

Neusner, Jacob, et al., eds. *Judaisms and Their Messiahs at the Turn of the Christian Era*. Cambridge: Cambridge University Press, 1987.

Oppenheimer, Aharon. *The 'Am Ha-Aretz: A Study in the Social History of the Jewish People in the Hellenistic-Roman Period*. Leiden, Netherlands: Brill, 1977.

Otto, Rudolf. *The Kingdom of God and the Son of Man*. Boston: Starr King Press, 1957.

Penella, Robert J. *The Letters of Apollonius of Tyana*. Leiden, Netherlands: Brill, 1979.

Perkins, Pheme. *Peter, Apostle for the Whole Church*. Philadelphia: Fortress Press, 2000.

Perrin, Norman. *The Kingdom of God in the Teaching of Jesus*. Philadelphia: Westminster Press, 1963.

———. *Rediscovering the Teachings of Jesus*. New York: Harper and Row, 1967.

———. *The Resurrection According to Matthew, Mark, and Luke*. Philadelphia: Fortress Press, 1977.

Phipps, William E. *The Sexuality of Jesus*. New York: Harper and Row, 1973.

———. *Was Jesus Married?* New York: Harper and Row, 1970.

Popovic, M., ed. *The Jewish Revolt Against Rome: Interdisciplinary Perspectives*. Supplements to the Journal for the Study of Judaism 154. Leiden, Netherlands: Brill, 2011.

Porter, Stanley E. *The Language of the New Testament*. Sheffield, U.K.: Sheffield Academic Press, 1991.

———, Michael A. Hayes, and David Tombs. *Resurrection*. Sheffield, U.K.: Sheffield Academic Press, 1999.

Raisanen, Heikki. *The "Messianic Secret" in Mark*. Edinburgh: T&T Clark, 1990.

Reimarus, Hermann Samuel. *The Goal of Jesus and His Disciples*. Leiden, Netherlands: Brill, 1970.

Rhoads, David. *Israel in Revolution: 6–74 C.E.* Philadelphia: Fortress Press, 1976.

Rosenblatt, Marie-Eloise. *Paul the Accused*. Collegeville, Minn.: Liturgical Press, 1995.

Sanders, E. P. *The Historical Figure of Jesus*. New York: Penguin, 1993.

Schaberg, Jane. *The Illegitimacy of Jesus*. San Francisco: Harper and Row, 1978.

Schoeps, H. J. *Paul: The Theology of the Apostle in the Light of Jewish History*. Philadelphia: Westminster Press, 1961.

Scholem, Gershom. *The Messianic Idea in Judaism*. New York: Schocken Books, 1971.

Schurer, Emil. *A History of the Jewish People in the Time of Jesus Christ*. 3 vols. Edinburgh: T&T Clark, 1890.

Schweitzer, Albert. *The Quest of the Historical Jesus*. New York: Macmillan, 1906.

Scobie, Charles. *John the Baptist*. Minneapolis: Fortress Press, 1964.

Shanks, Hershel, ed. *Understanding the Dead Sea Scrolls*. New York: Random House, 1992.

Simon, Marcel. *St. Stephen and the Hellenists in the Primitive Church*. New York: Longmans, 1958.

Smith, Morton. *Jesus the Magician.* New York: Harper and Row, 1978.

Steinmann, Jean. *Saint John the Baptist and the Desert Tradition.* New York: Harper, 1958.

Stendahl, Krister, ed. *The Scrolls and the New Testament.* New York: Harper, 1957.

Tabor, James. *Paul and Jesus.* New York: Simon and Schuster, 2012.

Talbert, Charles H., ed. *Reimarus: Fragments.* Chico, Calif.: Scholars Press, 1985.

Taylor, Joan E. *The Immerser: John the Baptist Within Second Temple Judaism.* Grand Rapids, Mich.: Eerdmans, 1997.

Tuckett, Christopher, ed. *The Messianic Secret.* Philadelphia: Fortress Press, 1983.

van der Loos, H. *The Miracles of Jesus.* Leiden, Netherlands: Brill, 1965.

Vermes, Geza. *Jesus the Jew.* Minneapolis: Fortress Press, 1981.

———. *The Resurrection: History and Myth.* New York: Doubleday, 2008.

———. *Who's Who in the Age of Jesus.* New York: Penguin, 2006.

Webb, R. L. *John the Baptizer and Prophet: A Socio-Historical Study.* Sheffield, UK: Sheffield Academic Press, 1991.

Wellman, James K., Jr., ed. *Belief and Bloodshed.* Lanham, Md.: Rowman and Littlefield, 2007.

Werrett, Ian C. *Ritual Purity and the Dead Sea Scrolls.* Leiden, Netherlands: Brill, 2007.

White, L. Michael. *From Jesus to Christianity.* New York: HarperOne, 2004.

Wink, Walter. *John the Baptist in the Gospel Tradition.* Eugene, Ore.: Wipf and Stock, 2001.

Wrede, William. *The Messianic Secret.* London: Cambridge University Press, 1971.

Wright, N. T. *The Resurrection of the Son of God.* Minneapolis: Fortress Press, 2003.

Wroe, Ann. *Pontius Pilate.* New York: Random House, 1999.

Zeitlin, Solomon. *Who Crucified Jesus?* New York: Bloch, 1964.

ARTICLES

Applebaum, Shimon. "The Zealots: The Case for Revaluation." *Journal of Roman Studies* 61 (1971): 155–70.

Barnett, P. W. "The Jewish Sign Prophets." *New Testament Studies* 27 (1980): 679–97.

Barr, James. "Which Language Did Jesus Speak? Some Remarks of a Semitist." *Bulletin of the John Rylands Library* 53/1 (Autumn 1970): 14–15.

Beavis, Mary Ann L. "The Trial Before the Sanhedrin (Mark 14:53–65): Reader Response and Greco-Roman Readers." *Catholic Biblical Quarterly* 49 (1987): 581–96.

Bokser, Baruch M. "Wonder-Working and the Rabbinic Tradition: The Case of Hanina ben Dosa." *Journal of Jewish Studies* 16 (1985): 42–92.

Broshi, Magen. "The Role of the Temple in the Herodian Economy." *Jewish Studies* 38 (1987): 31–37.

Bruce, F. F. "Christianity Under Claudius." *Bulletin of the John Rylands Library* 44 (March 1962): 309–26.

Buchanan, George Wesley. "Mark 11:15–19: Brigands in the Temple." *Hebrew Union College Annual* 30 (1959): 169–77.

Case, Shirley Jackson. "Jesus and Sepphoris." *Journal of Biblical Literature* 45 (1926): 14–22.

Casey, Maurice. "The Use of the Term 'Son of Man' in the Similitudes of Enoch." *Journal for the Study of Judaism* 7.1 (1976): 11–29.

Cohen, Shaye J.D. "The Rabbinic Conversion Ceremony." *Journal of Jewish Studies* 41 (1990): 177–203.

Collins, Adela Yarbro. "Mark and His Readers: The Son of God Among Greeks and Romans." *Harvard Theological Review* 93.2 (2000): 85–100.

Collins, John. "The Zeal of Phinehas: The Bible and the Legitimation of Violence." *Journal of Biblical Literature* 122.1 (2003): 3–21.

Davies, P. S. "The Meaning of Philo's Text About the Gilded Shields." *Journal of Theological Studies* 37 (1986): 109–14.

Dunn, J.D.G. "Echoes of the Intra-Jewish Polemic in Paul's Letter to the Galatians." *Journal of Biblical Literature* 112/3 (1993): 459–77.

Evans, Craig. "Jesus and Predictions of the Destruction of the Herodian Temple in the Pseudepigrapha, Qumran Scrolls, and Related Texts." *Journal for the Study of the Pseudepigrapha* 10 (1992): 89–147.

Fitzmyer, Joseph. "Did Jesus Speak Greek?" *Biblical Archaeology Review* 18/5 (September/October 1992): 58–63.

Fuks, G. "Again on the Episode of the Gilded Roman Shields at Jerusalem." *Harvard Theological Review* 75 (1982): 503–7.

Glasson, Thomas Francis. "Reply to Caiaphas (Mark 14:62)." *New Testament Studies* 7 (1960): 88–93.

Golb, Norman. "The Problem of Origin and Identification of the Dead Sea Scrolls." *Proceedings of the American Philosophical Society* 124 (1980): 1–24.

Green, William Scott. "Palestinian Holy Men: Charismatic Leadership and Rabbinic Tradition." *ANRW* 19.2 (1979): 619–47.

Hamilton, Neill Q. "Temple Cleansing and Temple Bank." *Journal of Biblical Literature* 83.4 (1964): 365–72.

Hewitt, J.W. "The Use of Nails in the Crucifixion." *Harvard Theological Review* 25 (1932): 29–45.

Hindly, J. C. "Towards a Date for the Similitudes of Enoch: A Historical Approach." *New Testament Studies* 14 (1967–68): 551–65.

Hollenbach, P. W. "The Conversion of Jesus: From Jesus the Baptizer to Jesus the Healer." *ANRW* 2.25.1 (1982): 198–200.

———. "Social Aspects of John the Baptizer's Preaching Mission in the Context of Palestinian Judaism." *ANRW* 2.19.1 (1979): 852–53.

Horsley, Richard A. "High Priests and the Politics of Roman Palestine." *Journal for the Study of Judaism* 17.1 (1986): 23–55.

———. "Josephus and the Bandits." *Journal for the Study of Judaism* 10 (1979): 37–63.

———. "'Like One of the Prophets of Old': Two Types of Popular Prophets at the Time of Jesus." *Catholic Biblical Quarterly* 47 (1985): 435–63.

———. "Menahem in Jerusalem: A Brief Messianic Episode Among the Sicarii—Not 'Zealot Messianism.'" *Novum Testamentum* 27.4 (1985): 334–48.

———. "Popular Messianic Movements Around the Time of Jesus." *Catholic Biblical Quarterly* 46 (1984): 409–32.

———. "Popular Prophetic Movements at the Time of Jesus: Their Principal Features and Social Origins." *Journal for the Study of the New Testament* 26 (1986): 3–27.

———. "The Zealots: Their Origin, Relationship and Importance in the Jewish Revolt." *Novum Testamentum* 28 (1986): 159–92.

Kennard, J. "Judas the Galilean and His Clan." *Jewish Quarterly Review* 36 (1946): 281–86.

Liver, J. "The Half-Shekel Offering in Biblical and Post-Biblical Literature." *Harvard Theological Review* 56.3 (1963): 173–98.

Meyers, Eric M., Ehud Netzer, and Carol L. Meyers. "Ornament of All Galilee." *Biblical Archeologist* 49.1 (1986): 4–19.

Rappaport, Uriel. "John of Gischala: From Galilee to Jerusalem." *Journal of Jewish Studies* 33 (1982): 479–93.

Reed, Jonathan. "Instability in Jesus' Galilee: A Demographic Perspective." *Journal of Biblical Literature* 129.2 (2010): 343–65.

Remus, Harold. "Does Terminology Distinguish Early Christian from Pagan Miracles?" *Journal of Biblical Literature* 101.4 (1982): 531–51.

Robinson, B. P. "Peter and His Successors: Tradition and Redaction in Matthew 16:17–19." *Journal for the Study of the New Testament* 21 (1984) 85–104.

Roth, Cecil. "The Cleansing of the Temple and Zechariah XIV.21." *Novum Testamentum* 4 (1960): 174–81.

Smith, Morton. "The Origin and History of Transfiguration Story." *Union Seminary Quarterly Review* 36 (1980): 39–44.

———. "The Zealots and the Sicarii." *Harvard Theological Review* 64 (1971): 1–19.

Suter, David. "Weighed in the Balance: The Similitudes of Enoch in Recent Discussion." *Religious Studies Review* 7 (1981): 217–21.

Tomasino, A. J. "Oracles of Insurrection: The Prophetic Catalyst of the Great Revolt." *Journal of Jewish Studies* 59 (2008): 86–111.

van der Horst, P. W. "Can a Book End with ΓΑΡ? A Note on Mark XVI.8." *Journal of Theological Studies* 23 (1972): 121–24.

Vermes, Geza. "Hanina ben Dosa: A Controversial Galilean Saint from the First Century of the Christian Era." *Journal of Jewish Studies* 23 (1972): 28–50.

———. "The Son of Man Debate." *Journal for the Study of the New Testament* 1 (1978): 19–32.

Webb, Robert L. "Jesus' Baptism: Its Historicity and Implications." *Bulletin for Biblical Research* 10.2 (2000): 261–309.

Zeitlin, Solomon. "Masada and the Sicarii." *Jewish Quarterly Review* 55.4 (1965): 299–317.

———. "Zealots and Sicarii." *Journal of Biblical Literature* 81 (1962): 395–98.

DICTIONARIES AND ENCYCLOPEDIAS

Analytic Greek New Testament. Grand Rapids, Mich.: Baker Book House, 1981.

Cancick, Hubert, et al., eds. *Brill's New Pauly Encyclopedia of the Ancient World: Antiquity*. Leiden, Netherlands: Brill, 2005.

Freedman, D. N., et al., eds. *The Anchor Bible Dictionary*. New York: Doubleday, 1992.

———, et al. *Eerdmans Dictionary of the Bible*. Cambridge: Eerdmans, 2000.

Green, Joel B., and Scot McKnight, eds. *Dictionary of Jesus and the Gospels*. Downers Grove, Ill.: InterVarsity Press, 1992.

Interpreter's Dictionary of the Bible. Nashville: Abingdon Press, 1976.

Louw, Johannes P., and Eugene A. Nida, eds. *Greek-English Lexicon of the New Testament*. Grand Rapids, Mich.: United Bible Societies, 1988.

Richardson, Ernest Cushing, ed. *A Select Library of the Nicene and Post-Nicene Fathers of the Christian Church*, vol. 3. Edinburgh: T&T Clark, 1892.

Schneemelker, Wilhelm, ed. *New Testament Apocrypha*, vol. 2. London: Cambridge University Press, 1991.

Stern, Ephraim, ed. *The New Encyclopedia of Archaeological Excavations in the Holy Land*. New York: Simon and Schuster; Jerusalem: Israel Exploration Society, 1993.

Thayer's Greek-English Lexicon of the New Testament. Ann Arbor: University of Michigan Press, 1996.

Werblowsky, J., et al., eds. *The Encyclopedia of the Jewish Religion*. New York: Holt, Rinehart and Winston, 1966.

Index

PHOTO: MALIN FEZEHAI

REZA ASLAN is an internationally renowned writer, commentator, professor, producer, and scholar of religions. His books, including his #1 *New York Times* bestseller, *Zealot: The Life and Times of Jesus of Nazareth,* have been translated into dozens of languages around the world. Aslan's first book, the international bestseller *No god but God: The Origins, Evolution, and Future of Islam,* was named one of the 100 most important books of the decade by Blackwell Publishers in 2010. He is also the author of *Beyond Fundamentalism: Confronting Religious Extremism in a Globalized Age* (originally titled *How to Win a Cosmic War*), as well as editor of two volumes: *Tablet & Pen: Literary Landscapes from the Modern Middle East,* and *Muslims and Jews in America: Commonalties, Contentions, and Complexities.* Aslan's degrees include a bachelor of arts in religious studies from Santa Clara University, a master of theological studies from Harvard University, a Ph.D. in the sociology of religions from the University of California, Santa Barbara, and a master of fine arts from the University of Iowa, where he was named a Truman Capote fellow in fiction. A tenured professor of creative writing at the University of California, Riverside, Aslan serves on the board of trustees for the Chicago Theological Seminary and the Yale Humanist Community, and is a member of the American Academy of Religion, the Society of Biblical Literature, and the International Qur'anic Studies Association. Aslan's previous academic positions include the Wallerstein Distinguished Visiting Professor of Religion, Culture, and Conflict at Drew University in New Jersey (2012–2013), and visiting assistant professor of religion at the University of Iowa (2000–2003). Born in Iran, he lives in Los Angeles with his wife, author and entrepreneur Jessica Jackley, and their three sons.

rezaaslan.com
Facebook.com/rezaaslanofficial
Twitter: @rezaaslan

Also available from the bestselling author of *Zealot*

REZA ASLAN

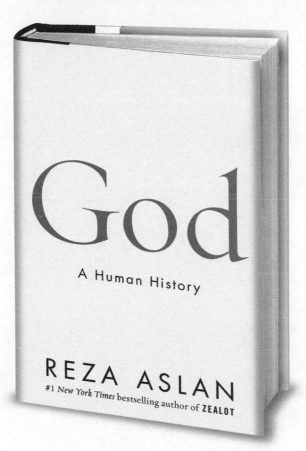